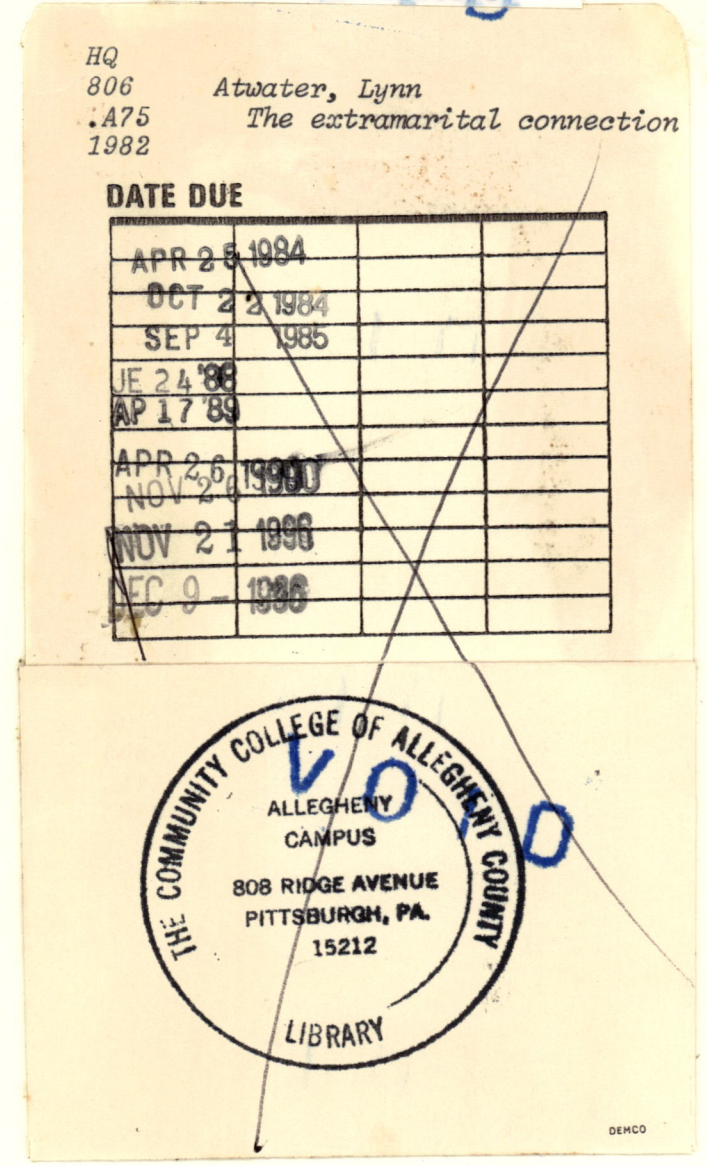

ALLEG HQ806.A75 1982
Atwater, Lynn.
The extramarital connection

3036000000068041

HQ
806   Atwater, Lynn
.A75   The extramarital connection
1982

DATE DUE

APR 2 5 1984			
OCT 2 2 1984			
SEP 4 1985			
JE 24 '86			
AP 17 '89			
APR 2 6 1990			
NOV 2 6 1990			
NOV 2 1 1996			
DEC 9 1996			

THE COMMUNITY COLLEGE OF ALLEGHENY COUNTY
ALLEGHENY CAMPUS
808 RIDGE AVENUE
PITTSBURGH, PA.
15212
LIBRARY

DEMCO

THE EXTRAMARITAL CONNECTION

THE EXTRAMARITAL CONNECTION

Sex, Intimacy, and Identity

Lynn Atwater, Ph.D.

IRVINGTON PUBLISHERS, INC.
551 FIFTH AVENUE NEW YORK, N.Y. 10017

HQ
806
.A75
1982

Copyright © 1982 by Irvington Publishers, Inc.

All rights reserved. No part of this book may be reproduced in any manner whatever, including information storage or retrieval, in whole or in part (except for brief quotations in critical articles or reviews), without written permission from the publisher. For information, write to Irvington Publishers, Inc., 551 Fifth Avenue, New York, New York, 10176.

Library of Congress Cataloging in Publication Data

Atwater, Lynn.
  The extramarital connection.

  Bibliography: p.
  Includes index.
  1. Adultery—United States. 2. Married women—United States—Sexual behavior. I. Title.
HQ806.A75   306.7'36   82-6561
ISBN 0-8290-0770-2   AACR2

Printed in the United States of America

Chapter 2 of this book was published in a different version in *Alternative Lifestyles*, February, 1979.

CONTENTS

Chapter

1	Extramarital Relationships	15
2	Getting Involved	30
3	Extramarital Intimacy	57
4	Open Marriage	82
5	Sexual Scripts and Sexual Behavior	107
6	After Involvement: Identities and Attitudes	142
7	Extramarital Relationships with Other Women	166
8	The Extramarital Connection	188
	Footnotes	209
	Bibliography	221
	Appendices	235
	Index	259

to
women and men

reaching
for
growth and intimacy

but
especially
to
my sister Eileen

and
especially
to
Gus

Preface

Extramarital relationships have become a commonplace feature of American marriage. According to the best available information, most people's lives will be touched by the experience of an extramarital relationship. It is now more likely than not that one spouse, or both, will become involved with someone else during the course of their marriage.

Besides the prevalence of extramarital experiences in real life, they have been a favorite topic in fiction. The mass media has also persistently focused on this area of human behavior, playing on our fascination with the subject. Despite this widespread exposure to extramarital behavior, most people are still personally uncomfortable with it at some level.

Social science itself has reflected the general uneasiness by largely avoiding, until recently, the scientific study of extramarital relationships. This book is part of the emerging focus on an ambivalently acknowledged aspect of American marriage. In it I explore the contemporary extramarital relationships of women, who are dramatically increasing their rate of extramarital participation. I also compare women's experiences with what we know about those of men.

This research differs from the style which currently dominates sociology. I did not survey large numbers of women and statistically analyze the results with a computer. Rather, I intensively interviewed a group of fifty change-oriented women to get an in-depth picture of extramarital involvements. Interviewing is an especially appropriate technique to study any behavior about which we know very little. I believe these respondents can provide insights, clues, and hypotheses about the meanings and consequences of women's extramarital behavior today and as it may evolve in the future.

This study is also part of the new scholarly attention to women which is filling the void left by a traditional sociology that studied a society dominated by men. Georg Simmel, a uniquely perceptive sociologist, noted this tendency in 1911. "Almost all discussions of women deal only with what they are in relation to men in terms of real, ideal, or value criteria. Nobody asks what they are for themselves. . . ." Only in the last decade have we begun to study women in this way.

Here women speak in their own words of what they are for themselves. What they say may sound provocative to the traditional ear. The accounts of their lives fly in the face of both conventional and moral beliefs about women and their sexuality. The remarkable uniformity of the meanings of their experiences suggests a new model of women's extramarital sexuality, one that has not been fully presented in the research literature before.

I do not claim these respondents speak for all American women, but that knowledge of their extramarital experiences can add to our growing understanding of the myriad ways in which women are transforming their lives. Not only do their accounts offer insight into extramarital activities today, but they also expand our vision of women's sexuality, and of the changing nature of marriage and the family. Although some social critics are now predicting a return to traditional family values, I stand with those researchers who feel that changes in the family and sexual lifestyles of the last two decades are irreversible. Women have always been the pivotal figures in the institution of marriage, and whatever they do to alter their wifely roles has implications for the future of marriage.

The findings and interpretations in this book should interest scholars, researchers, and clinicians. However, the book is addressed to two other important audiences. One is college students studying in the areas of sexuality, gender roles, marriage and the family, and alternative lifestyles. The other audience is women and men interested in the topic of intimate relations. Although general readers may find a few areas of the book offer more sociology than they need to know, I hope they will find the book informative and useful, for I believe that sociology can and should help deepen understanding of our own lives and the lives of others in society.

Lynn Atwater
South Orange, N.J.

Acknowledgements

As with any book, many people stand unseen behind the author's efforts. I am grateful most of all to the women who participated in this study and who were willing to share with me, and ultimately with others, one area of their intimate lives. All of their names and identifying characteristics have been changed to protect their privacy and anonymity. They volunteered for this project so that women could know the reality of other women's lives, believing that through sharing personal experiences women can learn from and help one another.

I also benefited from the many discussions I had with colleagues, students, and women and men I met during the course of researching and writing this book. I especially want to thank Laurie Davidson and Lucinda San Giovanni, both sociologists and friends, for their most helpful comments on Chapters 1 and 5 respectively. And I must acknowledge the unique influence of Harry C. Bredemeier of Rutgers University, my primary intellectual inspiration during my years as a graduate student there. I am also appreciative of Seton Hall University, which granted me a sabbatical leave in 1979, when this book first took shape.

Fortunately, there were a number of people who were unusually supportive during the long course of researching and writing. I enjoyed the unfailing optimism of Sam Cicalese whenever my spirits were lowest; the caring shown by my son Mark; the helpful interest of friends, particularly Howard Robboy, Marilyn Wollheim, Nancy Slack, and Bill Kolshorn; and the various contributions of my mother, father, and very special grandmother.

For typing services, I am indebted to the dependable and efficient skills of Stephanie Katz, Valerie Feltey, and Pat Parry, whom I also count as a warm friend. Two student assistants, Ellen Devaney and Susan Sanderson, gave important help in the tasks of transcribing and coding interviews. And lastly, I thank Cliff Snyder and Andy Birler of Irvington Publishers, Lynne Tillman for editorial work, and Eric Katz for preparation of the index.

L.A.

> "as for me, I am a watercolor
> I wash off"
> Anne Sexton

Composition, Series 1

We drew our strokes clear and fine
with brushes of imported camel's hair.
We were not the sort of monument
great museums are built around,
but pieces of flimsy paper
torn off a pad, one by one.

We mixed our palette in raw sienna
and greenearth, rich shades formed our impasto.
Overhead, a cerulean blue sky and titanium clouds
gave the impression of white space.

It took us two years to complete our wash;
her canvas was primed, the past eleven.
Her substance and durability, a thick gouache.
Your paintings with her are oil, or
frescoes suitable for cathedral walls.
Solid and enduring, socially acceptable,
children will be brought in to look at them
in groups bussed in from school.
She is a docent, she will lead their tour.

And you and I? We are pastels
fine, thin bougainvillea watercolors,
like *Winslow Homer in the Tropics*
a book I bought for you, but kept.

Our was a prettier picture
but thin paper doesn't last
and watercolors fade.

I was a sheet torn off the pad when
our sketch was done.
I look elsewhere for subjects
in a different landscape now.

Diane O'Donnell

AUTHOR'S NOTE

Because the topic of this book is a morally and emotionally sensitive one, I am pointing out at the beginning that it focuses on what women who have been extramaritally involved do, think, and feel. It is not a book about whether people should or should not get involved extramaritally, for that is a question of values that cannot be resolved through research.

Furthermore, this report is not a complete account of every possible aspect of extramarital relations, for such an exhaustive inquiry is beyond the scope of one book. Rather, it is designed to advance knowledge of extramarital behavior by asking certain questions that have seldom or never been asked before. In asking these questions, I have uncovered a predominantly positive reaction to extramarital behavior which may be unique to this time of social transition in marriage and women's roles. This positive view supplements previous research which has tended to focus only on negative qualities, thereby yielding an incomplete picture. Thus, this new knowledge not only adds to our logical understanding of extramarital relations but, by extension can also add to our understanding of marriage.

Lastly, I have studied and interpreted these reports of extramarital relationships from a sociological perspective. This perspective seeks to clarify and expose the meanings of social reality which are normally hidden from our everyday consciousness. In uncovering these meanings and connections, what is said may initially startle some readers who may be unfamiliar with sociological work and practice.

Chapter One

Extramarital Relationships

Sandra, a twenty-six year old social worker, is getting ready to go out for dinner with a friend. Before leaving, she stops to put the frosting on a cake she baked that afternoon for her husband's birthday. He'll be home later that night from a business trip, and she wants to surprise him with it. Satisfied with her efforts, she goes off to meet her friend Steve, a young law student. She plans to be home about the same time as her husband.

In another part of town, Alex is kissing his wife goodbye as he heads for an early evening meeting with some friends to wrap up a business deal. He hopes the meeting will be short, because afterward he's looking forward to stopping by to see his friend Ann. Ann is divorced and has her own apartment.

Both Sandra and Alex are involved in extramarital relationships. They are like most Americans who are, or will be, involved extramaritally at some point in their married lives. They are also like most Americans, who, when asked, say they disapprove of extramarital sex. In the latest available survey, 87% said that extramarital relations were "always wrong" or "almost always wrong."[1] But attitudes about extramarital relations tell only half the story. The other half of the story is what people do, not what they say.[2]

When Dr. Alfred Kinsey and his associates published their groundbreaking study of American male sexual behavior in 1948, they documented that half of all married men had extramarital relations at some point in their married lives. This figure of one in two men with extramarital experience was confirmed by surveys published in 1977 and 1979. Although the number of involved married men has remained steady over the years, these surveys indicate that the frequency with which men participate has apparently increased.[3] Moreover, younger men report they are more likely to engage in extramarital sex than older men. Seventy percent of all men under the age of 40 said they could see themselves getting involved in an extramarital situation, compared with 53% of men over 55.[4]

Women are also changing their rate of extramarital behavior. Extramarital relations are not the object of equal opportunity laws, federal suits, or demonstrations against discrimination. Nevertheless, women are quietly but steadily finding increased opportunities for sexual expression outside of their marriages. In 1953, Kinsey reported that 26% of married women had extramarital experience by age 40. In 1975, a generation later, the figure had risen to 38%. The most dramatic increase has been among the youngest married women, under age 25, where the rate has risen from one in ten to one in four.[5] As these young married women move through the life cycle, it is projected that one in two will have an extramarital experience.[6]

The evidence suggests that we are sexual schizophrenics. We say one thing and do another. We are still emotionally attached to traditional beliefs of sexual exclusivity, while we live with the needs and desires provoked by contemporary values which hold sexual expression to be a new social frontier. We have inherited a repressive set of legal, moral, and religious codes that we still use to guide our attitudes, yet these codes were never designed to meet the problems of modern intimacy that confront us today.

How did this chasm between our beliefs and our practices come to be? Part of the answer lies in the strength of our inherited attitudes. The proscription of extramarital sex is one of the most ancient and stringent cultural rules regulating family life. In Western civilization, it can be traced back at least to early Hebraic society.[7] This prohibition did not develop because of concern about sexuality as such, but because of the threat extramarital intercourse represented "to the stability of society; most specifically, male property rights."[8] The rule against extramarital sex originated in the concern of powerful males to preserve the economic system of private property, and it forbade extramarital relations absolutely for women and relatively for men. This double standard required premarital abstinence and postmarital fidelity for women while leaving men free to pursue sexual variety with female slaves and prostitutes. By bequeathing property only to the sons of their wives, men could be certain they were passing on their inheritance to their legitimate heirs. An economic system built on the concept of private property required sexual faithfulness within marriage for its survival.

Although prohibition of extramarital sex originally functioned for economic reasons, it was incorporated into religion, law, and public attitudes of morality. Christianity, and particularly

Puritanism in the United States, was markedly repressive of sexuality. Strict efforts were made to control premarital, marital, and extramarital behavior. These restrictions served to protect the institution of marriage as it then existed. In an earlier, primarily agricultural era, marriage was the principal way men and women joined with each other for mutual physical survival, as well as for whatever sexual expression was approved. Later, laws were passed reflecting Puritanism's anti-sexual attitudes and, over time, morality became largely synonymous with sexual behavior. Today, adultery is still illegal in many states.

Modern American society is dramatically different from the eras in which marriage was institutionalized. Marriage is no longer primarily for the creation of legal heirs, nor is it intrinsically linked to physical survival and well being. For many, the primary purpose of marriage is the care and meeting of emotional needs. Deviations from sexual exclusivity no longer endanger our economic system, nor do they threaten our physical well-being. Consequently, public punishment has largely disappeared, and people are no longer branded with a scarlet 'A' nor prosecuted for adultery. Yet old attitudes still remain, largely intact.

In addition to the reduced social need for monogamy, many societal changes have occurred which tend to encourage non-exclusive behavior. In an urbanized and industrialized society, men and women come into contact with many more people each day than when America was rural. An individual can often meet hundreds of potential sexual partners in the course of a normal day's activities. This mobility, as well as population density in urban areas, contributes to a social anonymity, which makes it possible for unapproved behavior to remain unobserved as it never could in small town America. Furthermore, our increased longevity means that marriages have the potential for lasting longer, lengthening the period of susceptibility to others. A century ago, death broke up as many marriages as divorce does today.[9]

With the relaxation of control over exclusivity and increased opportunities for many more sexual outlets has come a predictable increase in extramarital behavior. What has not come is any appreciable increase in our approval of what we are doing extramaritally. We have made a hyprocrisy of our belief in fidelity. We continue to cling to the ideal, because we believe it to be the best way to meet all of our personal needs in an intimate relationship. We have transformed what once was an economic necessity into an emotional one. We blindly believe that if only our love partners are faithful, all of our emotional needs will be satisfied.

There are several myths that contribute to our unrealistic faith in sexual exclusivity. They include the following:

Myth: One person can and will supply all of another's emotional, social, and sexual needs.

Reality: This may well be our most unrealistic expectation. It is never possible for one person to meet all of another's needs, for each human being's needs are complex and are also constantly changing. We have also raised our expectations for satisfaction in marriage to extremely high levels. As Americans, we now feel *entitled* to a happy marriage. If our first one is not happy, we feel further entitled to divorce in order to continue our pursuit.

Myth: People grow to love each other more as years go by.

Reality: The rate of divorce and research studies on happiness in marriage indicate otherwise.

Myth: Sexual exclusivity comes easily and naturally.

Reality: There is no evidence to indicate that human beings are "naturally" sexually exclusive. Exclusivity is not easy, as any married person (or any person who has promised exclusivity to another) can testify. It is likely that maintaining exclusivity will be even more difficult in marriages of the future because of the social trends already discussed.[10]

The extent of extramarital relations suggests that sexually exclusive marriage fails to meet the intimate needs and capabilities of many married people. Clearly, we have seduced ourselves with the myths of monogamy. We retain romantic attachments to these myths despite the pain and disillusion these unexamined beliefs are bound to bring us. If we are lucky enough to avoid divorce, we must still confront the strong probability that our marriages will be touched by an extramarital relationship at some point, either our own or our spouse's. When that does happen, the effect is often negligible until the other spouse becomes aware of it. This fact has largely failed to enter our consciousness. As far back as 1953, Kinsey reported that "extramarital relationships had least often caused difficulty when the spouse had not known of them."[11] Most women in his study reported their husbands presumably did not know of their involvements. In a 1979 study of men's involvements, three-quarters of wives remained unaware of their husbands' activities.[12] It is only when a spouse's extramarital involvement becomes known that difficulties are likely to occur, which suggests that we react more to traditional meanings than to the actual impact upon us of our spouse's involvement.[13]

Most people tend to react to knowledge of their spouses' involvements with feelings of anger, jealousy, lack of trust, and sometimes the impulse to divorce because these are the "feeling rules" built into traditional attitudes about extramarital sex.[14] In other words, whatever the meaning of the outside relationship, whether it be casual or serious, regardless of when the relationship occurred, in the distant past or the here and now, the tendency is to react with the same set of emotions. We do this because in our culture, these are the only correct emotions to feel when discovering our spouses' infidelity. We do not yet have any feeling rules to cover the changes in the incidence and meaning of modern extramarital sex. Clearly, our feeling rules, built upon traditional attitudes about extramarital behavior, have a great deal to do with our perception of damage to us. This structured emotional reaction and our continuing disapproval of extramarital relations, despite the rising incidence, suggest that Americans are still unwilling or unable to come to terms with the reality of extramarital relations.

There are several possible approaches to employ in resolving this gap between our ideals of exclusivity and our extramarital behavior. Using a *moral* approach, we can continue to condemn extramarital relations and make more zealous attempts to live "faithfully" for life. While this will be successful for some, and possibly desired by most, it is unlikely to be a workable solution for the majority of Americans. In terms of the personal satisfactions we are looking for, our expectations of marriage are too unrealistic to have them all be met in an exclusive framework. And the diverse social forces propelling us toward new marital traditions are too strong to be repelled solely by the force of moral conviction.

Recognizing the impact of these rising personal expectations and changing social pressures, a group of scholars on the family recommend a *'futuristic'* approach.[15] They advocate a new marital ideology that would, in effect, change our ideals to conform with our behavior. They see the need for a new marital ethic which recognizes the value of alternatives to exclusivity. They do not feel we should abandon monogamy, but that we shold recognize its inadequacy as a life-long marriage plan for most people. They propose a new ideological perspective on marriage, one that includes the possibility of choosing from a variety of exclusive and non-exclusive alternatives over a lifetime.

Another approach, a *psychological* one, has been used, especially in the past, to lay the blame for the causes of extramarital behavior in individual weaknesses and deficiencies. There is, undoubtedly, some truth to this explanation, but it can hardly explain all incidences of extramarital involvement. In 1967, psychologist Albert Ellis distinguished between healthy and sick reasons for having extramarital sex, thereby beginning to remove moral taint from psychological understanding. While not all psychologists would agree with a nonjudgemental view, the trend is in this direction. For example, psychologist J. D. Block, in a recent book entitled *The Other Man, The Other Woman,* offers therapeutic suggestions for understanding and coping with the emotional needs and reactions associated with extramarital involvements.

A *sociological* perspective, used in this book, complements the psychological focus on the individual by exploring the *social* factors associated with extramarital involvements. When large numbers of people are engaged in any behavior, it ceases to be strictly a private issue. It becomes a public and social concern. From a sociological perspective come such questions as: "What changes in society that are beyond the control of the individual contribute to the rising incidence of extramarital sex?" "What common patterns are to be found in extramarital involvements?" "Are there differences in the extramarital relations of women and men?" "What are the consequences, good and bad, of extramarital relations on marriages and on individuals?" "Are the feeling rules we have still appropriate to the incidence and meanings of today's extramarital sex?"

A sociological focus attempts to move individuals beyond thinking that personal problems have only personal causes, to a consciousness that their problems are similar to what others are experiencing and why. Sociological information can aid us in understanding behavior by exposing and clarifying the connections between individuals and the society they live in. A sociological approach does not evaluate what is right or wrong behavior, but it can help us grasp what it means to be living at a particular time in human history. It can help us understand that what we are doing and feeling and thinking has roots beyond our personal motivations, desires, and values. A sociological understanding can aid us in decoding the meaning of our existence.

One of the conditions of modern existence is that we have become increasingly freed from the control of church and state, and as a consequence of this freedom we are personally responsible for more and more decisions that shape our private lives. We no longer are told whom to marry; instead we choose a mate that we hope will prove pleasing to us. We are no longer confined to the some occupation as our parents had; instead we select a career that we believe will prove satisfying and lucrative. We no longer are expected to belong to one religion; instead we can change it as we mature, or even reject religion entirely. We no longer must become parents after we marry; instead we are free to choose whether to have children or not.

And now we no longer are forced by external constraints to be monogamous in marriage. It is now something we must choose instead of having it imposed upon us. President Carter recognized this in his famous *Playboy* interview, when he admitted to lusting in his heart after other women. We have this choice "to be or not to be monogamous," whether we want it or not. Ironically, one advantage modern life does not give us is the choice of not having to make choices.

In having to make choices in so many areas of modern life, we often depend on available information. But we need accurate information to make responsible and intelligent decisions in the situations which confront us every day. The custom of dating arose so that we could get to know people and gain information about them in order to decide whether to marry them or not. We try to find out what various jobs are like and what our own interests are in order to choose the right career for ourselves. Often contemporary married couples read articles and books on the pros and cons of parenthood before deciding whether or not to have children.

Similarly, knowledge of people's extramarital behavior can help us understand this contemporary addition to the institution of marriage. Learning about others' extramarital experiences, and the positive and negative consequences of that behavior, may help us assess these experiences for our own marriages. If we are never tempted, or are at most uncertain, knowledge of others' involvements can confirm the validity of our own decisions. If we, too, have had or think about having extramarital experiences, then that knowledge can deepen understanding of our own decisions and behavior by being able to compare them with others.

Whatever the extramarital decisions individuals make, when they exhibit enough similarity to constitute a pattern, and when they show enough continuity to endure over time, they will become part of the mosaic of modern sexual morality. As our ancestors developed a code of strict monogamy to fit the social needs of their era, so, too, are we developing new traditions to mirror the many possibilities in marriage styles taking shape today.

One example of this creation of new cultural patterns of intimacy is in the area of premarital sexuality. For many years the same hypocrisy characterized attitudes toward premarital sex as currently exists with extramarital sexuality. Gradually, over a period of decades, this attitude-behavior gap is being eliminated. Starting with the 1960's, attitudes became more permissive, so that by 1978 only 41% of a representative sample of Americans thought that premarital sex was "always wrong" or "almost always wrong." Those who disapproved were mostly in the older and less well educated segments of the population. Eighty percent of the 18-29 age group approved of premarital sex.[16] According to the most recent study, 80% of that same group have also experienced premarital sex.[17]

While there is an unmistakable trend toward convergence of attitudes and behavior in the area of premarital sex, there is as yet no firm evidence for a similar trend in extramarital sex. One clue to the possibility of this happening lies in the attitudes of highly educated young adults, a group that often suggest trends indicating where the rest of the population will be going. Of this group, age 18-29 and with more than twelve years of formal education, 40% approve of extramarital sex.[18] This is insufficient data on which to base a prediction, so we must wait for the future to reveal how the tension between extramarital attitudes and behavior will be resolved.

The purpose of this book is to report on and discuss extramarital behavior as it is occurring today. The intent is to further understanding, free of past mythologies and traditional moral condemnation. Many will disagree with interpretations of this study, but that is to be expected on any controversial issue, especially in the area of sexuality. Studies of sex, from Kinsey to Masters and Johnson, have stimulated powerful responses because of the conflicting sexual attitudes Americans hold, and because sexuality is such an emotional topic in our society.

Any interpretation of extramarital behavior reflects, and is colored by, the viewpoint of the onlooker. I am no exception. I view extramarital relations from a feminist perspective, and I'm doing so for several reasons.[19]

First, this research and analysis will focus mainly on women, for it is among women, more so than men, that rates of extramarital participation are rising dramatically. Second, feminism is often the inspiration behind the spectrum of change being painted across the lives of women today. Women's renewed interest in social equality has gained them new opportunities in areas as diverse as work, education, religion, politics, and sports. Women are redesigning their lives and redefining their selves. This pervasive new consciousness affects every facet of living, and sexuality is no exception.

Third, women's sexuality, both in its physical and social expression, has long been shaped by stereotyped ideas. Although these myths and ideas are rooted in the anti-female bias of early Western culture,[20] writers, researchers, and scholars have supported and perpetuated them into the present. A number of familiar beliefs make up the social construction of traditional female sexuality. Among these is the idea that female sexuality is rooted in emotions rather than sexual desire, activated by love rather than physical attraction. Another idea is that women's sexuality takes years to develop and reaches its peak when women are in their late thirties or forties. By contrast, male sexuality, it is said, reaches its peak in adolescence. Women have also been thought to be less interested in sex than men. And in the ultimate of myths, Freud sought to physically relocate women's "mature" orgasm from the clitoris to the vagina.[21]

Beyond these physical "facts" about their sexuality, there is also a traditional model of the social aspects of women's sexuality. This model assumes women are passive sexually, lack autonomy in sexual decision-making, equate sexual expression with love, and perceive sexuality as a form of service to others rather than something they do for their own enjoyment.[22]

It is impossible to know precisely how many women have tried to live up to these culturally dominant notions or how many have succeeded in living up to them, and at what cost to themselves.

Feminist theorists, new research findings, and women themselves are all challenging these traditional sexual stereotypes. Masters and Johnson's work in 1966 on *Human Sexual Response* showed there was no physical evidence for the theory of separate vaginal and clitoral orgasms. Moreover, they found women to be more sexual than men if the capacity for multiple orgasms is used as a measure. Mary Jane Sherfey, a feminist psychiatrist, concludes from Masters and Johnson's evidence that women have the capacity to be sexually insatiable.[23] Women have also begun to rely on their own experience to define their sexual capacity and preferences. *The Hite Report* gives self-accounts of the sexuality of some 3,000 women.[24] Such books are necessary in this transitional era to provide information on what those experiences are, both for women who want to know about and compare themselves with others, and for scholars who wish to understand the phenomena of female sexual behavior.

The relatively small amount of research that has been done on the extramarital sexuality of women has tended to reflect the traditionally dominant beliefs. For instance, Kinsey attributed the lesser number of women's extramarital partners (as compared to men's) to their lesser needs, explaining it biologically by referring to innate differences in the nervous system of women.[25] Morton Hunt, a journalist who published his extensive exploration of extramarital "affairs" in 1969, reported that women are "less prone to react quite so strongly" to successful experiences outside of marriage. He implied that cultural definitions are responsible, since "sexual ability is not so closely identified with success as it is for men."[26] In a discussion of reasons for extramarital relationships, sociologist Robert Bell saw the process of aging and its associated need for evidence of physical attractiveness as a motivation for females, but not for males.[27] Overall, the stereotypical model of women's extramarital relations has been characterized by falling in love, motivated by unsatisfactory marriage, rationalized as being beyond personal control, and accompanied by considerable guilt.

But feminist sociologists have taken a different view. They would agree with Jessie Bernard, an eminent woman sociologist, who commented that

> it seems to me that a new kind of woman is emerging...and one of the distinguishing characteristics of this woman is that she can be casual about sex...as casual about sexual relations in or out of marriage as men. They (women) can accept sex at

some point without conflict. Even a regular extramarital relationship does not faze them or in fact interfere with their marriage.[28]

Which of these two opposing pictures of women more accurately captures the reality of women's lives today? Do the increased numbers of women having extramarital relations do so because they fall in love with another man? Because they're unhappily married and seeking an easy way out of their dissatisfation? Do they feel too guilty to enjoy the extra sex? Are older women doing it only because they fear they're losing their physical attractiveness?

The most recent research suggests that the stereotypical view of women's extramarital behavior is mistaken or at least out-of-date. In 1975 one study of 2,262 women by sociologists Bell, Turner, and Rosen reported that women with low-rated marriages were most likely to have extramarital sex, *but that many happily married women also had sex outside of marriage.* Therefore, they concluded, "this would suggest that for many women extramarital coitus is influenced by a number of personal or social values that go beyond how they evaluate their marriage."[29] One of the personal or social values they found associated with extramarital sex was a liberal sexual attitude. By that they meant women who enjoyed oral-genital sexual contact, and women who often initiated sex within their marriage. Thus, a tendency to engage in extramarital sex may be part of the liberalization of the entire package of women's sexual behavior.

Some similar findings emerged from a study of 100,000 women who answered a questionnaire published in *Redbook* magazine. More than half of the women who had extramarital sex said they were happily married. When Robert Levin, an editor of the magazine, analyzed the data to determine why these happily married women were involved extramaritally, he found that

> when the satisfied-experimental wives were compared to *all* women who took part in the survey in terms of education, income, political outlook, employment status, religious affiliation and even intensity of religious belief, *the statistical differences are negligible.* From a sociological point of view, the average satisfied-experimental wife does not seem too unlike the average women who answered the questionnaire.[30]

Sociology traditionally relies on demogaphic variables like education, income, employment, and religion partially to explain human behavior. But the *Redbook* magazine results suggest that we have to look elsewhere for explanations of contemporary extramarital behavior. That "elsewhere" is not to be found in the happiness or unhappiness of marriage, according to the Bell and *Redbook* studies.

Then why are many women having "affairs" or extramarital relationships today? What do these relationships mean to them? What kinds of feelings do they have toward "the other men" in their lives? How does having an extramarital relationship affect their behavior toward their husband and children? What is sex like for a woman having an affair? How does a woman feel about herself afterward? What about women who share their sexuality with other women, as well as other men? What does all this mean for the future of marriage and the family?

Doing This Study

To seek answers to these questions, I decided to interview women about their extramarital relationships. This was an exploratory project in an area of human behavior where there is limited information. Intensive interviews were necessary in order to obtain in-depth information from each woman. One of the deficiencies in present knowledge of extramarital behavior is that most of it has been gathered through questionnaires or surveys. While surveys have the virtue of giving information on many individuals, they give only a few pieces of knowledge on each one. That knowledge also tends to be quantitative, with numerical answers to questions like "How many extramarital partners have you had?" or "How many times did you have sex with each partner?" The reason for the emphasis on numbers is that they are the easiest answers to tabulate and process.

We need qualitative data to balance our numerical knowledge. We need to know, for instance, what the meanings of extramarital involvements are to individuals. Intensive interviews are an ideal way to gather that data, but they take a great deal of time to conduct and analyze. They are economically feasible only with small groups of people.

Since I was most interested in the changes women were making in their lives, I decided it was vital that the women interviewed be feminist-oriented. I selected a group of 50 women to interview from approximately 300 in 47 states who responded to an ad placed in *Ms.* magazine.[31] The ad requested that women who were presently or recently engaged in extramarital relationships write to me. The women were selected for variation in background characteristics, so as to represent a broad spectrum for analysis.[32]

The women lived primarily in urban/suburban areas, coming from 17 different states. Their ages ranged from 23 to 59 years and their education from high school to post-graduate work. Occupationally, about one-third were homemakers; one-third held full-time clerical/secretarial jobs, and one-third were in managerial/professional occupations. The sample somewhat over-represents middle to upper-middle class women, but these are the women more likely to be in the vanguard of social change.

Sixty-five percent had intact marriages at the time of the initial interviews; the rest had separated, divorced, or been widowed some time after their first involvement ouside of marriage. Seventy percent of the women had children, varying in age from infants to adults. More than one-third had been extramaritally involved with only one partner; the rest had had two or more partners. (More extensive information on these background characteristics and on the entire methodology of the study can be found in Appendix 1.)

The interviews were gathered in two different ways because of the geographical distances involved. I talked in person with 30 of the women who lived in the New York/New Jersey/Philadelphia area and tape-recorded their interviews. I used a nine page guide consisting of a series of open-ended questions (see Appendix 2). The guide was developed during a number of exploratory interviews with other women on the subject of extramarital relations.[33] Women also were encouraged to bring up topics they considered important but which were not already in the interview guide.

The remaining 20 women were located in 14 other states and one province in Canada. They interviewed themselves, using the same interview guide. They tape-recorded their own interviews and mailed them back to me. Subsequently, I contacted each woman by mail or telephone to clarify any questions raised by her interview material. These interviews were even more candid than those done face-to-face.

The initial interviews were begun in late 1974 and continued through most of 1975. Each one took an average of three hours, with many lasting even longer. Since that time, I have been in additional contact with many of the women as a follow-up to the initial interviews.[34]

These interviews provide the basic informtaion for the analysis in this book. In addition, the interpretations in this book draw on personal conversations I have had with hundreds of women and men during the course of teaching, giving community talks, traveling, and attending professional conferences and meetings. Finally, this work also considers other research on both women's and men's extramarital relationships published through the first part of 1980.

It is important to note that the experiences of the interviewed women do not represent all American women, or even all American women who have had extramarital relations. There are several reasons for this limitation.

First, as in most sexual research, this study is based on people who volunteered for interviews. Volunteers were used because selecting women randomly (which would be scientifically representative) requires identifying *all* women who've had extramarital relations, clearly an impossible task. It is not known exactly how much those who volunteer to be respondents differ from those who are randomly selected. Indications are that the more effort it requires to participate voluntarily, the more likely it is that those who do so are sexually liberal.[35] In a study of extramarital sex, however, only those who are more sexually liberal are likely to have had such experience, so volunteer bias is probably of less significance in this project.

There will be objections to the feminist orientation of the women in this sample group. However, in research seeking to explore the impact of social change, this choice allows us to understand women who are open to personal and social change. Feminist-oriented women, as a bellweather group, can give indications of the quality of women's extramarital participation in sex.[36] Although women who read *Ms.* magazine are a small minority, the number of women who support goals of equal rights has increased to a large majority over the last ten years. There is every indication that this trend will continue in the future.[37] Although these women were recruited through the magazine, they were, with only a few exceptions, moderate on feminist attitudes and beliefs. They are very similar to a national sample of American women when comparing attitudes towards equal rights (see details in Appendix 2).

Finally, there is the usual question about whether a small group can tell us anything worth knowing sociologically. The answer is an emphatic "yes," as long as the goals of the research are appropriate to the size of the sample. Here, the goals are very apt. They are to gain in-depth information on extramarital relationships by asking questions which have seldom or never been asked before; to use this information to apply certain sociological concepts and theories to help us understand extramarital relationships; and to generate ideas and insights about extramarital relationships which may be explored and tested further in future research.[38]

This inquiry treats extramarital relations as both social and sexual behavior. Too often the preoccupation with sex in our culture has led to an over-fascination with the sexual aspects of extramarital involvements, and a corresponding neglect of the social. In this book, I am trying to focus a sociological eye on the extramarital experiences of women, exploring the social and sexual connections they have with their extramarital partners.

I am also trying to explore extramarital behavior from the viewpoint of the individual women who have had these experiences. This is an alternative to past research which has often assumed either a marriage perspective or a traditional perspective. The marriage perspective has emphasized studying extramarital sex for its effects and consequences on marriages. This is important and necessary, but it overlooks significant questions about the meanings and consequences for the individuals who are extramaritally involved.

The traditional perspective has allowed the moral bias of society to color the questions asked, so that research focuses on negative aspects of involvements. One example of this was the study which found that individuals with low strength of conscience were more likely to become extramaritally involved than those with high strength of conscience.[39]

In contrast to these perspectives some readers may feel this book, with its focus on the individual and with its effort to be morally neutral, takes a positive bias. If that is the impression given, it may partly be because we are more used to viewing the extramarital relations negatively. It may also be that women who have positive extramarital experiences are more likely to volunteer for this kind of research, so that more positive experiences are included than may randomly occur.

In any case, if there is a positive bias it comes out of the research findings this book presents. These findings represent the extramarital experiences of a group of women as they lived them and as they reported them to me in great depth. I believe their experiences represent a pattern of extramarital behavior that is increasingly prevalent in the changing lives of contemporary American women.

Chapter Two

Getting Involved

Any woman has the potential for engaging in an extramarital relationship at any point in her married life. While this is sociologically true, it is not necessarily the case that individual women feel this way. In fact, almost all the women interviewed for this study did not make this assumption.[1] They had no thought of becoming involved at the time of their marriages. They defined extramarital relationships, if they thought of them at all, as something that happens to someone else and never expected it to happen to them. These women were like any other women who accept monogamous marriage. As two sociologists, Judith Long Laws and Pepper Schwartz, have noted: "Most women do not debate whether (monogamy) is the right sexual style for them. They do not know it is a debatable issue."[2]

Yet anywhere from one to twenty-eight years after they were married, all these women had become involved in their first extramarital relationship. Three-quarters of them became involved within six years after marriage. What common sequence of events could have occurred in the lives of these women to shape their paths to the same destination?

In an explanation of the transitional process in other kinds of unanticipated sociosexual behavior, one sociologist has identified three principal phases.[3] First is a passive phase, in which individuals initially learn of the prospective behavior and then move on to thinking talking about it. Second is an active phase, during which persons inquire about opportunities and may actually test out the behavior. Finally, in the committed phase, they define the new behavior as acceptable to their self-image through reassurance by other participants and through self-rationalization.

Most of these women have gone through that process, although not necessarily in that precise sequence. Here we will look at these women's transition to first extramarital involvement in approximately chronological order, to capture the sense of their experience as realistically as possible. For this purpose, we can divide the journey to involvement into four steps. The first step "preinvolvement," approximates the passive phase described above. The second and third steps, "actual involvement" and "first extramarital sex," correspond roughly to the active phase, and the fourth step, "rationale for behavior," approximates the committed phase.

STEP 1: PREINVOLVEMENT

Premarital Sexual Behavior

The impact of premarital sexual experience stands out as the first factor in the path to extramarital involvement. Previous research indicates a woman is more likely to have extramarital sex if she has had premarital sex,[4] and these women followed that pattern. Eighty percent had sex with their husbands before marriage, and half of these had additional sexual experiences with other men. These women were in the vanguard of the era of sexual permissiveness, since an 80% rate of premarital sex was probably not reached until the 1970's. But in the number of premarital partners, they exactly match other women who now have premarital sex.[5]

As a whole, this is a group of women who early in their lives began making their own decisions about sexual behavior. They gained experiences in handling whtaever problems their sexual activities engendered, such as the need for secrecy, the avoidance or solving of unwanted pregnancy, and coping with the guilt that often accompanied the change in sexual identity from virgin to non-virgin. Several women, in the course of their interviews, directly compared their first premarital and first extramarital experiences. They viewed both instances as a kind of sexual transition or marker event, "a hurdle to be gotten over." Although this was not a focus of any specific interview question, the fact that women voluntarily made such observations suggests a definite linkage in the meanings they assign to these two similar situations. Women's consciousness about their sexual development is increasingly becoming embedded in a sequence of events that occur both inside and outside marriage, whereas traditionally, of course, all the important happenings—loss of virginity, intercourse, childbirth—took place within the confines of marriage.

First Opportunities

As mentioned earlier, these women made a conscious break

with their premarital behavior and resumed sexual monogamy at marriage. For those women who had sex only with their husbands before marriage, this transition was perhaps only a matter of automatically resuming the sexually acceptable behavior all women have been carefully taught since childhood.

What, then, determines the path to sexual unconventionality after marriage? The experiences of these women suggest that the first tentative step begins with the personal awareness of opportunity for involvements. Virtually all of the women reported they were aware of opportunities before they became involved in their first relationship and before they seriously entertained the idea of having a relationship. These opportunities consisted of sexual invitations from men, ranging from vague suggestions to unmistakably direct propositions. The reactions to these opportunities ranged from outright refusals to ambivalence to shock and disbelief:[6]

> I would just turn them down gently.
>
> I panicked.
>
> I really didn't pay too much attention to them, probably because the men involved were not appealing.
>
> I had been in situations where a couple of people had made passes. I always ignored it and thought it stupid. Finally I said to myself, "Maybe it wasn't such a bad idea after all. Maybe this is what I *should* do."
>
> I was stunned when a former boyfriend called me up after I had been married for about a year to ask me out. He knew I was married but he acted as if my marriage didn't even exist! I always thought that after you got married other men never even looked at you again, let alone asked you out.

Women traditionally have been taught not to initiate sexual encounters with men, and in keeping with the sexual conformity they reembraced at marriage, these women felt they did not suggest or invite these first opportunities. What seems to happen is that men continue acting out the aggressive sexual role they have learned before marriage. It is difficult for them to suddenly, at marriage, drop all their old behaviors, just as it has been difficult for women in the past to change overnight from premarital purity to postmarital sexual responsiveness. These abrupt changes in social expectations present discontinuities in learning new roles, especially when the new role contradicts past ones.

Family sociologists Nye and Berardo discuss this discontinuity in the male role:

> Boys are socialized to take sexual initiative toward the other sex. At marriage the norms proscribe sexual advances to women other than the spouse, but the resocialization of men at marriage is not entirely effective. Other women continue to appear attractive, and social control to prevent husbands from following some of these sexual interests is not very effective in a mobile, urban society.[7]

Men, by continuing behaviors they have been taught so well, become unwitting socializing agents in the transitional process to the first extramarital involvement. Women are not completely passive in this process, of course. But male sexual initiative, especially to the degree that it is forthright rather than ambiguous, raises the opportunity for extramarital sex to a woman in a way that she must consciously be aware of and respond to. As other researchers have suggested, people will become involved in extramarital sex to the degree they perceive opportunities for involvement.[8]

Some women reported difficulty in learning how to handle these invitations smoothly, and in a few instances become involved partly because they did not know how to gracefully counter the expectations of an aggressive male. Two women recalled:

> In some situations I've allowed these things to happen because the man was very persistent and I didn't quite know what else to do. I'm really kind of chagrined about that now.

> Twice in particular I've had a sexual experience that I definitely did not want. One man verbally coerced me and not wanting to hurt his feelings, I gave in.... Another time I firmly refused and the man tried to physically restrain me. I threatened to scream...and vowed never to get myself in such a situation again.

Several women in this study also recalled problems of "not knowing how to refuse" or of men "refusing to accept their refusal" as an important reason for their involvement in premarital sex. One study of premarital sexual behavior revealed similar consequences of unwanted sexual encounters when the negotiating skill of the female was ineffective.[9] In the premarital studies the women were much younger and less socially (and sexually) experienced than the women in this research, but it is interesting to observe the continuation of the behavior despite the additional experience.

The concept of gender roles—of what is appropriate behavior for males and females—can partly explain women's continued ineffectiveness in communicating "no" in sexual interaction. One assumption of conventional sexuality is that women have the responsibility for refusing unwanted invitations from men. Gender role socialization, however, includes distinctive styles of speech for the sexes. Women, far more frequently than men, use a verbal pattern which allows listeners to view women as indecisive, hesitant, and uncertain.[10] Thus, women's failure to communicate their sexual decisions effectively and men's refusal to accept those decisions (men are taught to interpret indecisiveness and hesitancy as a cue to continue rather than stop) can be traced in part to differences in symbolic communication between the sexes.

This gender difference in speaking will be even more important in the future as sexual behavior is increasingly freed from the control of social rules. As individuals make decisions in sexual situations according to their own personal code of ethics, effective skill at negotiating will help to determine whether or not a sexual encounter takes place, and whether or not it is completely intentional and voluntary for both men and women. At this point in the social reconstruction of gender roles, it is women whose sexual autonomy is more at issue, for they have not yet solidified the right *not* to say yes. First, women had the duty to say "no," then increasingly they have asserted their right to say "yes." The final achievement in sexual dialogue will come when their right to say "no" is accepted as a personal decision and not because it is backed by the force of traditional beliefs about what women shouldn't do. Similarly, as women increasingly initiate negotiation of sexual encounters, men will have to become verbally adept at refusing invitations they do not want. Otherwise they will face the prospect of loss of control of their sexual behavior and become heir to all the feelings that sexual coercion has produced in women.

Returning to the discussion of these first extramarital invitations women encountered, it is clear that they imposed the need to confront and negotiate unexpected sexual opportunities personally. Another consequence was that they may have also served as preliminary socializing experiences for subsequent involvement, or as a way of testing the acceptability of the idea of becoming extramaritally involved. A fifty-year-old woman whose husband refused a divorce decided to become involved with other men and found herself having to relearn certain behaviors:

> I think just dating is a tremendous ordeal. I mean it's a hurdle that—marriage is so different from dating and when you've been married for thirty years, you don't know how to date. You're like at the dance, the sock hop, against the wall—you don't know how to talk with another man readily.... It was also my first experience with any kind of touch from another male—you know, kissing and whatever. It blows your mind. A kiss like a grade B movie—I mean, you wake up and it's all going to be a funny thing, but yet—I enjoyed myself.

In several other cases, women reported significant social and emotional relationships that did not go on to include sexual intercourse:

> I did have an opportunity before I engaged in my first extramarital relationship. But we didn't go through with it because we were both held up in the same morality, I think, religiously and psychologically. Somehow we could get over our guilt of falling in love with someone who was not our spouse if we didn't consummate the relationship sexually. And I think it was stupid.

> We worked together...we were very intellectually involved and it sort of evolved into a great deal of physical and emotional attraction too. Finally he just kept telling me, "No, he couldn't go to bed with me" and that was that because he felt too guilty about doing that to his wife.

In these relationships it was not until extramarital behavior had reached the threshold of genital intercourse that it was defined as an act of betrayal to the spouse and, therefore, not acceptable. When *does* an extramarital relationship begin? Because of the salience of sex in our culture, most would probably agree that genital intercourse with someone other than your spouse constitutes extramarital sex. But what about behaviors up to that point? Kinsey found that 20% of women had engaged in "petting" outside their marriage, in addition to those 26% who had intercourse. Apparently people define the meaning of extramarital petting for themselves, since we have no agreed upon social definitions. Perhaps this vagueness allows the freedom to test what is acceptable to us personally, for how else can we be sure of what our own standards are? Possibly more women today than in Kinsey's era have relationships that include extramarital petting but stop short of intercourse. Why they stop is an interesting question for which there is no complete answer at present; it is one that needs further inquiry.

Knowing Someone

Another contribution to the transitional process leading to the first extramarital relationship was knowing a person who had already had one. Very often people who are about to take on roles about which they know little, whether it is becoming a college student, mother, or disco dancer, will use as models, consciously or otherwise, people who they know to have already had a similar experience. About one-half of the women knew such a person. Most of these "role models" were friends or people they worked with, but in some cases they were parents or other relatives, raising the possibility of intergenerational influence. The models women reported to have had strong influences on their behavior were always friends, however. One 35-year-old woman recalled:

> My girl friend in Texas—she's a gal who's had great influence on me. She's the most unleashed person I know of. Four years ago when I first met her—we were all out there together, without our husbands and children—she proceeded to pick up a guy about ten years younger than herself and trot right off to bed with him and brag about it the next morning. I had never met anybody like this, who was so open about it...it was just unreal, I never met anybody like that. So she was influential in my coming around; I knew it could be done.

This woman's comments illustrate one aspect of the way role modeling works, that it is persons most similar to ourselves that have the greatest impact.[11] In this case, both shared the social statuses and identities of woman, wife, and mother. In a subsequent interview in 1979, this woman revealed that she had in turn had a similar role modeling impact on two friends. They were all on a short trip for a few days, staying at a relative's condominium, and after dinner one evening the conversation turned to extramarital involvements:

> They were talking about how they wished they could have an affair, but they never could. Finally I turned to them and said, "Well, I have had..." I just shocked the teeth out of them, but subsequently they also got involved.... They said, "It's all because of you." And I said, "Well, it started with my girl friend in Texas."

Talking To Someone

Often knowing someone overlaps with the impact of talking to someone, but the experience of talking to someone about extramarital relationships is different qualitatively. It has additional significance as an element of anticipatory socialization (ie., a kind of mental or behavioral rehearsal) for the individual who enters into an unfamiliar role. Talking to a person apparently contributes to moving previouly unthought of behavior into the realm of the possible, more so than just knowing someone. Over half of the women recalled specific conversations about relationships before their involvements, and most of those felt the conversation to be "significant" to them. For instance, one woman recalled:

> I was with a friend who...finally got involved in her first affair... it just got me very excited and, just as with my first sexual experience where I said 'Well, it's my turn,' I said in her kitchen the same thing. I said, 'Well, you've got one going. It's something I've never tried. There's nothing I'm really afraid of jeopardizing in my marriage, and I'll be damned, I'm going to have one, too!' And I sat in her kitchen, and it went through my mind, men that I had contact with, and—oh—who I thought I could get in that position.

This particular situation provided the woman with an intimate friend for discussion of the acceptability of untried behavior, the presence of a role model, and the opportunity to link mentally the woman's decision regarding premarital sexuality to her current situation. Her interpretation indicates that a recognition of past behavior that was similar and successful probably eases the transitional path.

A twenty-six-year-old woman reported:

> By then, after talking about it a year and half I couldn't stand it anymore. I was just going to go out and do it. I was just—you know, it seemed like this thing I just couldn't ever do. And yet my husband and I had agreed upon it. Before I slept with this individual, I told him (husband). And I was very scared, and I said, 'Look, I can't go through with this.' And he said, 'Oh sure, go ahead.' The big liberal. It was absurd...he was sort of comforting me. It was a little bit of a strange thing.

In this case lengthy discussion beforehand seemed almost to propel the woman to action. Her husband also provided encouragement and support, which was the usual case where the married partners both desired a sexually open marriage. It should be noted that two of the women interviewed began involvements because their husbands had persuaded them to change to an open marriage relationship, so that talking for them was obviously of particular significance. Once that decision had been made, however, it was the woman's ' responsibility" as to how she would go about it. All of the other women interviewed began their first relationships without the knowledge of their husbands.

Approximately one-fourth of the women talked about extramarital involvements with their husbands before engaging in them. This included the two instances of open marriage, general discussions of the topic of extramarital relationships not related to intentionality, and a few cases in which women decided to "pretest" their husband's reactions with hypothetical questions. Most of the other people women talked to before getting involved were friends or work peers. Usually these were conversational situations in which the topic came up for general discussion, but which ultimately came to have a more specfic meaning for some of these women by enhancing the probability of their subsequemt involvement.

Thinking Before Involvement

Whether a woman thinks about getting involved before doing so is important in understanding not only the transition to unconventionality, but also the meaning which women assign to their behavior. As John Gagnon has pointed out, if women are changing their lives to place more emphasis on self-determination, an "affair" will no longer be something that "just happens,' but will become a more consciously planned activity.[13] There is also a similarity here with the situation of premarital sex as many young women still experience it today. Much premarital sex occurs unprotected by birth control, because to plan for its use requires thinking about the event beforehand and implies intentionality of behavior. Apparently many female virgins are readier to change their sexual behavior than they are to accept responsibility for their sexual decisions. This dissonance implies there are still ample vestiges of traditionalism in the meanings young women attach to premarital sexuality.[14]

There was ample evidence that women did not just drift into "affairs" or enter them spontaneously. Three-quarters of the women thought about becoming involved before doing so. For most of the women, the self-reflection was precipitated by a particular person with whom there seemed a possibility of involvement. Women thought primarily about whether this was something they really wanted to do and what the possible negative and positive consequences might be. Thinking, in that it constitutes a mental rehearsal for a role, serves as another element of anticipatory socialization for the individual. It helps also to move the new behavior into the realm of the possible, as the following comment by one of the women reveals:

> Yes, I thought about it a great deal before I got involved. I had to because this was such a change for me. *So really unthinkable before this* (emphasis added). (Thinking time about two months).

The length of time women thought about becoming involved before acting varied from several weeks to several years. The most frequent thinking time was about one month, and this time frame was usually associated with women thinking about a specific individual. Where there was no intended person in mind, the thinking phase lasted from three to six months for several women and as long as a year for a few. The following comments are illustrative:

> I began to realize that I had made a mistake by not having sex before marriage. It suddenly hit me that I—who was only 28—would die having had sex with only one man. I decided that was not what I wanted to do with my body, and after that the idea of having sex with another man became something possible, even desirable. But I had nobody in mind at the time.
> (Thinking time about one year)

> I thought about it a great deal for a very brief period of time and there was not very much question on my part. I wanted the relationship and I was willing to do whatever that meant.
> (Thinking time about one month)

> I thought about it only slightly. I was very preoccupied with the other demands of life. My school, the kids, my husband.
> (Thinking time about three months)

In addition to the noted variation in thinking time, there was also a qualitative difference in thinking. For those women whose involvement represented a notable personal change from their previous behavior and standards, there was correspondingly more intensive thought. There also tended to be a more pronounced flavor of self-determination and autonomy in the reports of this subgroup of women, as is evidenced in the first two excerpts from interviews.

Finally, it should be noted that there was no discernible temporal pattern in moving through this preinvolvement stage. Some women were influenced by events that occurred several years earlier but still retained a vivid impact for them. Others, particularly the youngest women, passed very quickly through this preliminary phase of the transitional process. In fact, the biggest increase in the incidence of extramarital sex is precisely in this youngest age category. For married women under age 26, the rate has risen from Kinsey's reported 8% to 24% in Hunt's sample of 1974. It may well be that younger women today enter marriage less strongly committed to monogamy than their mothers were. If that is the case, they can and will make the transition to extramarital behavior more quickly and with greater emotional ease than women even in the recent past have done.

STEP 2: INVOLVEMENT

The second step of the transition to extramarital participation focuses on the situation existing just prior to first extramarital intercourse. To understand both the social and sexual dynamics of the event, we will explore certain critical factors. For instance, how and where did women meet the men they became involved with? How emotionally involved were the women? In deciding to get involved, were they responding primarily to their feelings for the man or were other motivations important? And who took the initiative in these relationships—when the women actually became involved—as compared with earlier opportunities that were rejected?

Meeting Situations

Women met the first men they were extramaritally involved with in a great variety of circumstances. Almost half of them met partners at work or school. A few were friends from before marriage, some were met at social organizations, several were friends of the husband and, in two cases, were brothers of the husband. There were a couple of instances in which women met men in the course of carrying out specific parental duties: in taking her child to the first day of kindergarten one woman met a man taking his daughter; and in taking her children to the neighborhood ice cream store, another woman, over time, became friendly with the owner.

Previous sociological studies have suggested that the "opportunity structure," or the number of chances for a particular behavior that are built into an individual's living patterns, can help explain why people do certain things. Thus, middle-class children, because they have a higher opportunity structure, are more likely to go to college than impoverished children. Physicians and nurses, because they have a high "illegitimate opportunity structure,"[15] in terms of their access to drugs, are more likely than other professionals to become addicted. Similarly, it has been implied that variations in extramarital participation could be explained, in part, by opportunity structures. However, there was such a pervasiveness of meeting opportunities in the course of these women's daily lives that this factor does not explain much about their involvement. In fact, the life style of women has changed so much from the days in which they would stay at home and meet only the mailman—who nowadays is a mail person, anyway—that it is probably the unusual woman who does not encounter opportunities.

There was also little evidence that the type of occupation was significant in affording opportunities for involvement. Only one woman was involved in a "high opportunity" occupation that involved considerable travel. Furthermore, because opportunities were so prevalent, there was also little evidence of women "creating" opportunities. The amount of repeated exposure was probably most useful in understanding the transition, for only a couple of women began their first sexual activity within days after meeting someone. About half of the women knew their partners for several months before beginning a relationship. In the other half of the cases, the partner was known for a year or more, and in a few instances, as long as ten years. Perhaps the element of *repeated exposure* not only makes it more likely that a relationship will occur, but also introduces a note of "gradualism," which serves to ease the transition to extramarital involvement.[16]

Feelings

A traditional assumption has been that women cannot get sexually involved unless they first fall in love.[17] If this is still true for most women, one would particularly expect to find it so in this first involvement, since in rejecting their past beliefs and behavior women might be presumed to need the legitimation of "falling in love." However, only a few women described themselves as being "in love" at the time of their first involvement. Approximately one-half reported they were "emotionally involved" with the person, and the other half considered their partner to be a "friend" or someone they "liked." This is strong evidence for the idea that contemporary women can and will redefine sex and love as separate entities. This redefinition has long been expected as women gradually internalize new findings on female sexual capabilities, and as the impact of the sexual revolution spreads to all segments of the population.[18] For women, sex and love will no longer always go together automatically like a horse and carriage, and they are demonstrating that revised belief in their extramarital behavior.

Even in the few cases of strong romantic feelings there was an element of rejection of conventional myths about love. Two women recalled:

> I immediately was attracted to him because he responded to an ideal I had built up during the years of my marriage, of what I wanted in a man...So he took me out for coffee I think three or four times, and I knew that I was falling for him entirely...Yet I was amazed because basically it's all in your mind. The moment you closed your eyes, it could be any man that is touching you. It's an awfully confusing experience. You have to look constantly to make sure it is that particular person you're with.

> We discussed things like the reason we were in the relationship, was it primarily because we were unhappy with our own husband and wife—I guess it was a combination that we loved each other a great deal, even when we were happiest in our marriage it was there.

In the first instance the woman found that even intense infatuation did not make the physical experience of touching unique, a feeling women have been taught as part of the sexual double standard; and in the second excerpt, the woman alluded to simultaneous feelings of love for both her husband and her lover, clearly contrary to the romantic prescription that it is possible to love only one person at a time.

Most of the women, at the time of their first extramarital relationship, described their feelings for their partner in the following ways:

> I'd say that we were just very casual friends, if men and women can be friends in today's society.

> We were friends at first. Much later we were in love, but always warily.

> Yes, I liked him. He seemed sensitive and vulnerable and

totally unphony.

It was really a friendship, and we never did get emotionally involved.

Of course, it is possible that those women who described themselves as being "emotionally involved" were merely using different words to describe the same old feelings of being "in love." However, since they specified in the interviews that being "emotionally involved" was, for them, a lower level of feeling than being "in love," this is not likely.

Person or Situation

Women reported that rarely was the "person" more important than the "situation" when getting involved. This is compatible with the finding that most of these women were not in love at the time of their first relationship. In most cases, it was a combination of the situation and the person or the situation alone that motivated these women to become involved. For about one-half of the women, an unsatisfactory marriage was part of the situational motivation, but reasons that pertain to personal needs for growth, knowledge, and sex were equally important. The following excerpts illustrate this combination of motivations:

> I was curious about other men. I was curious about who I had become. And I was angry with (my husband) and I'm afraid there was a certain revenge to this.

> My marriage was zero at that time...I felt ripe for the affair, but I don't feel it could have been just anybody. I feel it was just a perfect combination of my being ready, of both of us liking each other an awful lot.

> So, essentially, it was the situation that was more important in getting involved. I had decided that I was going to do it. I had picked the person that I was going to do it with, and then I went after it.

> It was simply the fact that I wanted to find out if I could enjoy sex as much as all the foreplay that had been going on for a year. I definitely think it was the situation more than the person.

> I knew I was a very sexual sort of person; I needed sex. Possibly if I had discovered masturbation at that point, I wouldn't have been so horny. But I think it was the person, too. It was just the quiet way he talked; he had a very sensuous voice.

At the time of first involvement, then, most women were not motivated only, or even primarily, by an unhappy marriage. Since Kinsey's era, researcher after researcher has reported that women have extramarital involvements for other reasons than unsatisfactory marriages.[19] That fact seems not to have entered into our ideology, however. These women, as another recent study of women's extramarital experience found, were also responding to positive factors, such as a "search for a wide range of experience, for personal fulfillment and for discovering or expanding...sexual potential."[20]

While these women abandoned their commitment to monogamy, they did not do so because they fell in love with someone, nor did they rush to embrace the first man or just any man who came along. There was an implicit meaning in their choice of partners that men were not to be used as impersonal "sex objects" or "relationship objects." Rather, women chose on the basis of their affinity for the person. As one 30-year-old woman explained:

> I picked out the—well, I thought, maybe I'd just sleep around. I mean, I've never had more than one lover at a time (before marriage), but I thought, "Ah! I'll just sleep with everyone in sight." I kind of intended to do that, at first, but I couldn't. I didn't, I— when it came right down to it, I didn't want somebody I didn't like inside my body. I picked out the fellow, the boy, who was the closest to me, as a person, who I felt the most affinity with as a human being, rather than the one who I initially desired the most.

Thus, women retained traditional feminine concerns for the person, but rejected romantic ideology and its belief in the uniqueness of the chosen one, in the transition to these first extramarital relationships.

STEP 3: EXTRAMARITAL SEX

Initiating Sexual Intercourse

In traditional sociosexual situations, women do not reach out to initiate sex with men.[21] Although almost all the women had defined the first opportunities they encountered as unsolicited on their part, by the time they actually engaged in their first extramarital relationship, they were less passive and were taking more initiative. One quarter of the women thought they were responsible for the relationship, about one-half felt it was a mutual idea, and the rest believed it was primarily the man's idea. For example:

> I think it was our idea. I think it was—ah—ah—I was not consciously aware of making a move toward him when I confided my recent—ah— experience (with a man who decided he didn't want to get involved). Although I must have. After I came home, after he had propositioned me—I came right home, I had to sit down and have two drinks right away. I was very nervous about it. I was not expecting it consciously. So he says that it was his idea and he was reluctant to say anything to me about it, and I can admit now that probably part of it was mine; so I'll say ours. (age 27)

> The idea to get involved was both of ours, except that I concealed my feelings as much as possible for as long as possible. (age 34)

> It was really his idea to get involved. I think it was in the back of my head, from the time we met, but he was the one who brought it up, he was the one who made the plans initially. And he and I have talked about that, that he was really ready and looking. I was obviously more ready than I thought I was. (age 30)

> We met each other and wound up talking in one of the places where people congregate around school. He offered to drive me home that night and he was making a pass at me before I knew it. So it was basically his idea. (age 28)

Even when the idea for the sexuality was defined as mutual, there often was a note of ambivalence on the woman's part in showing readiness, and in most cases the precipitating action was taken by the male. Males again here assumed their usual sexually aggressive role as their part of the transition process. Although these women were comfortable in acting upon nontraditional motivations for entering a relationship, most of them conformed to traditional gender patterns in initiating actual sexual activity.

Interestingly enough, in the situations when women did initiate action almost all of these involved a relationship with a younger man. The accounts of two such women follow:

> It was my idea to get involved...We had talks and then he took me—I expressed an interest in his parents' farm and he took me home to his parents' home to his farm, and I put new sheets on the bed, and went out and got some jelly for my

diaphragm, and I got him to take me out for supper. And when he drove me home I asked him if he would come and sleep with me. Very difficult to do, I've never done that before. I always waited to be asked. He was very surprised, of course, because I'm a nice married lady. (age 30; partner 24)

I really—I advanced (sic) him. I mean—because I was really going crazy one night; my husband was gone and I was just in that mood, and I did advance to him. I was afraid that he was going to turn me down. That's what was most embarrassing. That was the only thing I was worried about, to be turned down. That would be the most crushing— but he didn't turn me down. (age 29; partner 22, husband's brother)

These women usually experienced some difficulty in stepping out of the passive role and having to confront the more usual male gender role problems of aggressiveness and possible rejection. Probably the relative status superiority of these women over their relationship partners—in age, marital status (both men were single), and sexual experience—was an important factor in allowing this role reversal, for when men act as the sexual initiators it is usually with these status advantages on their side. No doubt women in general do feel freer today to initiate relationships, be they premarital, marital, or extramarital, as a result of the recent changes in women's position in society. To achieve a situation in which both women and men equally feel free to be initiators— certainly one of the conditions of sexual equality—requires that their social and economic positions be equalized first. And this, most people will agree, will take considerably more effort and time.

Reaction to First Extramarital Sex

Since this was their first extramarital sex, and a heretofore "forbidden" experience, were women able to enjoy it? Were they nervous, calm, apprehensive, or confident?

For most of the women, their first extramarital sex was a pleasurable experience. Very simply, they enjoyed it. The favorable reactions tended to vary from mild to intense in degree, while those few reactions that were unfavorable were always moderate. No one had a severe negative response. Of course, it may be that any woman who did have such a reaction would not be inclined to respond to a research project like this one, so there may be an unknown but unavoidable bias in these responses. The following excerpts illustrate the range of positive yet moderate reactions:

> My reaction during and after my first sexual relationship was satisfaction, a sense of pleasure, relaxation, total enjoyment. It told me that I could handle a situation like this.
>
> It was like, "Why did I wait so long?" It was very satisfying. I was also having sexual problems with my husband aside from everything else. And this was really a very, very good thing for me. I saw myself as a woman and sexually satisfying to somebody.
>
> It just always seemed there was a huge divide between the faithful wife and the unfaithful wife, and you know the divide is so insignificant in terms of emotional impact and in terms of actual procedure that it really—it was another dumb thing, like virginity...I feel like I am over a hurdle and I'm really liberated by it.
>
> I felt it was very significant. I felt all my old, puritanical things dropping away. I felt myself opening up much more as a person. I was able to please him, and I was able to please myself. I learned a great deal about myself.

Women's reactions contradict traditional myths that women can achieve sexual satisfaction only in marriage, and that guilt will ruin any sex that violates the marriage bed. Not only are these women capable of enjoying sex outside of marriage, but also the extra sex is often equally as good or better than marital sex. This was a finding as far back as Kinsey's time, and as recently as 1974, but again, it is not a belief that is dominant in our consciousness of female sexuality.[22]

An intriguing secondary theme running through the women's comments is a sense of learning, self-recognition, and self-discovery that occurs as a consequence of the new sexual behavior. "It told me I could handle a situation like this"; "I saw myself as sexually satisfying"; "I felt all my old, puritanical things dropping away." This kind of revelation and the perception that one *can* enjoy extramarital intercourse are the kinds of knowledge about the sexual self that can only be gained through direct experience.

The few cases of dissatisfaction resulted from either situational obstacles or, paradoxically, from the uneasiness of the male partner:

> My reaction was negative. There was too much of a return to adolescent frantic looking for a place to go to bed and always being afraid of being discovered.
>
> Disappointment. I feel bad saying that, but I hadn't realized

that he would be so inexperienced. And I'm not talking about technique; I think technique is revolting. I am thinking, though, that he seemed to feel so shy and self-conscious. I didn't have an orgasm but then, in all my love affairs, I never have the first time. So I felt disappointed, in a way, sexually, but closer emotionally.

It was like we were both so scared and so frightened and he was so straight and had never done anything like this before in his whole life. He was petrified. We sat on the bed and talked for two hours and finally I said to him, "This is ridiculous. I am not going to waste the whole night sitting here talking to you." And I grabbed him...

The behavior of these two men reminds us that men also can and do deviate from what is socially expected. Traditional gender roles may not fit the capabilities or preferences of all men any more than they do all women. We will undoubtedly see increasing variation in male sexual behavior as men become more interested in loosening constraints in their social roles.

The remaining one-quarter of the women described rather intense emotional reactions to their first extramarital sex. These were also mostly favorable, but they were also more likely than the moderate reactions to contain negative self-evaluation. It also proved to be an experience that provoked a mental rerun of some elements from their pasts:

> It was pretty traumatic the first time, because I couldn't believe that it really happened. I kept saying to myself, "I can't believe this is really happening. Maybe we shouldn't finish this." I must have really sounded like an idiot when I think back on it. I was thinking I was really cool, having my first affair, and then saying things like "Maybe we shouldn't finish. Why don't we stop now?" ...Afterward I felt kind of strange. I really felt that something was wrong with me. You know, I started thinking about the nuns saying, "Don't let those things happen!"

At the same time it tended to provoke an upheaval in their present identities:

> It was absolutely the most beautiful experience of my life. It was right out of the romantic novels of the 19th century. Oh, it was just fantastic! And he felt the same way; so much so that I came back the next night...
>
> At this point I was beginning to feel very guilty...I always

had this picture of my husband...that he was just as pure and chaste as the driven snow, and now here I am, a fallen woman. Again, you know, I thought all the blame was going to fall on me and I thought I just can't live like that any more. Even if it had never gone beyond that first kissing...at least it woke me up to the fact that I am alive, I am capable, I'm not dead. I really had reached the point where I thought sex is for the 20 year olds, and I was just settling very nicely into middle age at 35.

I was floored. I was more astonished at my reaction than anything else. Which was that I'd always been fairly passive in bed. I knew that. It was something I never dealt with but I just knew I wasn't particularly aggressive, and I just thought, "Well, that's how I am." And the first time we slept together, I found myself —it's hard to divorce the first time from the first couple of times—I found myself very, very turned on, and I guess because I was turned on for the first time that I became sexually aggressive, very much so, in fact, and it shocked me. It just seemed so natural and the sex was just unbelievable. It was a sexual experience that I don't think I'll ever have again.

For these women the intensity of the transition to the first extramarital involvement represented much more than just a sexual encounter. The intensity of their emotional reaction indicates the extent of disturbance in previously held beliefs about the self. By following personal desires into their first extramarital sex, they discovered selves that contrasted sharply with the ones they knew themselves to be in marriage, their socially approved relationship. The experience of these "intense reactors" accentuates the reports of the moderate group of women that extramarital activity can be a social event and a learning experience with consequences for sexual and self identity.

STEP 4: AFTERWARDS

Rationale (or Rationalization) for Involvement?

When people do things they hadn't expected to do, particularly when those things are socially disapproved, the rationale or "account" they give afterward often reveals a great deal about the meaning of their behavior. It specifically can inform us about the impact of their actions on the self-concept or identity.

Accounts have been classified into two basic types. "Excuses" are those accounts in which an individual accepts social definitions that the behavior is wrong, but seeks to eliminate responsibility for the actions. "Justifications" are accounts in which an individual assumes responsibility for the behavior but denies that it is wrong.[23] In another version of justifications for unanticipated behavior, a sociologist terms them rationalizations. That is, the explanations may not be entirely factual, but are offered so that persons can legitimate their behavior and keep their self-images intact.[24] In the case of extramarital involvement, the explanations offered can help us understand the effect on women's self-image, and whether or not women are redefining the meaning of this activity for themselves from deviant to acceptable. In other words, after the event, did women feel they had done wrong?

Approximately three-quarters of the women offered "justifications" for their involvement; that is, they assumed responsibility for their actions and denied the negative connotations attributed by society:

> It seemed like a sort of exciting and interesting thing to do. I have this sort of existential philosophy about things in general, that time is marching on and there are so many things to do and live and feel. This really, without too much thought to it, was just one more thing that would make me live and grow and give me a whole new dimension to life.

> It's really strange what kinds of needs will get people into relationships and mine was needing someone who shared my curiosity. I guess that's the best word for it. Curiosity—about the whole cotton-pickin' world. I was emerging again. I was breaking out of years of being the Brownie Scout mother and the cookie baker and the Sunday school teacher. And I was exploding with ideas, with all kinds of things which I wanted somebody to share with me, to kick around with me, and to explore and to debate, to get excited about.

> When the whole thing started I thoroughly convinced myself that it was for experimental purposes only.... I just wanted to see—well, if I did spend time with someone else, go to a movie or go out on a date—how would I react to that person? Would I in any way feel farther away from my husband or would I feel closer to him? Maybe I would just feel this is what I want again, to be out dating other people.

> Frankly, I realized very fast that love doesn't mean fidelity, and you can separate—sometimes sex and love go together and it's great—but when they don't, well, you have to take the moments you can enjoy.

Running through the justifications is a thread of what has been called a "peculiarly modern type of justification, namely, *self-fulfillment*."[25] The emphasis in sexual relationships on self-fulfillment and the reactions to the first extramarital sex contrast sharply with the traditional model of women's sexuality—as existing for the purpose of other people (men) and other things (procreation). These women have different beliefs about the purpose of their sexuality. Even in the face of such beliefs, however, it is still possible to experience conflict, anxiety, or guilt about extramarital sex, as about one-third of the women who offered justifications did.

Since some women did have a negative emotional reaction afterward, even though they said they felt justified in their behavior, is it fair to ask whether their justifications were really *rationalizations*? Perhaps only the women, or their therapists (if they had them), might know for sure. It is plausible, however, that doubting the truth of their justifications arises from a traditional morality that says women should *not* feel justified in having extramarital sex, for it makes all of us who retain some attachment to traditional beliefs uncomfortable.

But there is another sociological answer to this question of why guilt or anxiety may accompany justifications. The presence of these emotional reactions suggests a residual attachment to the negative value generally assigned to extramarital sex. It is evidence also of process in intrapersonal change. Feelings, belief, and behavior do not all change at the same rate. Ambivalent feelings about the negative value of an act can still be present even when a woman has reached a point where she thinks she is personally justified in performing that act.

Such ambivalence demonstrates that there is another kind of account for behavior in which people accept both the responsibility for and the negative judgement of their action. In the most extreme example of this type, one woman even labeled herself in traditionally moralistic fashion, as adulteress.

The other one-quarter of the women offered excuses, an account in which persons deny responsibility for their actions but accept the negative value of their acts. Their excuses implied a fatalistic cause for their involvement and represented a pattern of "it just happened" statements. Since about one-half of the "excusers" reported no guilt and gave no other evidence that they accepted the negative definition of extramarital sex, these reports represent a fourth kind of account, in which persons deny both responsibility and the negative value of the act.

For these women having their first extramarital involvements, guilt and other negative emotions were more frequently associated with excuses than with justifications, which means that women who "justified" probably are changing their belief systems more so than women who excused. To emphasize this, three-quarters of these women offered justifications for their first extramarital relationship. Such women may be adopting a new ideology about marriage, sex, and monogamy which says that extramarital behavior is acceptable.

Analyzing accounts of behavior not only has value for understanding its meaning, but it also may help to predict future actions and feelings. (See the figure for the four kinds of "accounts" or explanations we have identified.)

	RESPONSIBILITY	
	Denies	Accepts
NEGATIVE VALUE OF ACT Denies	Anomic	Justified
Accepts	Excused	Conflicted

(Figure 1: Typology of Accounts Offered)

For instance, a woman who offered an account which denied both personal responsibility and negative connotations—anomic in the figure—may be likely to continue extramarital involvements because there is no psychic cost such as guilt or anxiety. "It's just something that happened. Besides, it's over now." Such a woman would be least likely to adopt a conscious belief in her right to have involvements because she tends not to have internalized either negative or positive beliefs about it. Similarly, a woman who excused her behavior, but felt some guilt, is unlikely to choose consciously to engage in more involvements because she denies personal responsibility for her actions. She may revert to conventional behavior because she still feels extramarital sex is not acceptable, or she may continue it as a deviant activity, e.g., "I know I'm doing wrong, but I can't help myself."

A woman who justified is the most likely one to continue involvements, because she has already consciously chosen to have her first involvement and she rejects negative definitions, e.g., "I have a right to do this and I feel it is a good thing to do." Finally, a woman whose account was conflicted is most likely to undergo severe intrapersonal suffering. If she is able to resolve her conflict, and if she has appropriate options and personal resources at her disposal, she may emerge with a change in identity and/or life style as a resolution of the crisis.

An Uncommon Woman

To illustrate this "conflicted" reaction, as well as to highlight the transitional process, the experience of one woman will be presented at considerable length. Several years ago, Althea, then forty-two, high school educated, married, with four children, began working as a clerk at a resort in the West. She found herself unexpectedly attracted to the manager of the shop, who was thirty years old and married. Her account of this extramarital relationship is remarkable for its insight, emotion, and honesty.

> I had never had an opportunity for an affair before. It was a very narrow life that I led before; I was Raymond's wife, that was all over my life, it was stamped on everything. I was never aware that anyone was particularly interested in me and I was never particularly interested in someone else…
>
> I wasn't aware that I was dissatisfied with my marriage, I wasn't looking to have an affair at the time and then I met Kim and I found him very physically attractive, extremely so. I started fantasizing a lot and reaching out in ways—it was hard to remember how to do it almost. Then I began to see things in my life that I didn't like and I found excuses, maybe, for saying what I was doing was right.…
>
> I knew him four months before we got sexually involved, and yes, I still feel I was in love with him at the time. No, he was not in love with me.
>
> We had worked together for four months every day and one day one of the girls…was not working up to par…and he asked me what was wrong with her. (Her boyfriend had just gone back to his Army post.) I said, 'You know, girls need it, too. They miss it when they don't get it.' He laughed and said "The trouble with women is that they don't know enough to go get it when they want it." I laughed and that was the end of the conversation.
>
> That idea stuck in my head and stuck in my head and I kept thinking about it. 'Was that true?' And I said, 'Yes, I guess that was true for most of us.'
>
> Well, when the end of the season came…we had a party one night…and at that point I knew he was leaving and I was leaving and I wouldn't see him. So as people started leaving (the party) and we were left there pretty much alone I said to him, 'I'd like to talk to you.'

> We went over from the bar to a table and sat down and I said, 'Remember the conversation we had about Cathy?' and he hadn't, so I reminded him of the conversation and he said 'Yeah, that's true.' And I said, 'Well, I want *you*.' And he just — (laughs) — it was really — his facial expression was really tremendous and he said, 'Uh — do you know what you're saying?' And I said yes, and we talked about it some more back and forth and about what it involved, about husbands and wives. I told him I had never been with anyone besides my husband, which amazed him.
>
> He said something about going out to the car and we could make love in the car. I said that I had never made love in a car and I wasn't going to start then and so we ended up at a motel. It was really a beautiful thing. We had a good time. I remember when we got there we were kissing and things and I got sort of concerned about my physical appearance — my body isn't that great, I said, 'I'm not young and I'm not beautiful.' And he kissed me and said 'You're beautiful because you want me.' That's one of the nicest ways I can think of to start an affair.

Althea's is an example of an extremely dramatic and unanticipated path into unconventionality. Although she had read about "affairs" she felt "that was for other people. I'd never thought of myself in those terms." She had heard some talk in the neighborhood about women who had "affairs," but "just didn't understand it and thought the way I was living was the way you should live."

The only prior hint of her transition was to be found in a joking situation:

> We had one couple we were friends with that we used to joke and say that we would stay with our partners in this world but in the next one we would switch, but that was just a funny kind of ha-ha thing, I never thought in terms of.... I didn't fantasize or do any of that.

One of the functions of humor, of course, is to allow us to say or "test," without penalty, thoughts or ideas which would usually not be tolerated by ourselves or others.

The most outstanding factor for Althea, however, was the completely self-initiated nature of her transition. Without any social support she decided to throw over her past patterns of behavior and step out of the traditional female role, choosing a partner totally in violation of age and appearance norms and, furthermore, assuming the role of sexual initiator. The gender role-breaking nature of her behavior is clearly acknowledged in the disbelief and confusion of Kim's initial reply. Nevertheless, she did not waver when he questioned her intentions. She did not experience any remorse or conflict later, perhaps, in part, because of the support and acceptance by her partner.

> I had a great time in the afterward.... I didn't feel unhappy. I was really pleased with myself, I felt I had taken a giant step forward. I sound like the man who landed on the moon, but it was that big in my life.
>
> When I talked with Kim a couple of days later he said that going home he had been wondering what I was feeling and what I was going to do when I woke up the next morning when I realized what I had done. By the way, we were not drunk or anything like that. We had been drinking, but I was not drunk and I knew what I was doing. And I was happy with what I was doing; I never to this day regretted having taken that first step.

That first step, dramatic as it was, was taken not only at considerable upheaval in personal identity but also in the face of complex social entanglements—family and church—which locked her into a web of conformity.

> I realized that in what I was doing I had become an adulteress...but psychologically I didn't feel guilty...the situational obstacles were tremendous. How would I manage just to have time to be with him? And religion was a big thing. This was important at that point to me. And because I considered this so important to me, I felt in all honesty—because it was contrary to my religious beliefs—that I had to give up my religion and I have and I haven't regretted that. I haven't found it that much of a void, not spiritually. Materially I did because I was very involved in church activity and not having those activities, the committees, the Sunday School teaching, without that to do I found myself with a lot of time on my hands. Well, I got involved in a crisis hotline; it was a shifting of causes, so to speak. I handled it as I had to, by just working it out in my head.

The extramarital relationship and the related behavior of this woman became a catalyst for a transformation in her life style. Not only did she renounce her religion and substitute new voluntary activities, but also she went on to reevaluate her marriage and adjust her relationship with her husband and children to give herself some personal time and freedom. She abandoned old friends and acquired new ones, and in a sense, did the same with her personal identity. Symbolically, she dropped the "Mrs. Raymond Smith" name she had used and became simply "Althea," not even "Althea Smith," for a period of time until her new identity stabilized. She emerged as a person more fully self-fulfilled.

By the time of the last follow-up interview in 1979, Althea had utilized the experience of her volunteer work to obtain a full-time job she found very involving and satisfying. She has continued her marriage because:

> ...I do love him. I plan to stay (with him). I'm not looking for another husband or a way out. But I do feel that I need something more than he is able to give me, both—not physically and mentally, more mentally but physically, too. It's just a reaffirmation that I am alive.

Although the sexual aspects of her first relationship ended after a few months, Althea has retained a friendship with her first lover. She has also continued extramarital involvements with several other men in the intervening years.

Although this woman's experience was the most striking in the extent and suddenness of transformation, particularly since it occurred at a relatively late stage of adult life, it illustrates well the latent capacity for self-initiated change that probably exists in all of us, even the most conforming.[26] It underscores the fine and tenuous line that we draw in our lives to keep ourselves on one or the other side of convention. It is also an example of the kind of female independence that may be expected as a result of liberating influences in our culture. And it emphasizes the relationship of sexuality to other areas of women's lives. Women's sexuality has long been more rigidly controlled in the culture than men's and the way women used their sexuality—whether they married or not, whether they became mothers or not—has always been a major source of their social identity. Therefore, the more extensive and intensive changes are in their sexual behavior, the more likely that behavior will impact dramatically in other areas of their personal and social lives.

Chapter Three

Extramarital Intimacy

Some clues to the meanings of extramarital relationships to these women have already emerged in the accounts of why they first became involved. Only half of the women were reacting—in part—to unsatisfactory marriages. Most were also searching to fulfill their expanding potential for personal growth.

To explore more deeply the meanings of involvement to these women, I asked them questions in the initial interview about their most recent relationship. For 40% of the women, their most recent relationship was also their only one. Nearly all the relationships women talked about in response to these questions were ongoing at the time of the interview; the remaining few had occurred during the previous two years so that recalling events and emotions was not a difficult problem.

The shortest relationship still in progress was just two months old. At the other extreme, one was ongoing after sixteen years. (A few of the women had had "one-night stands" at some point, but none of these was their most recent relationship.) In some cases women saw their extramarital partners as often as every day—usually where they worked together.[1] Most of the women, however, saw their extramarital partners about once a week for several hours at a time. In a few cases women saw them only once a year for several days. These were "long distance" relationships in which the partners lived as far apart as opposite coasts, real life equivalents of the characters in the play and film *Same Time, Next Year*. In this plot the happily married participants in an extramarital involvement meet once a year, for a week, over a period of twenty-five years.

Although nearly all women had been pleased with their initial extramarital encounters, is it possible that their first reaction was to the glow of a new relationship? That the novelty of the experience was responsible for their positive evaluations? Perhaps, over time, the relationships or their partners disappointed the implicit expectations the women held?

Just about half of the women had rather definite expectations when they began their relationships. Most could be described as rather realistic and generalized—"fun," "a casual relationship," "an opportunity to know someone," "just an affair." What they anticipated turned out to match quite accurately the reality of their involvements.

There were several exceptions to this. Four women who anticipated light, short-term relationships, found they grew into deeper, longer-lived involvements, which, in one case, became a factor in the break-up of a marriage. Three other women with more specific expectations of extramarital intimacy found they were not met. Two were disappointed romantically:

> I expected it to be much more romantic (laughs). I didn't expect him to be exactly like his brother (her husband). I didn't expect him to take me anyplace because I knew he didn't have any money... It wasn't what I expected, but I don't know what I expected. All I know is that it wasn't all it's cracked up to be.

> I expected that there would be a lot of glamour related to it, certainly no problems (laughs). Fun, a lot of fun and a lot of time with the person. But there was not enough time, and we spent too much time on the "heavies," working out the relationship, on getting to know each other and talking about the problems.

And one who was disappointed sexually:

> I expected it to be exciting and sexually fulfilling. It certainly was exciting because of all the hassles, but sexually it was not as fulfilling as I had hoped, so it did not meet my expectations there.

Traditional elements of romance, usually found in the initial stages of first involvemet, were a very minor part of these relationships. Only four women had described themselves as being "in love" at the time of first involvement, and most of the other women did *not* fall in love as time went by, or when they became subsequently involved with other men. In response to questions concerning their emotional feelings, about two-thirds of the women said they "liked" or were "friends" with their extramarital partners. These friendship feelings generally occurred in short-term relationships, those of less than a year.

It was principally in the longer lasting relationships, those of a year or more, that love feelings surfaced. Approximately one-quarter of the women defined their feelings as "love," but only a few said they were "in love." Moreover, women carefully qualified the "love" responses to mean a "human" type of love, or a "person-to-person" love. They specifically rejected traditional romantic feelings, as well as the traditional words, "in love," to describe their feelings. They did not use passion to excuse their involvements. With but one or two exceptions, they were not "torn between two lovers" due to their extramarital involvements.

Women's descriptions constituted a new vocabulary of love or, at least, an attempt to describe an affection that is not the same as romantic love. Several commented on how difficult it was to find words that accurately conveyed their feelings. They were caught in the dilemma of language lagging behind changes in our emotions and behavior. Another example of this language lag is that we do not yet have a commonly accepted word to describe the partners of unmarried people who live together. Similarly, we do not have a non-pejorative term to describe extramarital partners, a problem I have experienced in this research. Although I will use the term "lover" at times, it does not seem to convey accurately the quality that the involvements had for most of these women. "Lover" has connotations from another time, not precisely suited for the meanings of extramarital relationships of the 1980's.

To uncover the qualities of these relationships, I asked the women directly, "What does having this relationship mean to you?" Most of the answers centered around one of two themes. The first of these concerned the kind of relationship they were having:

> This relationship means a great deal to me, as we explore our many differences and similarities, discuss a variety of issues, and express ourselves physically. It is a total trip, taken very slowly since we have as much time as we need to really get to know each other.

> It was my first open relationship. That was very important. I will do things that way in the future in spite of the pain.

> It meant learning about another person.

> It was a very long-term closeness with another person. I wanted to—and it seemed very natural to—to extend that closeness to include sex.

> It meant having another friend.

> It was like being with a soul brother. It was nice to be able to share intellectually, sexually, emotionally.

> It was very important. It started off just being sexual, but changed to a more encompassing relationship.

In their answers, these women clearly revealed a preference for extramarital relationships that rested on a complex of factors—intellectual, social, emotional—revolving around the sexual element. Only one woman gave her involvement a purely sexual meaning:

> I wasn't really interested in a relationship. I just slept with him for sex.

The second theme in women's responses was a frank reference to their personal needs and desires. For a few, particularly those whose marriage was at a low point, the extramarital intimacy helped to fill a painful void in their lives:

> It was an ego trip because I was feeling so down on myself. I had virtually no social or sexual activity for fourteen months.

> It made me happy at a time when there wasn't a lot to be happy about.

A few, very simply, just enjoyed additional attention:

> It was fun, the closest I ever came to being a kept woman. I got really spoiled by the whole thing. Going out to fancy lunches... and there's something very therapeutic about spending a couple of hours in a hotel room in the middle of a business day...just the attention of someone calling every day, and at the same time making no demands, like I've got to see you or something.

A third group, the largest of those who mentioned personal needs and desires, found self-expression to be the significant meaning for them:

> It meant I was a person, not an appendage of my husband.

> It makes me feel so completely a woman.

> It's made me a happy person because I'm doing what I feel without worrying about someone's rules. I'm the last person that people would think would break a rule...I don't believe in waking up at sixty-five years old and regretting the chances that you never took.

The majority of the responses, which alluded to the kind of relationship or to self-expressive needs, represent a distinctly modern vocabulary of meanings. Women, in talking about the kind of involvement they had, are saying they enjoy the pleasures of relating interpersonally to a variety of people. They are reflecting contemporary attitudes which emphasize adding greater personal contact and intimacy to our private lives as an antidote to the increasing isolation and impersonality of American life.[2] Whether individuals seek to find greater intimacy and to increase their network of associates through encounter groups, neighborhood centers, retirement community activities, therapy groups, or extramarital encounters is a difference of degree, not of kind.[3] The meanings of all human activity—whether it is work, education, marriage, or politics—are affected by central trends in cultural values. To interpret extramarital intimacy only in terms of its relationship to individual marriages is to overlook part of its meaning that is affected by changing cultural values.

The motivation of self-fulfillment that women cited also rests on a uniquely contemporary concept, that of knowing, developing, or rewarding the self through interaction with others.[4] The unprecedented affluence of modern society, distributed among many more people than ever before in our history, allows us the freedom and luxury to concentrate on self-development. For most of us, our lives are no longer limited by the sheer physical struggle to stay alive. Consequently, we can afford to devote more of our time and energy to the nonphysical aspects of living that make life more pleasurable and rewarding.[5] This psychic satisfaction is dependent on the quality of our relationships with others. We learn about others by interacting with them, and at the same time we learn about ourselves through the social reflection we get from others.[6] These twin pleasures, relating to others and learning about the self through outside relationships, were the dominant meanings of extramarital intimacy to these women.

Since it was surprising to find the social meanings of these relationships so overpowering the sexual ones, I continued to probe this point further. "What do you get from the relationship?" I asked the women. Here, again, about half of them emphasized the same meanings of relating to others:

> I guess essentially what I get is the companionship, the closeness and the ability to communicate with a male.
>
> The feeling of being treated as an equal; poems from him, all kinds of communication.
>
> Mostly I get the enjoyment of really getting to know another human being, and working out the differences into a mean-

> ingful relationship. That means just knowing that he cares, without needing him to remind me often, regardless of whether he calls or not.
>
> Essentially it was the pleasure of knowing completely a beautiful person who thought of me as being equally beautiful.

Their responses accentuated the mutuality of communciating and caring, while about one-quarter of the women focused on their receiving emotional and psychic benefits from the relationship:

> I get a variety. Other than that it was a real stroke, an ego boost, and one that I really needed right then, because I was doing a whole lot to hold other people together and had no support for myself—and this guy was really neat about that. Plus I knew how turned on he was to me, to my head.
>
> It made me feel really cared for; it made me feel I was special.

A prominent theme was a recognition that the emotional rewards they received contributed to their development as independent persons:

> I got self-confidence, a feeling of individuality, a self-reliance that I didn't have before, and understanding that I have resources and abilities, too, to meet my needs.
>
> I get the satisfaction of knowing that I could do it out of this relationship. I had often wondered if I could—and I did. I got attention, I got—ah—just a good feeling, satisfaction.
>
> He was very supportive; everything I did was good—uh—and I needed it—a lot. Along with supportive he also encouraged me to be my own person. He tried to develop that (independence) in me and he was highly successful. I was successful, but he helped me an awful lot in bringing out the independence.

Only one-quarter of the women talked about the dimensions of sex, variety, and thrills that one might more typically expect from extramarital activity. It cofirmed the pattern of the previous responses to find sex mentioned so rarely in answers to questions about what is commonly imagined to be a primarily sexual activity. Even the responses that reflected this typical image of extramarital involvements tended to overlap with the reward of interpersonal pleasure:

> Well, I get a kick out of the relationship. It's a thrill for me...

what I get out of the relationship is mostly the thrill of being with a man who wants me as a woman, in a sexy way.

The relationship, as far as I was concerned, although I was trying to rationalize that I cared for him, was mostly for sex. One of the things that intrigued me was—he said every time he did it, it was in a different way. I suppose in a certain way I was also fascinated by the fact that he was a black guy, too. I guess I was a little curious about that and whatnot.

It's a thrill; it's really a thrill. Also it's a way of knowing a serious, incredibly worthwhile person. And if I hadn't gotten involved with him, I wouldn't have known him as well. My life would be less if I had not met him and gotten to know him so well.

At first glance, it could be said that nothing is new in this pattern of social meanings, since women are expected to be more interested in the social rather than the sexual aspects of relationships. Both sociological and psychological theorists have described the female role as centered on relating to others.[7] Females are said to be "expressive" specialists, to be interested in nurturance and emotional support of others, to enjoy communicating words and feelings to people. Conversely, males are said to be "instrumental," to focus on things and goals and to be only secondarily interested in their relationships with people.

If women placed an overwhelming emphasis on the expressive aspects of their extramarital relatioships, they were just being traditionalists. It may be said that even this group of women who have embraced social change in their lives haven't really changed that much, although they may have dared to get extramaritally involved. But place a more discerning eye on their meanings— and note that women emphasized the mutuality of the expressiveness, or in some cases the getting instead of giving of emotional support, which *is* a significant variation on the usual female role. These women are not throwing away their traditional interest in expressiveness, but they do want to reshape and modernize it. They no longer wish to be part of the emotional "blood bank" system that we have set up between the sexes, in which women are consistently donors and men consistently withdrawers.[8] They want to be able to get back as much as they put in, and in some cases, they need, situationally or temporarily, to receive transfusions. So prevalent is this pattern in all the responses that the sole deviation shines like a beacon of traditionalism. Said a woman who became involved with the husband of a neighbor, "I felt like I was helping him."

Didn't they already get this emotionality and expressiveness from their husbands? Apparently not, for when asked what was the least satisfactory area of their marriages, all but one answered that it was in the area of communication. This pattern, a common one in American marriage,[9] originates in the different expectations, training, and rewards—the process of socialization—we teach to girls and boys while they are growing up. Put simply, to fill their future adult roles boys have been taught to be active, to be competent and goal-oriented—to be instrumental. Girls have been encouraged to be passive and to be attuned to people and their feelings—to be "expressive."[10] To be masculine and instrumental, then, is to be tough, competitive, quiet, and unemotional. To be feminine and expressive is to be gentle, cooperative, verbal, and responsive.

When they marry each other, this training served well in a world in which men used their instrumental ability to earn the family paycheck and women depended on their "people" skills to rear children and tend to their husbands. But that was yesterday. In today's world more than half of all married women are earning paychecks as well as running a home. Most men are now in jobs that require highly developed social skills to get along with their co-workers.

Marriage has always rested on men and women mutually exchanging skills, whether those skills are earning money, cooking, or taking care of one's spouse sexually.[11] When one partner starts to contribute more in one area, the other is expected to match that contribution in some way. Women, as a consequence of the additional economic resources they bring to marriage, and as a result of the contemporary reexamination of their roles, are raising their expectations of men in the expressive area. Although it seems likely that this is more true of middle-class marriages, family researcher Lillian Rubin reports that working-class wives also are looking for more expressiveness in their husbands. In return for their swelling economic competence, increasing numbers of women are anticipating a surge of expressive competence in men.[12] Emotionality, sensitivity, perceptiveness, and communication are going to have to go "unisex" to keep pace with this revolution of rising expressive expectations in marriage.[13] If we continue to socialize boys to be "expressive virgins" at marriage, they will have as difficult a time fulfilling the emotional expectations of their wives as women in the past, socialized to be sexual virgins at marriage, have had in meeting their husbands' erotic expectations.

Two male sociologists, Balswick and Peek, argue differently, however. They claim that despite the training men receive to be inexpressive,[14] they learn to be "situationally expressive" in marriage, and that emotional promiscuity with women in general may actually threaten the stability of a marriage.

There are a number of problems with this argument. First, there is as yet no research evidence to prove that men do become situationally expressive in marriage, or how they do it, if they do.[15] Furthermore, impressionistic evidence gathered from women in various life situations suggests that the expressively competent husband is a very scarce specimen. Second, it does not follow that an emotionally proficient husband will become emotionally promiscuous any more than a sexually proficient one will become sexually promiscuous. The possible misuse of a talent is a weak argument for not developing that talent.

A strong argument can be made, however, to destroy the traditional female monopoly on emotionality. Both men and women could benefit by making expressive competence a unisexual trait. Marriage satisfaction would increase for those wives who value this trait in a husband. Husbands would feel increased self-esteem for having met their wives' expectations, and it would also add to their share of power in marriage in the same way that wives' working magnifies their respective power. Spouses who prefer a monogamous marriage would have an improved probability of keeping it that way, for accumulated research on extramarital behavior suggests that "the greater the discrepancy between the personal and relational satisfaction a person desires and receives from marriage, the more likely is extramarital involvement."[16] In other words, the more closely we meet our spouses' expectations, the less likely they are to seek outside relationships.

Work is another area of life in which male expressive competence is not only desirable, but increasingly rewarded. It is a necessary skill for the successful performance of the more prestigious managerial level jobs. Whether one has to get along with co-workers, clients, or subordinates, interpersonal skills such as communication and sensitivity are the new tools men have to learn to use to be successful. It is the androgynous personality—one that possesses both feminine and masculine traits—that is most successful in interpersonal functioning, according to psychologist

Sandra Bem. There is even the possibility that inexpressiveness may contribute to the higher rates of heart disease in men.[17] If it costs men several years of their lives, the price of inexpressiveness is undeniably exorbitant.

Returning to the discussion of the extramarital involvements, it appears that they represent an opportunity for these women to obtain the expressive equality they are looking for in their relationships with men. These women are social innovators.[18] If they do not find what they want and need in a conventional male-female relationship, they improvise and form new relationships, in this case extramarital ones. This group is an example of women forging their own individual answers in the absence of social solutions to the current disequilibrium in male-female relationships. Sociologically speaking, their actions are a rejection of traditional feminine passivity, of women waiting for things to happen, and a substitution of activity and initiative, to take charge of the shaping of one's own life.

Not only are they implementing a new expressive equality in male-female interaction, but also they are renouncing the traditional moral code for women in order to do so. Breaking the moral code is at least partly culturally predetermined in the extramarital situation. If we examine the set of socially acceptable alternatives, we see that there are none for women and men who wish to enjoy friendly intimacy with each other. Such pairings are always assumed to include sexual expression, so there is a strong inclination for such cross-sex friendships to succumb to the self-fulfilling prophecy of this assumption. It is characteristic of our culture to eroticize the problems of intimacy. We direct nearly all our needs for human warmth to sexual interaction, neglecting the possibilities of friendship. It is necessary to recognize the complex intimacy needs of individuals today, so that we can begin to enlarge social scripts. By defining as acceptable male-female friendship combinations, before, during, and after marriage that do not necessarily include sexual expression, we can enlarge the available options for expressiveness.[19]

What factors made it possible for this group of women to be innovators and to achieve, if only temporarily, the expressive equality they desire in sexual friendships with men? Emerging as non-traditional women, they vigorously believe in male-female equality. That translates into a desire to transform the conditions of their relationship with men. These are women who had been developing a sense of personal power in their lives that carried over into their actions—shaping extramarital relationships according to their preferences.[20] Even in this era of social remodeling of roles in the interests of equality, it is far simpler to mold the form of an interpersonal relationship between two people than to transform entire institutions, such as schools or businesses, in which many people are involved in long-standing and complex patterns of interaction. One person's efforts obviously can have more impact on the interpersonal level.

Another part of the explanation is that extramarital relationships are completely voluntary, unlike marital ones, which most people feel pressured to enter and usually have a vested interest in maintaining. It is highly unlikely that a woman who is dissatisfied with the expressive area of her marriage would choose to begin and continue another relationship, completely voluntary and indeed carrying the risk of social disapproval, that would be lacking in the same area as her marriage. In the rare situation in which a woman was disappointed in this aspect of her extramarital involvement, she moved to end the relationship:

> I would have become more relaxed if he was the kind of person who would talk more, but he wasn't. He was afraid to let his feelings come out.... I don't believe in having a relationship and getting nothing back...that's why I just came to the point where I really couldn't see him anymore.

It may well be that the extramarital experience is the one in which women are freest and most successful in transforming their intimacy with men into a pattern that satisfies their needs and desires. Certainly the traditional patterns of marriage still prove resistant to equal partnership. And the premarital relationships of the 1980's, even though gradually moving toward equality, still offer males increased opportunities for casual, impersonal sex without the expressive context women prefer.[21]

Extramarital Expressiveness

Nearly all of the women did find their expressive needs met by their extramarital relationships. They explained what aspects of expressive communication they found so satisfying. A few were quite poignant when revealing the hunger caused by needs long unmet in their marriage:

> We talked about what happened during our day, stuff I was writing. But his life was very low-key at the time. There was nothing happening, according to him. So it would always be

my bubbling effervescence and he listened. Which was neat. No one had ever done that before. Just sat and listened to me.

Nothing very intellectual. We talked a lot about problems, decisions he had to make in his work. We talked a lot more about him than about me.... I really enjoyed hearing something from him. He could have talked all he wanted to. (laughs) It's just hearing response that I like. That was fun. My husband doesn't say too much.

This fellow I'm with now—he gave me a swat with a pillow the other night (laughs) and you know, I'm just eating it up. My husband never hit me with a pillow in his whole life. I mean that kind of fun—and I have missed thirty years of fun, so I'm just eating it up. This guy, he's a real male chauvinist, but he'll say to me, "C'mon, Ollie Mollie, how about getting supper on the table?" And I love this. Can you believe this? I love this! My husband never called me a funny name, ever, it's not him. Never...ever...I lay in there at night and sometimes I think, "You know, if I were to die tonight this would all be worth it."

Others found similarities with their partners to be the basis for the expressive quality of the relationship:

He is very much the same type of thinker as I am. We can have a topic, and we've gone at it for four hours, and be not near completing it, and I've taken the same question home to my husband and said, "What is love?" for instance. Within ten minutes he had answered it; it was complete, it was over. He didn't think of it any further and to me, that's a frustration. I just can't handle it...I think talking sometimes is much more consuming than sexuality because you have much more time to do it, in a much freer atmosphere and for me that's so paramount that I can't imagine being without it.

We talk about everything. Our families, in the past. We share growing up in the South and a very repressive religious background. We talk about where we want to go, values, is it all worth it. We read a lot of poetry to each other, our own and other people's. I think the superb level at which we communicate is absolutely the most important part of our relationship.

Pretty much human relations type stuff—which we are both interested in—how people deal with each other, philosophy, psychology, maybe a discussion of literature or movies. My husband is not a talker at all. When he talks about things he usually is telling jokes or talks about financial things or about sports. While I think these things are important, I don't think these are the only things, and he cannot carry on a discussion or conversation philosophically. He just can't do it. And so, in a way, this is a very important difference between the two men.

And occasionally, class differences with the partner opened up new worlds for some women:

> The communication is different in every way from that with my husband. I can say anything to him and he listens and understands. Unbelievable. In turn he can and does say anything to me, about his feelings, things he's done. Some things he's told me about himself he's never told anyone else, including his wife. He also writes songs to me—my husband can't even figure out what I'd like for my birthday.... I more or less teach him about feminism and other things he's unfamiliar with, and he's very eager to learn and know. He opens up to me the life of a blue-collar worker. Which he is, and isn't at the same time. He is a car mechanic while going to school at night. He's very creative, artistic, sensitive, and I enjoy experiencing that.

All of the women reported that the communication in their relationship was different from that in their marriage. Women valued diverse aspects of expressiveness. Some needed playfulness, small talk, sensitivity, or just to be listened to. Others preferred intellectual or philosophical discussions, but all knew what it was they lacked or wanted. They succeeded in getting it in their outside relationships.

While I have discussed how women managed to get this extramarital expressiveness, the opposing question—how men managed to give it extramaritally—has not yet been asked. Who were these lovers who seemed so expressively competent, who apparently didn't fit the stereotype of the inexpressive male? One explanation offered by a male sociologist, J.W. Sattell, is that male expressiveness in such situations is merely part of a sexual "con game." It is not so much that men are using a standard "line," but rather that they allow their emotional armor to drop temporarily, exposing their human imperfections, emotions, and concerns. By giving women what they want (expressiveness) men succeed in getting what they want (sex). In this scenario women are deceived into thinking they are getting authentic expressiveness, while in reality men remain in control and give only what they perceive is necessary.

Jack Balswick, a male sociologist previously mentioned, rejects this explanation as "unfair to those inexpressive males who are striving to become more genuine in their relationships."[22] I agree. While deception undoubtedly exists in male-female sexual relationships, I do not believe men and women coexist in such a totally exploitative manner. Further, most of these women were not engaging in "one night stands" when one would expect to find such exploitation. They usually had relationships of many months in which to evaluate their partner's expressive authenticity. It is implausible, I feel, that women, as expressive "specialists," would generally be incapable of detecting male insincerity, especially given this test of time.

The data from this project, based on several factors, sugests a different understanding from Sattell's. First, a number of the men— about a third—were single and young, in their twenties and early thirties. It is probable that maturing in the 1960's and 1970's, when social roles were being examined and modified, enabled them to move away from traditional traits of masculinity.

What about the married and older men with whom the women were involved? Were they other women's inexpressive husbands? Or were they men who somehow managed to escape the trap of inexpressiveness? If they were men who were exceptionally expressive, how did they get that way? One clue is that a few of the men were in helping professions that required high skill levels of communication. They may have selectively gravitated toward these professions because they already possessed expressive qualities, or they may have learned them as part of their professional training.

There is also a final possible factor. Men who are inexpressive in their marriage may be situationally expressive extramaritally, which opposes the assumption that men learn to be expressive within marriage. It may well be that the force of institutionalized marital roles and the burden of husbandly responsibility serve to inhibit expressiveness in marriage.[23] In fact, Balswick asserts that one way to foster men's expressiveness in marriage is to increase their participation in emotional roles such as child rearing. The more time spent on such emotionally involving work, rather than in the usual instrumental work involved in wage earning, the more likely a person will develop expressive ability.[24] Dustin Hoffman's personal transformation as he took on the role of full-time father in *Kramer vs. Kramer* is a good example of this.

With the majority of mothers now working outside the home,

they relieve fathers of part of their economic burden. The structural change required is already in motion in order that men invest more time in fathering and other expressive pursuits. As the provider role becomes interchangeable between men and women, so, too, it becomes possible for mothers and fathers to interchange the child caring role. In fact, it will be necessary for men to take on more fathering behavior in order to avoid overburdening women with two full-time roles. The key, of course, is how much men desire to change and to what degree they will do so.

Recent research offers clues as to which situational factors can foster men's participation in childrearing and probable subsequent emotional development. Those factors that maximize participation are similarity of wives' salary to husbands and the wives' negotiating and bargaining skills. The more powerful the woman is in economic and internal psychological resources, the more she is able to secure successfully her husband's increased involvement in fathering.[25]

The absence of economic responsibility in the extramarital situation may provide men with the necessary freedom to allow their expressiveness to emerge. Traditional monagomous marriage may not be the best vehicle for contemporary males to nurture and maintain expressiveness, especially if they are subject to demands for maximum performance in the instrumental or wage-earning area. Even today as women benefit from contact with a variety of men in developing their sexuality outside of traditional marriage, perhaps men also need expressive contact with a variety of women outside of traditional marriage to develop and display the full range of their emotional talents. The extramarital behavior of these women's partners may be partly in response to the inadequate structure of traditional monogamy, rather than the inadequacies of particular marriages or individuals.

Most past research and interpretations of men's extramarital behavior, however, suggests it is primarily for sexual purposes— to validate the masculine role which emphasizes sexual variety and achievement.[26] Traditionally men have not gotten extramaritally involved for expressive reasons. And certainly men do not yet have the freedom to legitimate their extramarital encounters for expressive reasons, as this group of women is doing.[27]

And yet an intriguing report from the most recent survey into male extramarital sex is that nearly half of the men reported as *one* of the reasons for involvement: "I enjoy relationships with other women, and sex is only part of that." Other reasons cited were desire for variety, additional sex, excitement and adventure, romance, and the wife being away and/or sexually inadequate.

Although this survey did not intensively probe men's feelings on this point, the author does interpret the responses to mean that many married men "seek the social and emotional companionship of other women even when they have a good relationship with their wives."[28] If this is accurate, it corroborates the women's descriptions just presented of a script for contemporary extramarital relations that is based on expressive or humanistic sex, rather than casual, impersonal sex. It also contradicts traditional images of masculine sexuality.

Do some men, at least, prefer expressive extramarital sex? Is this evidence of converging male and female preferences in sexual relationships? Such a convergence is contingent upon increases in male desire for expressive sex and female desire for less romantic sex. We have seen that this group of women, at least, is moving in that direction. If men are moving similarly toward more expressiveness, it suggests new possibilities for both sexes to relate on an equal and nonexploitative basis. Along with female sexuality, male expressiveness is a critical area for further study.[29] Because it is one of the most important influences on the quality of the premarital, marital, and extramarital relations of women and men, it is vital to understand further its present, changing, and future dimensions.

Marriage and Extramarital Meanings

Did the women make any attempt to change the emotional relationship in their marriages, or did they just seek to satisfy their expressive desires extramaritally? Nearly all the women had tried to improve the expressive relationship within their marriages, but met only varying degrees of success. An extensive exploration of the marriage relationships was not part of this project, but there are some reasons why women's efforts would not be totally effective.

I have already pointed to the burden of the husband's role responsibilities. Some husbands simply didn't wish to change. Others did, and managed to change to a certain extent. Even when people want to change, however, patterns established early in childhood are very resistant. We tend to have an emotional attachment to traditional ways of interacting, because it makes us feel secure to continue familiar patterns. Similarly, for a couple, change within an established relationship can be perceived as threatening to the relationship and something to be avoided; it substitutes unpredictability for the comfort and ease of repeating the past. So powerful is this pull from the past that even newly married couples who desire to have a nontraditional marriage find themselves reverting to old, familiar ways of marriage. Therefore, it was probably far easier for the women to begin a new, if only temporary, relationship and establish at the onset a pattern of equal expressive interaction, than to remodel the long-standing patterns of communication and interaction in their marriages.

Marital Meanings

Women identified the least satisfactory area of their marriage as the expressive area. But what did they value most about their marriages? For the women who were generally pleased with their marriages, security proved to be the most attractive feature:

> What I was getting out of marriage—what I wanted—was a sense of security, of not being alone in the world, some sort of stability.
>
> My marriage is sensible, structured, typical.
>
> I get respect as an individual, I care about him, we have a child together.
>
> I get security from my marriage.
>
> Security, financial and social. It's a comfortable relationship at this point. We understand each other very well. We don't have very many arguments. We agree on important things. We have developed a life style that is comfortable for both of us.

For those who were in low-rated marriages, the security began to feel like a trap:

> In my marriage I feel more responsibility for the day-to-day crap.
>
> My marriage is very dreary; everything is predictable and boring.

And for a group in the middle, the value of marriage seemed most enigmatic:

> Marriage is—uh—it's there. It's a mortgage and a child, and driving the nursery school carpool. It's paying for babysitters,

it's debts, in-laws. There's none of this in the relationship. When I see Jack it's just for kicks, good times, going out, reading to each other, smoking our pot—you know. It's a special, extra, exciting, on the side thing. And if we were married, it probably wouldn't be so super. It would probably be just like we are with our own (spouses).

It's not that it's bad; it's not that it's good. It's just the fact that it's there and that routine to me is hard in itself, because you're not unhappy, but you're not really happy either.

What these women all seem to be saying is that marriage fills that need for predictability and security which we all have, but that very stability then causes the desire for variety, change and risk-taking to emerge. Furthermore, there seems to be a tendency for marriage to become routinized by the burden of role responsibilities which paradoxly helps to create the stability we all desire. It is apparently extremely difficult to build-in the variety we crave and the stability we need within the same relationship.[30]

Since women were receiving different rewards from their marital and extramarital situations, they were asked to evaluate if being involved had affected their behavior toward their husbands. Nearly all of the women (85%) thought that it had, but of this group, more than one-half characterized it as a change for the better. Since these involvements were not conventional, romantic, "swept away," love affairs, but developed as friendship, liking, or "person-to-person" love, it follows that they would be less likely to affect the marriage relationship negatively. For a positive impact on marriage to be the result, it is imperative that emotional involvement in the extramarital relation be kept secondary to the marriage.

Women reported various positive effects. Some were more fulfilled because their needs were being met, and their behavior in general changed:

> Oh, yes, my behavior really did change. I bloomed. I became more interested in everything around me. I was on top of the world, and my family found me to be a much happier person, with much, much more to give them. My God, I was alive!

Other women used the rewards they were obtaining outside their marriage as a springboard to try to improve their marital relationship:

> Yes, being involved with someone else changed my behavior toward my husband. I think it opened me up a lot more

toward my husband. I know a lot of new physical stuff to try.

Since I have had this second relationship on-going, I have been able to draw my husband out more and get him to talk more and more and to be more open in expressing my feelings with him on a very gradual basis. I am slowly but surely trying to bring our relationship up to a level that meets more of my needs.

The most frequent improvement discussed was one uniquely rooted in the current transition in women's roles. Women valued the decrease in their dependence upon their husbands which came from having an alternate source of expressive rewards:

Yes, I'm not as afraid to say what I want to say, I don't think I kowtow to my husband as much as I used to, I don't let him hurt my feelings as easily as I used to 'cause I silently think that somebody else loves me. And if this man, my husband, is getting mad and raging at me, ridiculing me, then I don't bow and paw as much as I used to.

I think my relationships have changed my behavior toward my husband. With my husband—obviously before I started these relationships I still had a dependency to meet my needs and however meager his meeting of my psychological, social and physical needs were, or how inadequate I thought they were, he still was the only one I had to meet them. So, since having the relationship and being involved with them—uh—I have no need for my husband to meet any needs of mine.

Yes, it did change my behavior toward my husband. Initially, I was nicer to him because I think I was getting more than I needed and wasn't even conscious that I did need.... I used to always, even during the first few years of my relationship with Paul, I would always give in to my husband. If he would argue with me I would always sort of in the end let him have the last word. I felt on easier ground that way. I don't do that so much anymore. I never could walk away angry but now I can. I never could go to sleep without resolving something and kissing and making up. I can do that better now and I think that's good.

The women's husbands are not likely to agree with these evaluations, but one of the hallmarks of modern marriage is a trend toward equality between partners. Since men traditionally have held the balance of power in marriage, women who go outside the marital relationship and successfully find others who can fill their emotional needs feel an increased sense of power. They have discovered a new option that leads to a greater sense of independence and autonomy on their part. In a more traditional era, when wives were wholly dependent on their husbands for economic survival, most could not afford to have an extramarital relationship because their husband's disapproval would have meant the end of the marriage and a loss of their only means of support. Now that women have broader economic options, which lessen their dependent ties to their husbands, choices are also opening up in other marital areas of expressiveness and sexuality.

These are all pieces of a marriage relationship, in the past held together by economic coercion, that are now evolving gradually toward a partnership that can be held together by mutual choice. While the rate of divorce may be rising, those marriages that do stay together today are more likely to do so because both parties desire it. Currently, men can feel more certain that their wives desire them as people, rather than as economic passports, and women can feel freer to choose to stay married, rather than having to stay married to survive.

Not all the effects of an extramarital involvement upon a marriage were characterized as positive. About one-quarter of the women thought it had a mostly negative effect on their relationships with their husbands:

> The way that it did affect my behavior was to make me more hostile to him. Having to sit there and read a book or something under his watchful eyes when I knew I could have been out with someone else...made it even more attractive to be with the other person and made me more resentful of my husband.
>
> Yes, I was a little strained toward him at times, but I was also mixed up about a lot of other things beside the outside relationship.
>
> I became less tolerant of my husband. I would rather have been with Bill than at home. It did affect my relationship with my husband. I was irritable and tired.
>
> I ignored my marriage. I let it deteriorate while I had an outside diversion.
>
> Well, I was more considerate of his feelings in little things, but my general affection for him dwindled.

The negative impact tended to occur in marriages which were mostly unsatisfactory before the extramarital relationship began; or in which the woman was experiencing a period of turbulence in her personal life; or rarely, when the woman became emotionally over-involved extramaritally.

There were also a few women who thought their involvements had both good and bad effects on their marriages, and here again, the good effect was that of increasing personal autonomy and power as a wife:

> Sometimes it makes it less enjoyable being with him, when I'd rather be with someone else. But I think it's given me the strength to say, "Hey, that's not enough...I need more talking." I think at one time I wouldn't have been that strong about it.

Finally, a few women thought their involvement did not influence their behavior at all toward their husbands. This occurred primarily in long-term marriages that had fallen into less intense patterns which might be described as "passive-congenial" or "devitalized."[31] As one woman described it:

> No, it didn't, because my husband's relationship to me is in one compartment, my writing is in another, and so on and so on. My private life is in a different one completely from all else and I move within it and then come back to the house. I shut the door on it. I can do that. It works well.

The effect of extramarital involvement on a particular marriage is a complex issue, depending at least on the quality of the marriage, the quality of the extramarital interaction, and how a woman (or man) perceives, interprets, and values the rewards coming from each relationship. According to these women, the effects vary from mostly positive to decidedly negative to none, supporting the conclusions of other researchers since the Kinsey era. This reality contrasts with the traditional simplistic belief that extramarital activity is always injurious to a marriage. Continuing to believe this in the face of repeated opposing findings encourages a self-fulfilling prophecy. If people believe an extramarital relationship will break up a marriage, then it is more likely to do so.[32]

In these data, however, there were only four situations in which marriages were broken up because extramarital involvements evolved into a desire to live with the partner. None of these marriages were particularly satisfying to the women at the time they began the outside relationship. No second marriages occurred, and in only one case did a woman actually go on to live with her extramarital partner.[33]

Negative Meanings

Most women's responses to questions on the meanings of extramarital involvements were basically positive. To reveal negative meanings, I asked women: "What is the worst thing about having an extramarital relationship?"

About one-quarter of the women focused on various aspects of the relationship itself, such as not being able to be with their partners whenever they wished, concerns about personal reactions of pain over the ending of a relationship, or not treating their partner fairly (usually where he was single and, therefore, not in a symmetrical situation).

> The worst thing is—not being with him all the time. I would like to be able to give him everything, and be with him and take care of him and have him take care of me. So, I guess, not being with him is the worst part, and the constant thinking of him and dreaming of him.

> The worst thing is, I think, contemplating that it could be otherwise than it is right now, that it could end.

> The breaking off, which is painful, if it is not a mutually agreeable thing to break off.

> I was very unfair to him, because it was completely on my terms and I was very unfair, very unfair.

These responses evoke, in different ways, a traditional value system, one associated with the intensity and exclusivity of a monogamous relationship. These allusions to a romantic ideology raise the whole question of the effects of feminist beliefs on the ideology of romanticism. Most of the women in this group are moving beyond belief in traditional romantic love as a basis for male-female relationships, but there is still sufficient evidence of its existence here to pique curiosity about the effect of feminism on romanticism. It is a subject about which we presently know very little.[34]

Another quarter of the women gave answers which were a mixture of both traditional and modern thinking. A few voiced concern about what the relationship could do to their marriages, while a few were unconcerned about any aspect, as they were very negative about their marriages. Several other women mentioned the problem of insufficient time. The demands of modern life, with its multiplicity of roles and interactions with large numbers of people, left them with the feeling that being pressed for time was the major problem in having extramarital relationships.

Although only reported by a small number of women, this response is significant because it represents an excellent example of the "secularization" of sexuality.[35] Meanings of traditional sexuality are rooted in morality, and transgressions have usually produced emotional reactions such as guilt or shame. For the women whose worst problem was insufficient time, the meanings and consequences of extramarital involvements have been transformed into strictly pragmatic ones. They reacted principally to what is essentially a modern drama caused by temporal conflict among their many roles. For them sexuality, even "deviant sexuality," has become truly secularized.

Most of the women, about one-half, thought the worst thing about being extramaritally involved was the need to be secretive and dishonest:

> The worst thing is the deceit that's involved. I would rather not have to be deceitful. I would rather be open about the whole relationship... No, I don't want to marry him at all. First of all, he is happily married. I am (pause) comfortably married. I don't see breaking up two families to have what we've already got. We've got it anyway. So why destroy marriages and foul up children's lives and all the financial ends that go along with that just because we'd like to be together a little more? What I would prefer would be to be able to have this relationship with him and have my husband and his spouse approve of it. That's what bugs me. I think that I'm quite capable of living with my husband and carrying on a normal life with my husband and having a sexual relationship with this other man at the same time. And he is quite capable of doing the same and still have a good relationship with his wife and I don't see any reason why we should have to choose either/or.

> Oh, I suppose not being able to integrate the relationship into your day-to-day living. Again, we discussed this so as to decide whether we would get involved in each other's families, and we decided that we wouldn't. In retrospect, it was the right decision to make.

> Just the undercoverness of it, doing something deceitful. Here what I'm complaining about in my own marriage is a lack of openness and what I'm having to do is close up. It's a conflict.

> The worst thing is—you know—being involved with married

people and being married myself. You cannot openly share, and I hate the dishonesty and I hate the lying.

Women were obviously in conflict about the need for secrecy. It is important to note that the objection was to socially imposed secrecy; most of the women did not feel overwhelmed by guilt. They regretted the deception and dishonesty involved, which they perceived as unavoidable effects of the extramarital relation. It is worth noting that no one ended a relationship specifically because of this conflict. They just endured the dissonance, or at some later point, managed to be more open about their involvement, as we shall see in the next chapter. These women would choose to alter the extramarital role, not give it up. They are expressing a wish for social change, some more consciously and vigorously than others.

The woman who felt she did not want to destroy her marriage, but "would prefer...to have this relationship...and have my husband and (my partner's) spouse approve of it" because she feels "quite capable of living with my husband and carrying on a normal life...and having a sexual relationship with this other man at the same time" is feeling a deficiency in the structure of traditional monogamous marriage. Monogamy, defined as an exclusive and permanent relationship, will fail to meet the needs of ever larger numbers of people as our individual needs grow more complex and less stable. So far we have accepted only the variation of sequential monogamy to cope with these changing personal needs. We have opted to relax the demand for permanence but we still insist on the rule of exclusivity.

Our behavior shows more and more that exclusive monogamy is an institution that no longer can meet the needs of contemporary life. It is not just a few people who are venturing outside this institution. Sociologically speaking, we can no longer consider this behavior to be unequivically deviant, when half of all men, and soon half of all women, will experience extramarital involvements at some point in their married lives. People who do so and also manage their relationships in such a way as to invoke minimal costs to themselves and their marriages—and at the same time find rewards that enrich their lives and may even benefit their marriages—are in the social vanguard. They are demonstrating the possibilities of another alternative to traditional monogamy, of flexibility as a variation to exclusivity.

It is only by people testing out unacceptable or innovative

behaviors that new options for permanence come to be known. When these sexual pioneers report on the new marital terrain, we gain knowledge about which alternatives to traditional monogamy will work, and under what conditions, and for what purposes. Having an extramarital relationship solely because one is unhappily married, for example, is not a legitimate rationale for the open or flexible monogamy discussed here. Flexible monogamy is an alternative for those who wish to continue a satisfying marriage but find that exclusive monogamy frustrates their desires to know intimately other persons. The problem flexible or open monogamy addresses is the structure of marriage itself, not a particular, unhappy marriage.

These women who wish to add additional intimacy to their lives, and other married persons like them, are a group whose behavior and decisions add an important component to the variety of marriage patterns of the future. In the next chapter we explore how a sizable minority of this group—40%—attempted to transform their covert extramarital involvements into a more flexible variation on traditional exclusive monogamy.

Chapter Four

Open Marriage

During the last two decades marriage has been in a state of transition. As a result there are a variety of marriage forms coexisting. At the same time that conventional marriage continues to be the first choice of many, there has also been growth in the rates of sequential monogamy (marriage, divorce, remarriage), living together, and other forms of unconventional life styles. Some of the life styles we increasingly choose are extramarital relationships, "swinging," group marriages, communal living, and open marriage, the subject of this chapter.

Choice alone does not determine the marriage form in which we will live. Among the most important factors that influence ability to have the kind of intimate life style we prefer is the amount of power we have. Power has long determined the quality of marriage and other intimate relationships, although it is one of the less obvious factors to influence it. As a general rule, the partner with the greater amount of power is more likely to shape the relationship to her or his desires.

Where do we get power from? The most common source of power is the economic one—income—although power can also rest upon the ability to coerce the other person physically (more likely to be used by males) or emotionally (more likely to be used by females). Whoever has less interest in maintaining the relationship will also have a greater amount of power over the other person.[1] Other sources of interpersonal power are derived through expertise (principally through education or experience) or through identification (our desire to be like, or live up to the standards of, our spouse).. And lastly, there is a traditional cultural belief that males are the only correct sex to hold power. This legitimation of male power supplements and reinforces power from the other sources. In any relationship, all these sources of power will be blended and will tend to reinforce one another. For example, if Anne is a manager earning $25,000 a year, and her husband Bill is a graduate student totally dependent on her income, he will be more likely to want to meet whatever standards for the relationship she believes are important. His identification with her reinforces the economic power she has over him, and tends to lessen his legitimate power over her.

Historically, however, men as a group have had more power than women, and they have tended to be the dominant partners in marriage. In the recent past as well as today, women have been gaining more and more social power through education and employment. They have more to say today about what the rules of marriage are to be, and they are approaching equal partnership with men.[2]

In this research, one-third of the women changed the rules of their marriage from having extramarital relationships in secret to having them openly, with their husbands' knowledge. Women who did this were likely to be women who had greater amounts of power relative to their husbands. Of those who did make this change, all but two had completed college and half of them had gone on to graduate work. Education often liberalizes people's values and also gives them additional power, through expertise, to realize the life style they prefer. Education also increases wives' occupational options, lessening economic dependence on husbands, so that if women misperceived their husbands' willingness to tolerate an open relationship and marital disruption occurred, their education made it likely that they could survive, economically, outside of marriage. In addition to the social power derived from their education, most of the women worked outside the home full-time and a few part-time, so that all had independent sources of income. A uniform research finding is that wives who are employed increase their power in marriage.

Not all of the women interviewed about their extramarital activity wished to change the rules of their marriage to an open or flexible monogamy, despite their behavior to the contrary. Those who didn't usually were not ready or were having extramarital relationships primarily to aid an unhappy marriage. Two who actually had relatively high power and desired an open marriage but did not attempt to change matters did not perceive they had as much power as they did. In order to utilize power in any situation, it is necessary to be aware of the power that one does have.

More often, women who did not wish to be open about their extramarital behavior were inhibited by a marital situation in which they had very little power. Some characteristics which contributed to their powerlessness were absence of employment outside the home and the presence of preschool children. The responsibility of caring for small children contributes to a powerlessness by decreasing options for employment, as well as by reducing the amount of physical energy available for other activities.

The activity of women who had extramarital relationships with the knowledge, if not the complete approval, of their husbands represents doubly changed sexual behavior. It is not only a violation of the rules of conventional monogamy, but also a rejection of the rule of secrecy that has traditionally surrounded that violation. Secrecy has always been used to conceal sexual infidelity. But there is a strong suggestion that contemporary women are not only challenging the rule that marriage means sex with one man, but also challenging the secrecy that has traditionally veiled the breaking of that rule.

This emerging openess about extramarital sex is comparable to our changed awareness of premarital sex. Apparently a large increase in premarital intercourse for women occurred during the 1920's. As virtually no research documented this change until the Kinsey report in 1953, for a long time there was no awareness that premarital behavior was being modified. A condition of "pluralistic ignorance" existed in which most women did not know that others were behaving similarly. When this ignorance was revealed through research and media attention, we were surprised to find that a "sexual revolution" had taken place. The publication of the Kinsey research and the subsequent controversy it provoked—it did not validate what everyone thought was going on in the sexual lives of women—is a good example of this phenomenon. Similarly, with extramarital activity the first stage of change involves behavior. Next comes the knowledge of changed behavior; only then will there be the possibility of changes in attitudes, as occurred with premarital sex.[3]

To return to the discussion of open or flexible monogamy, how is conventional marriage transformed to this alternative? We have already seen the process by which women went from sexual exclusivity with their husbands to extramarital involvement. One out of three of these women decided they did not wish to stop at this first point, but wanted to take the process of marital transition further. How is the husband, also previously sexually exclusive, brought into agreement with a new basis for marriage? How did these women handle the delicate process of negotiating one of the major ground rules of marriage?

There are several areas of both practical and sociological

interest in this transition. One is the problematic nature of communication itself, of confusion embedded in the very words we say to each other to clarify matters. Communication theory tells us that every message from one marital partner to another, in addition to its overt content, contains an underlying definition of the two basic issues in every marriage, those of dominance and solidarity. Every time a wife or husband says something to the other, a dual message is being transmitted: "Will you take out the garbage?" is not only a message about garbage; it also says that the asker has the right to ask for the garbage to be taken out. Whether the other person agrees or disagrees will be a confirmation or rejection of the asker's right to do so. Thus, the issue of dominance is embedded in the most simple communication. Similarly, the question "What do you want to do this weekend?" contains the other underlying issues of how close or intimate each party wants to be.

Added to this is the complexity of the communication process itself, wherein every message has the potential for being ambiguous and contradictory because it is delivered with both verbal and nonverbal cues which can operate on several different levels of meaning. An "I love you" spoken from fiften feet away and delivered in a monotone may or may not mean what the words say. Or a spouse may declare "I want you to be independent and think for yourself." Such a message leaves the recipient in a double bind, for complying with the statement is to violate the intent of the statement.[4]

Another problem to be managed is that the process of transition to open marriage is basically devoid of known rules or norms that guide most other areas of social life. Rules exist to relieve the anxiety of not knowing what to do or say next. Transforming a conventional marriage to a sexually open one is a situation for which few precedents exist, or, if they do, are usually not known to the individuals who need to know them.[5] The necessary tactics to transform the situation have to be devised by each individual and depend upon the communication and negotiation skills they possess.

Finally, there is the critical factor called the "awareness context," or how much knowledge anyone has about the identity of others with whom she or he is interacting. There are ways that awareness or knowledge of the people we are close to can differ, all of which is relevant to marriage when there is an extramarital involvement. An "open" awareness is when each person "knows the other's true identity and his own identity in the eyes of the other." This is where these women wanted to move. A "closed" awareness in which one person does not know "the other's identity or the other's view of his identity," is what all the women (except three whose husbands wanted an open marriage initially) started out with, since their husbands did not know of their extramarital activity. Several women felt they were in a "suspicion" context, in which one person suspects the true identity of the other, or a "pretense" context, in which both people are aware of the other's identity but pretend not to be.[6] Many people find it easier to live in a suspicion or pretense awareness context than an open one, for it allows them not to confront a situation which may be threatening to deal with. All three contexts of closed, suspicion, and pretense have traditionally been associated with extramarital relationships. It is only the open context which is newly and more extensively associated with extramarital behavior.

Women used a variety of interactional tactics to begin the transition to an open marriage. A couple of them employed the traditional technique of crying in front of their husbands to initiate a confession of extramarital behavior. Crying can be used to coerce acceptance because many men find it difficult, because of their socialization against expressiveness, to tolerate such a naked display of emotion. Another tactic used to induce transition to an open relationship was discussion of hypothetical instances of extramarital involvements which, after the discussion, were revealed as fact.

To illustrate the nature of the transitional process, we will follow one woman's experience in considerable detail. It illustrates strikingly the developmental character of this kind of interaction, the complexities of a situation involving more than two people, the changing vested interests of the people involved, and the stunning transformations that can take place in the awareness contexts over time. It is ideal to study because it incorporates elements of traditional and modern meanings, and contains practically every element of interaction found in the other transformational situations in this group of women.

The woman—we may call her Carol—was thirty-five years old, married ten years, a college graduate, and worked full time as an accountant. Her age, education, employment, and the fact that both her children were in school assured her of marital power approximately equal to that of her husband.

Carol had rejected several opportunities before her first

extramarital relationship. Her motive for involvement was a combination of a discontent with her marriage, as well as need for her own personal growth that was characteristic of women in this group. Again, like most of the women, she preferred an extramarital encounter that had the potential to be expressively as well as sexually satisfying.

She described her personal and marital situation prior to her first extramarital involvement:

> I was at a low point in my own marriage, I was coming to terms with my own dissatisfaction as a person, I knew this guy would not go around and blab about it, I know he really cared about me as a person, it wasn't just going to be a night in the sack and that was it... My only hesitation was his wife (Alice) and I didn't want to hurt my husband (Bob); I thought he would be absolutely crushed. I didn't want to hurt him but I was going to have to if I was going to get what I wanted for myself.

Typical for these women, Carol began with a closed awareness situation. In order to conceal her new activity she resorted to the standard technique of offering normalizing excuses for her absences. This was more difficult because she had previously always informed her husband of her whereabouts. Coincidentally, however, the fact that she and her husband were not communicating openly about sexual practices in their marriage turned out to be a structural factor that contributed in making her excuses seem non-suspicious:

> And I made some excuse to get out of the house. I can't remember now what I said, because as much as I go out at night, Bob always knows where I'm going. I always tell him where I'm going...

> I went over to Ted's house and like with my husband I don't know whether it's just been an excuse that we never have intercourse when I have my period...I never really knew whether he didn't like it or whether it was all me. We just never did it when I had my period and that was it...

> And when I got over there I said to Ted, "What could be the worst possible news?" He said, "You got your period." I said, "Yes." He said, "So what!" Oh, how delightful!...

> And Bob said later to Ted (after her husband knew everything) in my presence, "Well, I knew nothing had happened because she had her period."

Carol's excerpt illustrates not only the complexity of the communication process, but also the way it serves to define the identity of those who communicate in ongoing relationship. Two married people have apparently talked enough to reach a rule that they will not engage in sex during the wife's menstrual period, yet the wife at least was uncertain as to whose preference was responsible for that rule. The husband, on the other hand, was convinced that part of his wife's identity was a woman who will not have sex during her period. Yet, given a receptive person, that is exactly what she did. This situation is an excellent example of family sociologist Arlene Skolnick's belief that:

> Sexual hangups between couples probably result as much from communicational knots as from purely sexual problems. One of the attractions of affairs may be escape from the old knots, and the exploration of a new set of rules and metarules for talking about sex.
>
> It is interesting that the Masters-Johnson therapy for couples having trouble in their sex lives is largely an attack on the couple's old communication or non-communication patterns.[7]

Carol's initial extramarital encounter turned out to be so satisfying that she continued it regularly, making it necessary to find a variety of plausible excuses for her absence:

> One time I remember telling him (husband) that somebody from the business had come in from California and had taken me out to dinner and he just swallowed it and I couldn't believe it. I think I told him I went up to a girl friend's house once. Oh, I know, I was racking my brain trying to think of what to tell him when it suddenly hit me, "You've had your night out for ten years and I would like a night out now." And he said, "O.K." and I went.

She suddenly percieved that she, as a supposedly equal partner in their marriage, was as much entitled to a night out once a week "with no questions asked" as her husband had been enjoying for ten years. When that realization occured, she had solved the major problem of maintaining a closed awareness. However, the growing pleasure over the relationship threatened the closed awareness context and made necessary the use of interactional tactics to disguise cues about her changed identity:

> It was very hard concealing my happiness. I just had the

feeling it was written all over my face and I had to play down the whole thing.

The structure of the situation also complicated matters. She and her husband were social friends of her lover and his wife. The frequency of the interaction among all four persons increased the possibility of accidentally changing the awareness context. This source of constant anxiety over revelation of her true identity led her to consider a new tactic:

> We were seeing more and more of them socially (after the relationship had started) and my husband just got to know Ted better and better and it was like something out of Peyton Place. We (she and Ted) just couldn't believe it. Like Ted would drop over after tennis on Sunday and we'd have breakfast and we'd wind up at their house that night and we'd smoke and it was just getting to be as thick as thieves. The two of us were going crazy. *Finally* I got Bob to the point of—I knew Alice was interested in him and I thought, "Wouldn't that just be the perfect solution to the whole goddamn mess," if he'd go after Alice, then I could have Ted and we'd have a great old time and just swap and do it and that would be it.

The "mate swapping" tactic came to mind partly because she already knew that Ted and Alice had in the past abstractly discussed and approved of outside relationships, and partly because she was feeling the urge to end the deception and transform the awareness context to what she percieved would be the increased ease and honesty of an open one. Maintaining a deceptive identity can be emotionally strenuous, as anyone who has ever done so can attest. The more intimate the situation, the more stressful the maintenance problem will be. Even with the knowledge of Ted's and Alice's preferences, Carol still felt the need to proceed in a circuitous and cautious manner because of her belief in her husband's faithful identity:

> So I started talking to Bob about this, all in an oblique way of getting around to the truth of what I really wanted to reveal to him. I wanted to tell him but I didn't want to tell him, so I wanted it to come out kind of—I don't know—and we talked into the night, *many* a night, all about extra relationships and what they meant and so forth, and he kind of agreed he wouldn't care as long as he didn't know about it.
>
> But he had always given me this impression of being *so* faithful and *so*— you know—just there's nobody else and all this

baloney. But I didn't like that conclusion of "as long as he didn't know about it." What I was trying to get away from was the deception.

Carol did not immediately achieve her goal and was still inhibited and troubled by her husband's faithful identity. She did at least gain some new knowledge about his identity, however. She learned he was not a person who would mind her having an outside relationship, as she previously had believed, but that he still preferred it enveloped in traditional closed awareness. Rewarded by this partial success, she continued to use the same technique of discussing possible reactions to a hypothetical extramarital involvement.

> So I kept pushing him toward Alice—she's a very attractive girl— but he had this thing where "I just can't go and do it with somebody, she's like my sister, what are you trying to get me into?" It was just laughable. "No, no, I know her too well, I never could."
>
> I think he just got tired of me talking about it...finally he said, "I can tell, you would like to do something with Ted." And I admitted it, "Yes, I would," as if it were all in the future. And he took that all right, he didn't crack at the seams like I thought he would so I thought, "Hmmm, let's push this a little further." At that point I began to wonder about all these years, maybe he wouldn't be so hurt, maybe he's not as pure as the driven snow and so forth...

The repeated discussions, as well as calculated partial admission of her own true identity in response to her husband's probing, produced new information about what kind of person her husband really was. This disclosure caused her to be suspicious of his "faithful" identity, a significant advance, in the transformational process

The continued talking in the "passive phase" of this gradual movement toward "swapping" mates served to escalate rapidly the participants into the "acting phase,"[8] when they actually test out the new behavior. The sudden turn of events is typical of human interaction, especially in unfamiliar situations. Even the participants are sometimes greatly surprised by unanticipated developments because they cannot always predict what they or even those persons best known to them will do.

Carol described how they actually came to act on what they had talked about so long.[9]

> Finally one night we were all four together at their house again and the conversation got around to swapping. Anyway my husband said, "Look, we have talked so much about this business of swapping, let's try it." Well, I was just aghast! I wanted to but not under the same roof—my old puritanical self, you know. So we decided we would pair off then and there, and they were very stunned that he should suggest it so openly. But that's the kind of way he is, he'll mull around for ten years and then drop a bomb like that.

Now Carol was shocked because her husband suddenly was moving ahead of her expectations of him and what she was able to be comfortable with. She found herself abruptly thrust into a situation she had never been in before, engaging in sex with another man while her husband was in the vicinity engaging in sex with another woman. It all became a bit too much to absorb comfortably when reflected against her conservative background.

> So Ted and I went out in the yard; it was the summertime and we proceeded to make love on a blanket in the backyard.
>
> The whole thing was awkward...When we came back in, like we didn't know what they were doing—should we go in or shouldn't we? We should have set up some kind of signal, to turn out the lights or something—oh, it was just like a three-ring circus, it was just unpleasant.

Since the couples had had no mate swapping experience, they neglected to plan ahead so that their actions could be smoothly synchronized. This became painfully obvious when Carol and Ted decided to rejoin her husband and his wife and realized they might be inadvertently intruding on their privacy. Since the alternative was to remain indefinitely outside the house, they were forced to confront the ambiguous situation inside.

As in many situations without guidelines, the absence of agreed upon rules produced considerable anxiety and discomfort for the participants. In addition to the anxiety, this part of the transitional process also was marked by the unexpected character of the interaction, the acting out of unfamiliar behavior, the newly changed identities of all those involved, and the problematic quality of the awareness context. Indeed, this served to propel all the participants into a subsequent continous sharing and verification of identities.

The changes in awareness now became so fast-paced that they seemed almost to acquire a velocity of their own.[10] Evidence of these changes is reproduced in full in the following excerpt:

>Finally we came home and I didn't know what had happened, and finally he said nothing really had happened and they just talked. She was a nice gal and he'd like to develop it further but there really wasn't much time—and he assumed nothing had happened with me and Ted out on the grass because I'm usually slow. (laughs)
>
>Finally he said, "What happened to you?" I said, "Do you really want to know?" He did, so I told him. Well, he *couldn't* believe it and he said he really wasn't hurt by it, he was shocked. I didn't say it had been the first time but I didn't say there had been previous times either at that point. I just talked about that it was very nice and I enjoyed it and would like to do it again.
>
>I guess the next thing was that Ted called the next day and said, "Listen, I've told Alice everything." I said, "You *what?*" I didn't mind, but I just wanted to be forewarned. And he said, "Yes, you won't believe it, Alice has had two lovers since we've been married. We told each other everything last night and I don't know what you've told Bob but I just want you to know—she's not upset with you and she's not upset with me and we're fine. But it's just been a blockbuster of a night with all these revelations." "Well," I said, "the only thing Bob knows is what happened last night , so we must go easy."
>
>So that afternoon I figured—"Listen, I might as well lay it on you, I've been seeing Ted for two months." Well, he got mad because he felt he'd been set up and used, because I'd been pushing him. So I had told him; Ted had told Alice; Alice had told Ted; they had told me....
>
>Finally the next morning, I was standing in the kitchen and it suddenly hit me—"Damn it, everybody in this situation has 'fessed up but you." And it suddenly hit me—here I am, the fallen woman, you know—and it suddenly hit me, "You haven't been honest with me and it's your turn." And he looked just as guilty as—I knew the minute I saw his face—
>
>He said, "No, you don't want to hear"—I said, "Oh, yes I do, because otherwise I look like I should be wearing a big "A" on my chest." So we sat down and we spent the whole afternoon and he told me a tale that I would not have believed if it hadn't come from his mouth. He's been fooling around for years, not with any attachment to anybody, and I've always argued that I couldn't do that. It doesn't have to be the love affair of the century but I do have to at least like the other person.
>
>It was like Dr. Jekyll and Mr. Hyde; this lump, this boring lump that I thought I'd been married to, suddenly—I mean,

he's had all kinds of homosexual experiences and heterosexual experiences which just floored me and everything. He said, "Does that bother you, is it upsetting you?" "No, just keep telling me. I'm just shocked."

And he said since he was a kid he always felt like he had a very high libido, a very strong sex drive, and he tried to control it and couldn't. He knew that about himself, that he needed a lot of outlets so he just proceeded to find a lot of outlets and keep his big mouth shut. Like I remember all the times when I would approach him and he acted as if he couldn't stand the idea of sex, and I've been so hurt and I'd say, "What's the matter with you? Don't you want me?" You know, he had the "wife" lines all the time. For years it was like this.

Well anyway, I couldn't—it was just so much to absorb in one weekend and I wasn't mad. As a matter of fact, my first reaction after the initial shock was, "Gee, maybe he's not so bad after all, he's got all these women falling all over him." (laughs) I began to see him in a whole new light. "You rogue, you"—I just could not believe it, he was so priest-like and uh—this all just kind of sunk in and it took a long time to absorb. I just couldn't swallow it all in one night and we kept talking and from that point on things started to get better principally because we were really being honest... It was just unreal, it was like something out of a novel. I didn't believe it was happening to me...He turned to me one night and said, "Did you ever masturbate?" Well, I nearly—I felt if he ever said that to me I would have fainted. And just to be able to say, "Yeah, you too?" We can talk about anything at this point which is really good.

Both Carol and Bob had been unaware of central features of each other's sexual identities during their marriage. Bob had defined Carol as a woman who takes a long time for sex because she had given him evidence of that identity early in their marriage. With another man, however, Carol discovered she was not necessarily slow to react. Bob had also continued to view her as sexually exclusive with him, despite the evidence in the "mate-swapping" situation and other hints that were there to be discovered. Openness, or knowledge of someone's correct identity, depends both on the person giving information and the person receiving it.

From Carol's perspective, she had been unaware of her husband's identity as a highly sexed person. He was afraid to tell her of his needs before they married because he expected she would have rejected him. Ironically, she came to prefer more sex as the marriage developed. Yet he had to refuse her to preserve his pretended puritanical image that he used to cover up his true identity—a person with strong sexual needs. Furthermore, Carol had never suspected her husband's bisexual behavior or his outside involvements despite years of his taking "a night out" once a week.

Perhaps the most surprising aspect of this entire situation is that it was possible for two people to live together for ten years in what is supposed to be the most intimate relationship society has devised—marriage—and for one person to be able to present and maintain a closed awareness concerning the true nature of his sexual identity during the entire time.[11] This couple's experience is an example of the long endurance of a closed context despite many structural factors—intimacy, repetition of interaction, the number of other participants in the husband's relationships—that would seem to be a constant threat to its stability. How many other American marriages exist under similar circumstances of closed context and concealment? How many other couples pay a similar price of strain and duplicity, spilling over and affecting the whole texture of the marriage?

If it had not been for Carol's perceptiveness that led her to question her husband, and her newly vested interest in equalizing a change in sexual identity between them, it is possible both would have remained closed about their involvements. As we see here, women's increasing desire to engage in extramarital sex and their contemporary progress toward equalization of power in marriage are two factors which may well influence a move toward greater openness about extramarital involvement between couples.

Carol's shocked reaction to her husband's revelations suggests there are human limits to the amount of changed identity we can accept about those close to us within a given period of time. To avoid this "future shock," paricularly in situations in which people are heavily invested emotionally, it is probably wise for the person revealing information to be particularly alert to the effects of that information on others. The effect of pacing information to transform awareness emerges as a significant factor which must be included in studies of how awareness contexts affect our functioning as social beings.

Finally, we must note the positive outcome of this transformation in terms of its effects on the marriage relationship. The husband's changed identity led to a reevaluation by the wife of his desirability as a mate. Since Carol now perceived him as more valuable as a prospective sexual partner—because of his being in demand by others—she felt more highly rewarded in being able to attract and keep him. She also got additional rewards through the improved sexual and social relationship in the marriage, and the marriage was moved to a more stable basis.[12]

At the time of the initial interview, about a year after the transition to an open awareness, she rated the marriage as much improved and very satisfying:

> For the first time in ten years we have put a lock on our bedroom door, and my husband has said, "I just can't believe that I really want you after all these years."...For the first time *I* feel like I'm staying with Bob because I really want to. It's not perfect; it probably never will be, but I don't feel—I don't feel like there's no alternative. At least we both know where we stand, we're at the point where we can really talk, where I can say my husband's my own best friend right now, which I never had before.

Both husband and wife planned to continue to have relationships outside the marriage aware of each other's involvements.

When reinterviewed four years later, Carol reported they were still satisfied being married and still both having extramarital relationships. Of their own marriage and her husband, she said:

> I know I want to stay with Bob and I know I love my kids and my family and what we have together. I also am realistic enough to know that I wouldn't find this with too many other people.
>
> And even if I did find someone else, I don't want to start a whole new relationship and go through divorce. And besides, in time, I know I'd just get itchy again. It's just too good—a family that's working—to break it up.

She valued the quality of the marriage and family life they had and recognized how relatively rare this was. Additionally, she rated her husband as high in expressive skills, talked about what she had learned from him, and gave him high marks for his fathering:

> Bob's a good person to bounce off of. He's a good listener. Friends always drop in with their problems, saying "I knew I could talk to you two."...
>
> He's also a fantastic father, a much better parent than I'll ever be. I came from such a strict upbringing. I've learned a

lot from him about what's important and what isn't important. He just has a beautiful relationship with the kids (currently 13 and 14 years old.)

In her marriage Carol valued the same qualities that women had been looking for in their extramarital involvements—expressive satisfaction and the opportunity to learn from another person. These rewards, along with her husband's outstanding fathering, caused her to rate her marriage very highly. Friends also rated their marriage highly, often saying "I wish I could work something out as well as you two have."

> What the friends don't see is that it's taken five years and many sleepless nights and screaming matches. It didn't just—bing—happen. It hasn't all been roses. There were times when we said, "The hell with it. Let's split." But then we've said, "We really don't want to. We really get along well in so many areas."
>
> We talk a lot and laugh a lot together. We both have the same quirky sense of humor. That's what people comment on, that we obviously enjoy each other.

In order to integrate smoothly the extramarital relationships into their marriage, they had worked out a common understanding of implicit rules:

> We're pretty open with each other. But we kind of have a rule that we don't rub it in each other's noses, you know. This has just evolved over the years. If I've pushed too far, or he's pushed too far—we've figured out what is too far for both of us. We've pretty well worked that out.

This working out what was comfortable for them resulted in her husband continuing his pattern of casual involvements, both hererosexual and homosexual, of which she was understanding and accepting. She had had a series of "comfortable long term relationships," which usually ended through a gradual reduction in the frequency of contact. Only once had she had "a one-night stand," and only once had she "fallen in love" during a three year relationship, which the man had abruptly terminated:

> I learned a lot from that. It was so painful—I don't know why I did it. My husband saw me through the throes of it. I don't know how he put up with me. I don't know if I could have done the same for him. Maybe I could, I don't know. I just haven't been faced with it...Now, I try to consciously avoid falling in love. It just works better that way. I also try to go out

on a night when he's already out, so he won't have to come home and see me getting dressed to go out. I hate that—he doesn't make it hard—it's more me.

Another rule they had worked out was that "you don't screw up your kids." While their children were taught that they "don't condemn that sort of thing," Carol and Bob preferred to avoid directly confronting their children with their extramarital activities until the children were at least into late adolescence. At that time they felt the children would be able to understand and not be negatively affected by knowledge of their parents' extramarital preferences.

In this account of one marriage, we have traced the successful transition from covert extramarital sex to an open awareness of involvements, or what could be called open marriage. This process of change was typical of the other marriages in which women preferred to convert to an open marriage. Not all the other results were as successful, however. In three marriages that were floundering, the transition to an open marriage did not improve the situation, and the marriages were ended. In a fourth case, the wife ended her brief extramarital involvement when her husband found he could not accept it although at first he had been encouraging. And in a fifth situation the husband was tolerant of his wife's activity but wanted her to be discreet so he would not be aware of her relationship. These situations will not be examined further since they do not represent actual open marriages. Before analyzing the remaining nine marital situations, let us look at some information about the concept of open marriage.

Open Marriage

The idea of flexible or nonexclusive monogamy captured public attention with the publication in 1972 of *Open Marriage* by George and Nena O'Neill. The O'Neills advocated maximizing the growth of each spouse through equality and flexibility of husband and wife roles within marriage and emotional openness toward other persons and interests outside the marriage. They avoided the whole question of outside sexual relationships despite the fact people have come to associate that idea with the O'Neills' model of open marriage. The desirability of emotional but nonsexual relationships outside of marriage is also a significant issue in contemporary monogamy. As I have mentioned elsewhere in this book, it deserves further study and exploration as a possible way to enhance marriage.

Several scholars of the family have presented rationales for sexually open marriage before and after the O'Neills" book,[13] but there have been only two researchers who have studied people actually living in open marriages. Robert Whitehurst studied 35 couples from across the U.S. and Canada, and Jacqueline Knapp focused on 17 couples in Florida and Kansas. In discussing these studies, Bernard Murstein, a psychologist who specializes in the study of marriage relationships, comments that "only in marriages in which the woman is very strong may it be possible for the woman openly to demand and achieve equality. Not surprisingly, such women turn out to be more successful in their extramarital interpersonal ventures than their husbands."[15] Power, as discussed earlier, appears to be a vital factor in a woman's ability to have an open marriage or even an extramarital relationship if she wants one. Without it, women have no recourse but to accept, as they have in the past, the double standard of monogamy, in which men are more able to satisfy their extramarital desires. The trend toward equalization of power within marriage, along with the movement toward sexual permissiveness in our culture, is likely to result in at least a modest increase in the number of sexually open marriages in the future, all other things being equal.

The "all other things being equal" usually includes conditions of economic affluence, but it is unlikely that anything short of a severe economic downturn would interfere with this trend. As Americans, we have become accustomed to ever higher standards of personal satisfaction. If we are deprived of some of this satisfaction through a reduced life style—because of the energy crisis or rising inflation buying fewer material luxuries—we may very well seek more rather than fewer satisfactions through interpersonal relationships. It is possible that fewer opportunities for expressing masculinity in the traditional areas of economic success, acquiring material possessions, and manipulating energy-consuming machines such as cars and boats could also serve to make the acquisition of expressive competence more attractive for men. It hardly seems likely that husbands would be content in the long run to have their wives be more successful extramaritally than they are.

Although we know very little about open marriage, a significant new variation in traditional monogamy, the findings from this group of women very closely match the results of the Whitehurst and Knapp studies. With this agreement in mind it is possible to make some preliminary conclusions about flexible monogamy.

In order to make flexible monogamy work for both parties, certain basic factors are necessary. First is equal power between spouses. This in turn generally produces a role flexibility, a movement away from the traditional assignment of duties by gender. The sexually open marriage demands the ability of a couple to negotiate and create new rules. If they have not been able to move away from prescribed husband/wife roles in other areas of marriage, it is not likely that they have the personal beliefs and communication skills necessary for sexually open marriage.

It is in this area of nontraditional roles that the practice of "swinging" or "mate-swapping" is distinguished from open marriage. In swinging, participants tend to be conservative in other areas of their married life and to be interested only in a sexual exchange accomplished by both partners at the same time and place.[16] In flexible monogamy, people are as interested in emotional involvement and interpersonal sharing as they are in sexual experience, and spouses operate independently of each other in their extramarital relationships.

Another requirement is that couples should already have a satisfying marriage relationship before reaching out to others. If not, there will be a tendency for the additional relationships to add to the already existing marital conflict. Flexible monogamy, in and of itself, will do nothing to improve an unsatisfactory marriage, and it also diverts attention from work on the marital relationship by providing alternate satisfactions. As one woman in this position noted:

> We do have an open marriage...we now are free to see persons as we choose, to set our own hours, and to pretty much live our own lives... I really think in our case open marriage is just another name for pretty much being roommates, and I think I am more satisfied with it than he is. It works fine, but I think that the desire to stay married had probably already disappeared before the arrangements were made.

It is also necessary that both marriage partners be emotionally ready to move to a flexible basis. In this group there were two women with open marriages whose husbands unilaterally decided to open their marriages, and they felt coerced into going along with the idea. These were the only couples in this study who decided to open the relationships before having secret extramarital relationships and the only instances in which women were not the initiators of the open marriage idea. One attempted to protect herself by becoming involved before her husband did:

> I didn't like this idea but with the accommodation and the malleability that I mentioned earlier, I didn't have the sense that I could say, "No, let's not do it." I felt that I had to accommodate to what he was suggesting. So I gulped and I gritted my teeth, and I said that I would do it...There was a provision that if either of us found that it was too painful and we couldn't adjust to it, we would say so, but of course, that was a provision I could never take... In particular, I wanted to sleep with someone before he did, in a way to protect myself, to minimize the pain.

Another was able to accept the open relationship initially because she knew the other woman (her girlfriend) was not seriously interested in her husband:

> My husband had spent one evening with a girlfriend of mine with my knowledge and I had discussed it with my husband and he had been trying to get me to see the point of view that if you really found someone else that you really liked a lot and cared for and wanted to get into something with them, if you're close enough in your marriage another person would be able to be accepted. Of course, I had heard that point of view and it seemed very logical. But emotionally I don't think I was quite ready to accept it, though I did manage to accept him with my girlfriend because I knew she really wasn't interested in him.

Unilateral decisions and/or coercion in any marriage obviously mean problems and conflict. Although both women did eventually accommodate to the new marital lifestlye, in both cases it was the husbands who eventually suffered attacks of jealousy and insecurity when the women moved more enthusiastically into further relationships. The husbands finally broke their own rules; they could not tolerate their wives in other relationships, and both marriages were eventually terminated.

In conducting flexible monogamy, it is of course necessary that all parties agree with and follow the rule of not becoming overinvolved emotionally. Two other cases of open marriage existed for two years more or less successfully, but eventually one marriage ended and another was threatened because the outside partner and/or wife became too emotionally involved:

> Ed (the outside partner) also agreed (with our rules) and was all into this nonmonogamy...but he didn't know what he wanted because he hadn't had enough experience...Plus, you know, you sleep with someone three times. If you continue

liking him, do you continue sleeping with him, and if you continue do you become involved? It's difficult... But the worst for me is becoming involved with someone else and then being hurt because you have to break it off.

Right now I feel the marriage is going to break up and I don't really want it to. I wish there were some way—I think if my husband and I still lived on the East Coast I would not feel so much like my marriage will break up—but I'm having difficulty living away from Peter. It may mean my husband and I working out some kind of long- term separation, or short-term, where we still love and see each other but where we don't live together and I live with Peter and my husband lives with whom he wants to.

In both of these situations the outside male partners were single, which decreased the structural barriers to their getting over-involved emotionally. Also, it must be noted, socialization for romance in our culture carries with it the expectation that relationships will progress into something more intense, more committed, more exclusive. If the extramarital relationship does not fade of its own accord, the expectation of progress is a formidable one to counter with new rules of behavior. A solid marriage relationship serves as a barrier to desires for over-involvement with the extramarital partner. It is also helpful if the extramarital partner chosen has a primary relationship of his or her own.

Of the eight remaining open marriages, only four could be characterized as successful at the time of the interviews, attesting to the difficulties of this new and more complex marital form. All had been converted to flexible monogamy about three years earlier, and in all there was a gradual entry into open marriage. Several brief extramarital relationships had provided a progressive testing of the new behavior, which in turn had precipitated considerable discussions of the concept of open marriage. These discussions served as a partial anticipatory socializing device toward changing emotional reactions from traditional jealousy to calm acceptance. What is critical here is that changed behavior and cognitive beliefs did not too quickly outpace emotional reaction, thereby avoiding the creation of an "emotional lag."[18] Knapp also discusses how couples "seemed to go through a period of striving to bring their emotional acceptance of co-marital sex up to a level equal with their intellectual acceptance." The couples in her study who most benefited from their flexible marriage "achieved intellectual- emotional integration with relative ease."[19]

The following selection from an interview reveals how emotional acceptance can crystallize at an unexpected moment. The situation described is that of a couple in their early thirties who had already etablished a norm or rule that each must inform the other of sexual activities with another person. In following this norm a gradual change in belief systems occured:

> He didn't come home one night until very late and when he came home I said something about where was he, and he said well, he was lying down in bed, down in Maxine's bed. And somehow we thought it was *funny*. It just struck us both as funny and it didn't bother either of us. That was the beginning of a whole change in our marriage, the idea, from my point of view, that you didn't own the other person. We had pretty well established that other activities, like doing things by yourself and having activities that you want to go out and if the other person doesn't want to go he doesn't have to go. Some things you just like to do by yourself. We had always done that pretty much. But the whole idea of sex being also your own body and not the other person's, your spouse's body, was slow in coming to our marriage. We'd been married a good five years by then.

Another common factor in three of the four successful open marriages was that the couples were highly educated professionals. The fourth couple was high school educated; he was a truck driver and she was a part-time secretary, yet they succeeded in working out an open relationship. On the whole, however, open marriage probably is a phenomenon more associated with the upper middle class. This class has had the helpful advantage of being educated to liberal values, and also has more extensive parsonal contacts, discretionary time, and income to pursue this way of life.

The type of occupation engaged in may also indirectly facilitate an open marriage. In this study, one of the partners in each of the couples was in helping professions. In being trained for their professions they developed sophisticated communication skills and a talent for recognizing emotions in themselves and others. This verbal ability and emotional awareness enabled them to work out fairly complex sets of rules to govern their outside encounters as well as to provide a satisfactory way to resolve conflicts about the outside reltionships when they occurred. For example, a forty-one-year old woman, who was a health counselor, was involved extramaritally with a professional associate who was a psychologist. She reported one difficulty she and her husband had resolved:

> My having a relationship with someone that both of us know—my husband and I—has been a problem once because of my husband's stated feelings that the person was not good enough for me or might mistreat me. He was not the kind of person that I deserved.
> At that point we had to deal with the fact of our separateness, the fact of our being responsible for ourselves, that my husband was not my father and that whatever risks I chose to take were mine.
> It was tense—we did work it out and because of working it out felt much better about each other. It's hard to really know that being a couple doesn't mean some kind of "baby possum riding on the momma possum or daddy possum's back all the time." That experience helped us to get to that place.

Another woman, thirty-seven years old, was an office manager and was having a relationship with a clergyman. Her husband was also a member of the clergy. Both their occupations required frequent business trips. They had developed a rule to cover the frequent separations in their marriage:

> One thing is that we try to provide time alone together when either of us returns from a business trip. The re-entry is fantastically important. I think the timing is—we've had some bummer experiences where we've learned—not just because of the open marriage, but coming back from a trip and being picked up at the airport and going right on to a dinner party when you know—you haven't even had a chance to reacquaint yourself with each other.
> My husband in particular has a fantastic need to know, which is alright with me. We talked about how much he needs to know and how much I'm willing to talk about and he's willing to say, "You're telling me more—or less—than I need to know." But we need that time together.

Both couples had developed complete sets of guidelines covering a variety of situations arising out of the open marriage. These guidelines included the handling of expenses, being available by phone in case of family emergency, division of time between family and personal relationships, and the introduction of the outside partners to the spouses. In both marriages, the men and women found it easier to deal with the reality of an outside partner through informal meetings or occasional dinners together rather than fantasize about the imagined perfection of some "superperson" who was their spouse's friend and lover. In this way they also felt enriched and rewarded by getting to know another peson whom they usually found they liked and enjoyed. Again, Knapp's couples also found themselves making similar ground rules to cover extramarital situations.

None of the married pairs in Knapp's sample had made their nontraditional life style known to their children because they were too young, but they intended to do so when the children got older.[20] The couples here with successful open marriages (one couple was childless) had even enlarged the awareness of their marital style to include their children of adolescent and pre-adolescent age. Two women spoke to this point:

> My children know that I have friendships with other men. They know my feelings about sexual relationships being a matter of choice. I have not discussed explicitly the content of my sexual behavior with other men with them because I don't expect them to tell me explicit details of their sexual behavior.

> They (her children) are very familiar with the fact that we both have friends...it's amazing how perceptive the kids are...they are aware of both of us getting calls and letters from others.... One day unexpectedly a woman friend of my husband was in town from New York, and he called up to say he was going to take her to dinner.... I said OK, but I was kind of griped about it because some other things were bothering me at that time and my daughter saw that and said, "What's the matter?" I said, "Oh, this woman Doris is in town, and Daddy's taking her out to dinner." She said, "Well, when you go visit Tom, does he take you out to dinner?" and I said, "Yes." "Well," she said, "what's the difference?"

Not only are these children becoming sensitized to alternate forms of marriage and sexual interaction, but also the latter example portrays a reciprocal socialization process. Instead of only the parent teaching the child, in this instance the child also teaches the parent. As a development of the interaction, the daughter contributes to the socialization of the mother to the open marriage. We can expect that children socialized in an open setting will be less prone to possessiveness and jealousy in their own mariages in the future. Indeed, research on childrearing indicates that we can expect change in the emotional makeup of future generations of children.[21] As we move away from the patriarchal toward an egalitarian family structure, children will be less subject to the insecurities and jealousies that are necessarily a part of a marriage system built on dependency and exclusivity.

Conclusion

What can be determined from the experience of these women in open marriages? First of all, it is possible to redefine marriage apart from its traditional monogamous base. Flexible monogamy is still in an experimental stage of development and is a more complex form of marriage than exclusive monogamy. Because of this the failure rate will necessarily be high. Nevertheless, four couples did succeed in open relationships for several years.

There are a cluster of factors, some obvious and others not so obvious, necessary for success. These include: mutual agreement of the marriage partners; a gradual process of self-socialization to a new marital belief system based on non-exclusivity; a constantly developing structure of explicit rules; adherence to the rules by all involved persons, including the extramarital partners; sufficient experience with intimacy to have eliminated gross reactions of insecurity; a high tolerance for conflict; and well-developed communications and negotiating skills.

An assessment of the most significant costs of flexible monogamy include managing jealousy, problems of allocating time, and the inability to share knowledge of one's life style with more than a few very close friends for fear of condemnation. Problems can also arise if one partner has more extensive outside involvements than the other. On the other hand, participants who manage a successful open marriage feel that the benefits far outweigh the costs. The most frequently mentioned benefits are increased self-knowledge and growth, intimacy with others, the excitement of new experiences, diminished jealousy and possessiveness, and improvement of an already satisfying marital relationship. This list of potential gains coincides with the reasons given by persons who deliberately decide to remain single.[22] Open marriage is an attempt to combine the best of marriage with the best of a successful single existence. At the same time it tries to reduce the less attractive elements of each, such as the one person isolation of singlehood and the two person dependency of couplehood. Paradoxically, in an open marriage, "the primary bond (with the spouse) became simultaneously more *and* less important. Contrary to usual Western-type thinking about love and the experience of polarities, these couples reported a concurrent development of both intensification of closeness and a sense of apartness with the primary other."[23]

It is likely that of the sequence of marital lifestyles that begins with traditional monogamy and moves through secret and consensual extramaritality, flexible monogamy, group marriage, and communes, open marriage may be the most comfortable for persons dissatisfied with conventional monogamy. That is because open marriage is based on the already familiar marital couple. It avoids the difficulties of trying to mesh the emotions and activities of a number of adults who would comprise a group marriage or a commune.[24]

It is also likely that couples may prefer the lifestyle of open marriage only at certain phases of their married life. Newly married couples in this and the other research to date waited until they were married several years to open their marriage. From what is known, then, open marriage appeals mostly to couples in their middle years. We can probably assume that elderly couples would not be interested in open marriage, but as sexually permissive married couples move along the life cycle, that assumption may be less likely to be true.

In fact, how many people live this option right now, or have lived it, or would like to live it, is not known. We need to have more information on the extent of open marriages; we need to study such marriages while they are in progress, to see how feasible a marital option it is. I have focused on the transition from having extramarital relations to an open marriage and looked primarily at the social aspects of this kind of intimacy. Let us now turn our attention back to extramarital relations and look specifically at the sexual side of these involvements.

Chapter Five

Sexual Scripts and Sexual Behavior

Sexual activity can be thought of as occuring within the framework of a script.[1] A sexual script tells people how to behave and think in particular situations. The traditional Western script for women, which might be called "chastity and monogamy," has long been taught to women through the institution of the family. It is by growing up in a family, and later by creating one of their own, that women have learned to repress their sexuality, to save it for marriage, and to use it for producing children. Throughout history, if women did not learn their lesson well in family life, the institutions of law and religion stood ready to punish any sexual infractions with either legal or moral sanctions.

Even in modern times, various scientific experts have supported the traditional control of female sexuality. Freud and his followers, in particular, have had a tremendous impact in defining and regulating female sexuality in our culture. Following Freud's writings, most psychologists have determined the female sexual character to be passive, masochistic, often nonorgasmic, and family-centered.[2] Sociologists Gagnon and Simon, in discussing the way in which we socially construct human sexuality, have summarized the key elements of the traditional script as follows:[3]

> For females the acting out of sexuality occurs much later and in response to the demands of males and within the framework of societal expectations. For the female sexual activity does not occur for its own sake, but for the sake of children, family and love. Thus sexuality for the female has less autonomy than it has for the male, and the body (either of the self or of others) is not seen by women as an instrument of self-pleasure. This vision of sexuality as a form of service to others is continuous with the rest of female socialization.

Radical elements have affected our ideas of female sexuality recently. Although some early findings of Kinsey that contradicted stereotypical notions of women's sexual behavior were mostly ignored,[4] the research of Masters and Johnson has gained greater acceptance. Through their work we know that the potential for sexual expression is virtually unlimited for women. This research and the 1960's cultural climate of sexual permissiveness are potent sources for contemporary understanding of female sexual potential.

The force of feminism has also made women more aware of many new possibilities in all areas of their lives. Feminist scholars, anticipating the consequencs of these events, have predicted an unprecedented redefinition of sexuality for women.[5] They believe that women will develop their sense of a sexual self based on their own sexual drive rather than on accepted definitions of what they should do. They expect that women will grow more casual about sex, that they will seek more sexual relationships, that they will marry less or later, and have fewer children.

A sexual script that has been taught for centuries, however, is not so easily or quickly changed in a decade or two. There is a tendency for new behavior and thoughts to emerge gradually and only in certain groups of the population at first, generally those that are younger, urban, and better educated. Thus, the first significant break in the traditional sexual script occurred among younger women who are increasingly engaging in premarital sex. Although a large majority of unmarried women are having premarital sex, this does not mean they have left behind traditional motivations for it. Some no doubt are having "modern" casual sex; for others the old drama still lives within their minds and bodies. They have sex primarily because they want to please their boyfriends, or they fear losing them if they don't.[6]

Similarily, although married women are also revising their sexual script and engaging in more extramarital sex, it is not known what the specific nature of this sexual activity is. Do women break out of the script of monogamy only to revert to traditional sexual behavior? Do they have sex to please their lovers or themselves? Are they inhibited because they are having sex with two men at the same time? How much do they enjoy the extra sexual activity? To get some insight to these questions, we will look at what women said about the sexual aspects of their extramarital involvements. In this discussion, women talked about their last relationship, which, for about one-third of them, was also their only one.

Evaluation of Extramarital Partner and Comparison with Husband

Almost all of the women said that they were satisfied with their extramarital partners as lovers. Their responses to questions in this area were decidedly enthusiastic. They used words such as "a skilled and beautiful lover," "great," "very tender," "fantastic," and "excellent." Very few women were disappointed, but when they were they pointed to deficiencies such as "less demonstrative" or "didn't put much feeling into it." Here, again, women were emphasizing the importance to them of the emotional qualities of the relationship. Whether women were evaluating the verbal or physical qualities of extramarital involvements, it was the expressiveness that mattered.

When asked to compare their lovers with their husbands and state which one they preferred, no one refused to andswer the question or hesitated to respond. Women talked comfortably about their extramarital sex and readily made comparisons between sexual partners. Replies to the question indicated that somewhat over one-half of the women (60%) enjoyed sex more with their extramarital partner; slightly less than one-quarter (24%) found sex equally enjoyable with both; and the remainder (16%) felt that they had more sexual pleasure with their husbands. Of the group prefering sex with their lovers, only half of the marriages were intact at the time of the interviews, whereas 82% of the marriages of the other two groups were ongoing. It is possible that deteriorating marriages affected the preference of the women for their lovers, or that the experience of better sex outside the marriage affected the evaluation of their husbands, or, even more likely, that both factors were operating at the same time. By now it is obvious from past research that the condition of the marriage is only a small part of the explanation of extramarital involvements.[7] Concentrating only on that factor is too superficial. We need to examine the quality of the extramarital interaction itself if we are to advance our understanding.

What was it, then, that made most women prefer extramarital sex with their lovers? The most prevalent response of women in this group focused on the difference in sexual experience:

> Our sexual relationship is totally different. I guess that's where the crux of it is. It's certainly where it initially was and although all other things with Peter are wonderful, too, it's still the main drawing card to stay involved in the relationship. I'm orgasmic with both. Sex with my husband is straight fucking and oral-genital contact which is all nice, but it's not passionate. It's pretty much all we do. My husband and I almost never, ever kiss. There is little time spent in bed

before we fuck. We don't fuck very often.... It's not really a turn-on like it is with Peter. I think Peter is the greatest lover in the world. That's obviously subjective, but I will bet that other women who've made it with him will say that, too.

Oh, Christ, I could write a book! Ah, comparatively he is a fantastic lover.... The physical thing, you know, between Jim and I is absolutely incredible. It's probably—it's the major thing even with all this intellectual closeness, it's primarily, you know, a good fuck.... He has really opened me up as a lover even more than my first. I do things with him that I can't do at home. It's funny to have a hang-up just because to me he is my husband, you know, so like—that's something else again.

He is a lot more tactile than my husband. He enjoys the extras more than just the intercourse thing. He is particularly good—I don't know is I should use the vernacular, but he eats pussy really well. And that is something I don't get at home.

I guess we made love about twice a week, but one of those times would be an all night session. His favorite fantasy was making love until he just couldn't make love anymore and that never happened to him and that was a fantasy I was quite willing and able to satisfy.

One of the things that intrigued me was—he said every time he did it he did it in a different way and—uh—I suppose in a certain way I was also fascinated by the fact that he was a black guy, too. I guess I was a little curious about that and what not.... It certainly was a lot more diversified and of course I guess partly being forbidden fruit or "the something different" kind of aspect—it was certainly more exciting. My husband and I had come to a point of not being able to get through to each other very well and—uh—it seemed like the more I suggested different positions or new ways of doing things, the more resistent he became.

All of these women, with the exception of the last one, had intact marriages at the time of the interviews. In part, women found their extramarital sexuality to be different because their lovers gave them specific sexual experiences they did not or could not get at home. Interestingly, a few women felt a sexual constraint with their husbands that they did not feel with their lovers. This reaction is not unusual. Kinsey reported some women were also more responsive in extramarital than marital sex.[8]

Beyond specific differences in the content of sex, women responded to differences in various qualities of their extramarital partners. A couple of them, as noted above, were fascinated by sex with men of a different racial group. Other women reacted frankly to the physical appeal of their lover's body. While at times this reaction was because women chose lovers who were their physical "type" and their husbands weren't, often the attraction was to younger men or to those men who were more "into" keeping their bodies "in shape." As one women explained it:

> Sexually it was really great for me. He was more sexually satisfying, more physical. I was more physically attracted to him, I was just absolutely in love with his body.

Because our culture has not emphasized the beauty and desirability of the male body as it has the female body, women have been widely believed to be sexually immune to the erotic lure of the male physique. Women have been socialized to ignore the physical attributes of men and to stress economic achievements in selecting partners. Even overweight or plain men have not found their appearance to be detrimental in attracting women. But the woman above doubtless speaks for many others who have discovered the physical qualities of a man to be an increasingly important part of what turns them on sexually.[9] Some men obviously have tuned in to this knowledge by placing increasing emphasis on body-revealing clothing and cosmetics for the face and hair. Just as women are raising their expectations of emotional competence in men as a consequence of women's improved economic resources, so, too, it becomes necessary for men to counter in the sexual bargaining market with improvements in their physical assets. John Travolta said it eloquently in *Saturday Night Fever* with his body. Which of the young women who admired him cared that he was only a clerk in a paint store when he looked and danced like a disco Valentino?

Not only are contemporary women reacting sexually to men's bodies, but they are also enjoying other charms of younger men. One 31 year-old wife reported on her relationship with a man five years younger than she:

> My sexual relations with Brett, as compared to my husband, is—uh—I am open, I can relax—uh, he's really into me, physically, and he's got my tempo down and what pleases me. I can tell him to stop, continue, do something new, just in response to my nonverbal clues. It amazes me how one man can be so sensitive and into a woman's being, as a woman, as compared to another man who is so completely ignorant and is very

> uninspired lover. The only thing my husband's got going for him is a large penis. If he only knew what to do with his hands and mouth, we'd be all set. You know, for years I felt very—for awhile there, with all the pressures my husband had, as I said, sex was once a month. Now, very, very rarely, it might be once a week; very, very seldom ever more than that.
>
> From my relationships, I do realize that I do crave a sexual relationship. Brett is just a fantastic lover. He's considerate; he's kind; he's into me as a woman, and it makes me feel good. And he's not clumsy, and for somebody who's twenty-six, it—um—maybe it's the younger generation—but he's really with it and he's in tune with his body and mine. Compared to my first relationship with somebody who was thirty-four, and my husband, thirty-two—maybe a stifled generation where lovemaking wasn't too inspired, at least not with the people I got stuck with.

Contrast this young man's sensitivity and intuitiveness to the following description by a 59-year-old woman, who preferred her 56-year-old lover to her husband, despite some problems:

> My sexual relationship with 'X' was, as I said, the most exciting thing that ever happened to me. As a lover he was not what I would call the world's greatest. He had great staying powers and we would go to bed, get up, have wine, listen to music, go back to bed. It was great fun.... Although he pretended or acted as though he was concerned with my total pleasure, he did not make any great attempts t see that this was accomplished. Mainly, I think because he didn't care that much, and I myself had no real desire to—well, I never had an orgasm with him, and it just seemed like too much work. I doubt if I could have since the psychological barriers were great. There was never an opprtunity for complete relaxation. We seldom had more than a few hours together.

Although this woman partially excused her lover's perceived deficiency on the basis of lack of time, women who had younger partners did not observe the same deficiencies and yet had only the same few hours with their partners. Pairings with younger men in general gave women increased access to the type of "new," sensitive, and expressive men many women preferred, since it is the younger men who are more likely to be in the forefront of modifying stereotypical masculine roles.

One 42-year-old woman had had a number of extramarital involvements, all with younger partners. Since she easily looked ten years younger than her age, she consistently attracted younger men. She spoke of her current involvement with her 28-year-old lover:

> He was one of the best. He was super enthusiastic about making love and making love to me. He was very loving, affectionate, tender. And so willing to please! He had had sex only with his wife and one other woman, so he was relatively inexperienced but a very quick learner. He had never done oral sex to a woman because his wife wouldn't let him. Anyway, I love it so I taught him and he became very proficient. I in turn did it to him—his wife wouldn't do that either—and he couldn't believe how good it was. He always said that I taught him practically everyting he knew about lovemaking. Oh, one other thing—he used the term 'oral love' instead of oral sex. I never had heard anyone say that before, and I really liked that. It seemed a much better description of what was going on.

More than one-third of all the women interviewed chose extramarital partners younger than they by four to fourteen years. Since the women's husbands were the conventional several years older than they, this meant their lovers were much younger than their husbands. This age difference added another element to the diversity women found in extramarital sex. Although the myth is that men are not attracted to older women, the reality appears to be otherwise. Kinsey reported in 1953 that a number of married women (he didn't specify how many) had extramarital involvements with younger men, adding that many men "prefer to have coitus with middle-aged or older women." The reason was not that older women were more grateful, as Ben Franklin humourously but chauvinistically expressed it, but that men found "older females not so likely to become disturbed (over extramarital sex) and often have a better knowledge of sexual techniques."[10] Of course, Kinsey's explanation also reflects a traditional understanding of sex, for although his research was on women, he sought to explain why men would enjoy older women rather than why older women might enjoy younger men. In any case, his finding of the desirability of older women to younger males seems not to have become as well known as other of his findings, probably because it did not coincide with established myths of male-female sexual interaction.

Beyond the Male Myth, a 1977 study of the sexual attitudes of 4,066 American males, reported that only one-sixth of the men interviewed "insisted that their sex partners be no older than themselves."[11] It was mostly older men—over 55—who demanded younger women. Age was of least concern to those men who were divorced or widowed and those who were college educated. Thus, the increasing trends in our society toward more marital breakups and toward higher levels of education may be contributing to a change in the age standards by which men and women evaluate each other as prospective sexual partners.

Currently, older women/younger men couples are more prevalent than in the past, even in marital or cohabiting relationships. Numerous Hollywood couples are an especially visible example, but probably most people can see examples of this trend among their friends. Census data indicate that about 15% of marriages now takes place between couples in which the woman is as much as five, ten, or even fifteen years older.[12] It is likely that among nonmarital pairings there is an even larger proportion of these "new" couples, because the issue of permanence is not as much a factor in these relationships. Indeed, the degree to which marriage itself is no longer a permanent relationship is undoubtedly significant in the number of marriages between older women and younger men.

This traversing of traditional age norms, in which women were expected to choose only men older than themselves, has consequences for both men and women. Younger men will benefit more so than older men, for they will have access to a wider range of women. They also gain access to sexual partners who are likely to be more understanding and more skilled sexually because of their greater experience. Women in their thirties, forties, and fifties, at the height of their sexual interest and capacity, can be more active than passive sexual partners, which many men say they now prefer.[13] The 42-year-old woman mentioned that her 28-year-old lover had said to her, "Why should I have to wait until I'm 42 to enjoy a 42-year-old woman?"

Older men may find less to enjoy in this new age trend, however. For one thing, their monopolistic access to older women will be broken, as they will face greater competition from younger men. Older men will probably become more conscious of their age as a factor in their sexual appeal and may increasingly resort to artificial aids like plastic surgery to retain their youthfulness as long as possible. One can already read various media reports on the growing number of male plastic surgery patients. While the American obsession with youth has been rightfully deplored by many, it is an integral part of a consumer society, and male-female relationships will continue in various and changing ways to reflect that fact.

For women, the rejection of traditional male-female age norms promises benefits beyond those already mentioned. It considerably increases the number of poetential sexual partners for women if they are freer to select both older and younger men. This growth in the number of potential partners will have more impact on women than younger men, for the population of adult males at all ages is always smaller than adult females since life expectancy differs by sex.[14] Older women can reduce the demographic shortage of men in their age groups by choosing younger men.

Additionally, the self-esteem of women cannot help but be enhanced by the knowledge that they are desirable to younger men. Traditional myths of sexual desirability have served only to derogate women's self-esteem as they grow older. The increasing prevalence of extramarital sex, as well as sex occurring after marital breakups, are two important areas of interaction in which women can gain social points for increased age. As another fortyish woman, who had several relationships with younger men, remarked, "I think it's fun to play the role of the older woman." There are few other areas of American social life about which women can make that remark.

Returning to the discussion of women who preferred sex with their lovers, a secondary theme among these women was the opportunity to continue to develop their sexuality. Women in general still have less premarital experience than men.[15] Particularly for the women here who have only had premarital sex with their husbands (40% of the women interviewed) or who have had no premarital sex at all (20%), there has been little opportunity to explore the sexual potential. They have had to define their sexual selves on the basis of experience with only one partner. As one 26-year-old woman explained:

> It's silly to say, but I knew that I was in no way turned on to my husband. I knew that he could be very much turned on to me, but I couldn't (be turned on to him). And so in that sense I thought there was something missing. I didn't know that our sex wasn't good. I just assumed that's the way it is. Screwing those five minutes—you know—and that was it. I didn't realize you could spend hours in bed and I guess I made up for lost time. So I spent a year and a half in bed. It was really excessive, I guess.

Interviewer: As you said, you were making up for lost time.
Yeah, and that's how I felt. I felt like someone had starved me. And it wasn't just for sex. It was the whole thing of reaching out for another person. You remember I told you that with my husband I felt always afraid to be touched. And here I was not just opening up sexually but just being able to go up to Evan and hug him and kiss him and feel warm and loving kinds of feelings. Which I'd never been able to do before. And I think I'd never been able to do that in my relationship with my husband even early on in the marriage. So in many ways, not just sexually, I felt it was a very liberating kind of thing and to that end I'm not sorry it happened at all. Because I would never have known that part of myself.

And another 30-year-old woman recalled:

I had figured once we were married, there were no restrictions, but the night of the wedding, my husband was in the missionary position, period. I already started feeling the shackles. It was terrible. On a scale of one to ten, I would rate my husband a one and David eight and one-half. It haven't met a nine or ten yet.... Sex with David is nice. I'm still not sure I'm having orgasms, but it's brought me places I've never been.

Since the sexual experiences were so different from those with their husbands, women gained sexual feedback different from what they had received before. Often women discovered through extramarital sex that they were capable of more passion, more aggressiveness, more interest in previously little performed activities than they had suspected.

Women who engage in extramarital sex can open up new avenues of social learning about sexuality and their sexual selves. Not only do they experience different sexual situations, they also experience themselves differently in these different situations. They get alternatives in sexual feedback, and they can compare and evaluate this feedback and choose the most positive evaluations from among them. Instead of accepting their husband's definitions—that they are too passive, too frigid, or too oversexed, as several of these women had—women with diverse extramarital experiences gain more autonomy in the creation of their sexual self-images.

A third focus of the women's reactions who preferred their lovers was on the opportunity it gave them to evaluate their marital sex. They may have had an excellent sexual relationship with their husband, but they had no way of knowing for certain that it was as good a relationship as they could have had. Conversely, if marital sex was disappointing, they may not have known that anything better was possible. Some of the previous comments have hinted at this evaluational component to extramarital sex, but the following woman's remarks illustrate it quite clearly:

> With my husband, I just felt there was so much that I could be satisfied, and Allan does that for me.... For me he's the kind of lover that knows more about me than I know...he's a more enthusiastic lover, more inventive, more spontaneous, much more spontaneous...a much more physical person...hand-holding, cheek-rubbing, Allan does that for me. Sexually we can be together for three or four hours, without even knowing that four hours have passed...maybe if I were living with Allan it would not be as exciting, I don't know. (Age 32)

Women Who Preferred Husbands

In the group of women who found sex more enjoyable with their husbands, there again was a difference in the experience between lover and husband. These women had a less complex response than those who preferred lovers, but they still reacted to the learning aspects of the experience. One woman discovered what was sexually dissatisfying to her:

> He was quieter, less demonstrative, and much more gentle, almost too much so. So gentle that I really needed much more stimulation, especially clitoral stimulation. I told him and he tried to have a little harder touch, but I guess he was afraid of hurting me becaue he still didn't touch me hard enough to really stimulate my clitoris to the point of orgasm. (Age 32)

Another learned that she had difficulty in articulating her sexual needs, a form of communication she had no need to practice at home:

> In my judgment my husband and I have an excellent sexual relationship in terms of satisfaction...then when I began relating to other men I didn't have an orgasm. I know part of it is I know what I need to have an orgasm but I'm timid about saying it still. And the nature of most circumstances are usually very different—somehow I'm just not very open about that.... That's my particular hangup. If I'm not sexually satisfied, it's my problem, because I haven't told anybody of my needs. So—uh—Ray, bless his heart, was the first person who ever directly asked me what I wanted. If they asked me, I

could tell them. So he's been the only person I've ever had orgasms with, in addition to my husband. (Age 37)

And a third found that a man's inexperience can be sexually stimulating and enjoyable because he had a personal manner she found very touching and sincere:

> It was not as good with Fred as with my husband. And yet, I had orgasms with Fred, also. Fred was not used to this—just kind of reveling in the body of the other person. Lying around, and feeling each other, and kissing each other. I don't know; it's hard to explain. So I did not enjoy it as much with Fred. But there was something about the way our bodies came together that I had orgasms anyway. And I found his inexperience touching. (Age 30; partner, age 24)

One woman preferred her husband for emotional reasons:

> My husband was much better, I think the other person didn't put much feeling into it.... I didn't have an orgasm with him and I did with my husband. (Age 25; partner, age 35)

In other cases, it was being sexually accomplished that was responsible for the woman preferring her husband:

> He is very satisfying, but my husband is much more of a sexual athlete. Sexually, I have taught my friend more. (Age 42; partner, age 53)

A few women, like the one below, were not specific about why they preferred their husband sexually but just indicated that the sex was "better":

> One of the proposals in this agreement I had with my husband was that we would never compare, but of course I always would. When sex with my husband was good, it was better than I ever had with Frank. But I really did enjoy him as a lover and the longer the relationship, the more compatible we were (Age 28; partner, age 28)

Women With No Preference

What about women who enjoyed both their husbands and lovers equally? Did they perceive any differences in their experiences? Here's what some of them said:

> The first couple of months it was fun because of the excitement. It was great because I did care. At home I have a lot of orgasms, especially recently. I can't even say sex was better. It's not. It's just as good at home as it is out, except we give in to

> fantasies much more with the other guy than I do at home. (Age 31; partner, age 33)
>
> I think both of them are very good lovers, sexually. Actually, on a scale of 1 to 10, I ive them both a 10. (Age 29; partner, age 29)
>
> They're about the same. I enjoyed it as much, maybe a little bit more. Not that it was any better, just that it was forbidden. You know the whole thing was exciting and different. (Age 29; partner, age 22)

These women had a tendency to give less elaborate responses than those in the previous groups, especially when they viewed the sexual experience as being not only equal with but also similar to that with their husbands. With a couple of exceptions, the content and length of their briefer comments suggest that the sexual activity has not been as great a learning experience because of the similarity between partners and husbands. They responded primarily to the excitement of doing something that has traditionally been forbidden and to the opportunity of enjoying sex with a different partner.

One exception was a woman who found herself enjoying sex with a lover who was impotent. She (and probably her lover, also) had discovered the myth of the "rigid penis":

> The guy's impotent, which made him a fantastic lover. He was just— sex with my husband is fabulous, but one thing we've never—until recently, it would be a fantastic fifteen minutes of sex and that would be it and with this other guy we could spend like five hours in bed, just kind of cuddling and holding and being soft and warm and not worrying about this tremendous tension that was building. (Age 30; partner, age 52)

Here physical expressivity—speaking with the whole body—replaces traditional goal-oriented orgasmic sex. What is usually thought of as foreplay becomes the entire sexual script, an end in and to itself. The man enacted a physical counterpart to the verbal expressiveness that women prefer. The sexual script that demands men satisfy women only through genital intercourse is thrown out the window—or out of bed, in this case. This is a different sexual experience that most males would probably not believe could please a woman. Yet this man was sufficiently innovative to supply tremendous warmth and extensive body contact, making him "a fantastic lover" despite the cultural label of impotence we have learned to attach to this kind of performance.

Another exception to this group of no preference between husbands and lovers was this woman:

> He's very similar to my own husband. But I really like the way he screws. He was just—very animal, and I really like that a lot. It was just like—it was almost like seducing a young virgin or something. He's older than me by about twelve years, but I almost felt wicked in seducing this virginal type creature....
>
> And the thing that had prompted our sexual fervor was a discussion of Masters and Johnson. And I was telling him (a doctor) that I thought he did a really fucked up job of sex counseling with patients and he had very little data. He had refused to read Masters and Johnson, thought they were really kind of perverted people.
>
> I really laid into him, and that got us really started thinking sex, and I guess it was experimental on his part, because I was able to show him dimensions of sex that he had only dreamed existed. Of ourse, by that time, I was pretty damn good in bed, and sort of would rival The Happy Hooker in many respects, I think. It just blew his mind that he was able to come that many times. It just really blew his mind. (Age 40; partner, age 52)

She became a "seductress" and reacted to the "virginal" quality of the man, teaching him from the perspective of her greater experience, despite her lesser age. Although the appeal of the sexual innocent has been a centuries-old theme for men, it has always been focused on very young and, therefore, usually socially powerless women. This woman's response, in contrast, relocates virginal appeal from differences in power to the interplay of the repressed and abandoned sexual roles. It does not rest on social dominance, neither by age, nor occupation, since this woman was a nurse and her partner was a physician. Moreover, this woman's pride in her sexual competence is quite evident, despite our traditional belief that such a feeling for women is unacceptable.

While nearly all the women in this "no preference group" enjoyed sex with both partners, one had no preference because neither was very "exciting":

> They're very similar, I guess, actually. Neither one is terribly exciting. But again, you know, maybe I've got this myth going—like I had about virginity—about adultery. Maybe that excitement doesn't exist. (Age 32; partner, age 32)

She is still puzzled over what to expect from sex. Clearly, neither marital nor extramarital sex has met her expectations, which presumably have been fed by conventional myths. She wonders, by way of explanation, if the problems lie in her high expectations. A partial conclusion here is that she still has unanswered questions about the possibilities of sexual gratification, questions that might in part have been answered had her extramarital (or marital) relationship been of a different quality. Thus, the opportunity for sexual learning in extramarital situations is only a potential, not a certainty, and depends upon the quality of the experience.

To summarize the reactions of these three groups of women, almost all found their extramarital experience to be satisfying. There was no evidence that sex outside marriage was intrinsically dissatisfying (except in the rare case of time being too limited); indeed, at times the excitement of its forbidden quality seemed to increase gratification. The "forbidden" quality of extramarital sex is more traditional than new, however.

What is noteworthy is that a great part of the enjoyment stemmed from the differences in sexual experiences between husbands and extramarital partners. Women enjoyed variety in their sexuality, and this variety arose partly from specific techniques, but also from different personal qualities of the extramarital partner, such as variations in age, physique, and sometimes social class and race.

Women also were gratified by the opportunity to play sexual teaching roles and by the freedom to continue to discover and develop their sexual selves. The perception of differences in sexual experience and the fostering of self-growth are inextricably linked in the chain of rewards which extramarital sex affords. Since much cultural emphasis today is placed on adult development, the rewards of extramarital sex stand out as a primary contemporary theme.

Differences in Sexual Activity with Extramarital Partner and Husband

As differences in the marital and extramarital experiences were so salient in women's descriptions, I questioned them further on specific differences in activities. Thirty-eight percent of the women said there were specific activities they had done with their lovers but not with their husbands. There was no consistent relationship between less satisfactory marriage and greater or lesser variety in sexual activities with their lovers, even though there was a tendency for these same women to prefer sex with their lovers. There was, however, a countertrend among women with higher rated marriages to use more variety of techniques with lovers than with husbands. It is unclear exactly what this means. It does support the previous assertion that the quality of extramarital relations is not necessarily dependent on the quality of the marriage. Beyond that, it may be that the finding is unique to this particular group of women, or it may mean something about women's extramarital sexuality that will take more research to understand.

The technique most frequently used in extramarital, but not marital, situations was oral sex:

> Anything different? O.K., as far as Frank—we do more oral sex. As far as Joe—we would have these marathon sessions where we could just go on and on for hours.... How come? It was because of my husband. He was neither interested in lasting as long as Joe and has hang-ups about oral sex, especially doing it. He didn't mind having it done to him at all. (Involved with two men concurrently) (Age 31)

> And he was interested in pleasing me that way, orally, which my husband wouldn't. He was the first man to ask me what I wanted.... He took the time to make me feel good, by stroking my skin and like being happy with the things I talked about and accepting me so completely that I could open up and say, "This feels better" and "Do that." He would immediately be accepting and responsive that way. (Age 53)

> There are a million things that I do with my partner that I do not do with my husband. Mainly because my husband won't do these things. My husband is a little robot and you put in a nickel and you push buttons and he goes through the motions. Uh—my partner is much more of a sensual man, for whom intercourse is not merely having an ejaculation, who can prolong a sexual encounter for two to three hours just with generally pleasuring each other many, many different ways. He also happens to be really turned on to oral sex which I am too, which my husband thinks is disgusting and can't do. (Age 36)

> Different things? Yes, oral sex, we do that. I don't do that with my husband. It turns him off.... The other thing I should say here is that my husband has not kissed me romantically on the lips for many years. I feel that's a real cheat. I love to kiss and he just does not respond to me. I mean, maybe the difference is that I'm a smoker and he's a non-smoker. You know, before

I get into bed, I'd just brush my teeth like crazy. Doesn't seem to matter, he's just not interested in kissing me. That's a big plus with my lovers, both of them; they both are very oral people. (Age 29)

Yes, positions differ; we have oral sex.... That is something I don't get at home.... It's not an important reason, but it is an important part. (Age 46)

The reported reason for the lack of oral sex in the marriage situation was the husband's unwillingness to perform it. In other sexual research women respondents have also reported the rejection of cunnilingus by some men.[16] Masters and Johnson, when they compared the lovemaking techniques of heterosexual men with lesbian women, observed that heterosexual men in their sample "were not as effective with cunnilingal stimulation as the lesbian stimulators." When husbands were interviewed on this matter,

> The consensus opinion returned...was that they had usually viewed cunnilingus as a means to an end (coitus) and simply had not devoted as much concentration on effective stimulative techniques as they might have if they had viewed cunnilingus specifically as an end point in itself.[17]

Here the myth of the "rigid penis" rises again. Cunnilingus, if used at all, is defined as preliminary, rather than the main event. This narrow definition of the way to orgasm results in constricting erotic possibilities. For a vivid example of this, we have only to recall and compare the portrayal of marital and extramarital sex in the film *Coming Home*, as Jane Fonda interacted first with husband Bruce Dern and then with her handicapped lover, Jon Voight. Sex with her husband, portrayed as an inexpressive person, was quickly and efficiently accomplished. He alone seemed involved in the act, and he proceeded directly to orgasm without any apparent concern for her feelings or physical satisfaction. Sex with her lover, a paraplegic incapable of "normal" genital intercourse, was tender, affectionate, and intimate. Engaging in oral sex, he brought her to a state of obvious involvement and orgasm.

In addition to the importance given oral sex, women mentioned variations in position:

> It was mostly different positions, mostly on that level. My husband wasn't interested in trying that. (Age 26)

> Yea, the main thing that I do with him that I don't do at home is — performing oral sex on him. I just can't do it at home. As

for positions there's a body difference there. My husband is very angular and bony, and it hurts me. So we pretty much do it sideways or a couple of other ways, because of that. Whereas Jim is—kind of—flabby, I guess, around the middle, and it doesn't hurt, you know, it's just really cuddly and super, so we do anything because his bones don't get in the way.... (Age 32)

Anal sex was rarely mentioned, and not especially favored when it was:

The only thing I did with David that I didn't do with my husband was anal sex once, but I didn't like it so I didn't do it again. (Age 34)

And, of course, different settings emerged due to the conditions under which extramarital sex is often conducted:

A lot of different stuff, of course, has risen from the situation. I mean when you're married to someone, and have your own bedroom and your own house, you don't have to go out and sit in the front seat of the car or make love on the beach or anything like that. So, these crazy things with Jim have come about because of the situation—like—we will go here to the beach and do it in the dunes and—you know, there's a great risk of getting caught, but we'll do it anyway. We've done it in their house, like when she was out of town. And, of course, this was a huge kick. (Age 33)

This last comment illustrates that excitement of risk and discovery can enhance the enjoyment of sex, a point which individuals could consider adding to marital sexual situations. It may well be that sexual scripts in marriage rely too much on the security of the home setting to give husbands and wives optimal sexual enjoyment.

Interestingly, two women felt inhibited about performing fellatio at home, but did so willingly with their lovers:

Yes, the main thing that I do with him that I don't do at home is—performing oral sex on him. I just can't do it at home. (Age 32)

He can—he gives me oral sex. I've let him come in my mouth and it hasn't bothered me. I guess I'm very abandoned with him because I feel so relaxed and he's so comfortable with his own sex.... And again, I did things with my—my friend that I wouldn't do with my husband, mainly because I just feel so inhibited with my husband, and my friend made me feel so good.... (Age 34)

Is it possible that some husbands who would not perform cunnilingus at home would also be more sexually free in an extramarital situation, as these women were? It is quite common to get locked into a sexual script because repeated and similar interactions build up behavior patterns that are difficult to break. One of the advantages of an extramarital situation is in being with a new person, as there are no previous agendas to overcome, and it is easier to try out new behavior.

In general, in this group of women whose extramarital sex was more varied than their marital sex, the importance of oral sex cannot be overlooked. Women also stressed other variations from a simple and goal-oriented intercourse, however. They preferred more complex sexual scripts, with emphasis on touching, extensive body contact, kissing, and more lengthy sexual encounters. What these women valued was a sexual spontaneity and expressiveness not controlled by rigid cultural notions of appropriate foreplay, positions, and timing.

Surprisingly, there were almost as many women (30%) who engaged in more sexual activities with their husbands as there were women (38%) who did more with their lovers. A few decided to reserve oral sex or other techniques only for their husbands because of their feelings for them:

> Yes, there were things I did with my husband that I didn't do with Tom because my husband means much more to me.

> Well, I did oral sex with my husband, but not with Chuck. I thought it was appropriate only with my husband.

What we see here is the development of greater complexity in scripting as extramarital sex becomes a more common experience. Oral sex is now very much a desirable part of sexual activity for these women. But by keeping their sexual contact with their lovers to genital intercourse they can reduce the level of intimacy with their lovers and maintain, to a certain degree, a measure of sexual exclusivity with their husbands. Thus, even though they were having extramarital sex, some women manipulated the meaning of it by limiting activity with their lovers. Much as premarital virginity was socially defined as unviolated by petting, so marital exclusivity and intimacy can be redefined according to the specific behaviors involved.

Sometimes the shorter length of the extramarital relationship was the reason for fewer activities:

> In fact, I think we're more conservative, because—well, I

guess I know my husband better after all these years and we've developed kinds of positions and behavior that we haven't gotten around to in the other relationship.

I have oral and anal sex with both men. There are things I don't do with my lover that I do with my husband just because of having more time, more furniture around, more floors, etc. My husband and I have made love in a swimming pool and my lover and I have never had that opportunity.

And, in two cases, the extramarital partners would not perform oral sex while the husbands did:

As for actually things different, I did fellatio on Bob but he did not do cunnilingus on me; that hung him up. And I can understand that, because I don't find fellatio that easy. When I'm really in the right mood, it's terrific, but sometimes I feel frightened by it. I don't—some guys force you to do it to them. Bob wasn't like that at all. But anyway, I could sympathsize with him that he found cunnilingus scary and he didn't want to do that. (Age 30; partnner, age 23)

He has tried cunnilingus, but I know he does not like it at all. It turns him right off. It's maybe doing too much for the girl in his little blue collar way, or whatever, I don't know. I've tried to say to Mac, "Look, for every time you like me to do it for you, I like to have it done to me, but if it doesn't go, you know, it's like beating a dead horse." There comes a point where you just have to say, "forget it," and I've reached that point with Mac. (Age 54; partner, age 58)

In these situations, age is the most likely explanation for the men's refusal to perform cunnilingus. One was probably too young to be comfortable with it, and the other in an age group—and social class—in which it has not been customary for men to practice oral sex.

In summarizing these specific differences in marital and extramarital sex, there are three tendencies reported in almost equal numbers. One is use of more and different techniques in extramarital sex; the second is less use; and in the third there is no difference. There is no simplistic relationship between techniques used and preference for either lover or husband. While there was a strong tendency to prefer oral sex in their erotic activity, very few women in this study placed emphasis only on the technique of the partner. It is not that technique is unimportant, but rather than women tended to judge technique within the context of the relationship. Sex for them was an experiential package that could not be separated from its emotional and social wrappings.

This definition is similar to that offered by women speaking about sexuality in general and differs from men's definitions, at least as they are perceived by women. Many women apparently see men as being genitally-oriented and interested specifically in orgasms.[18] Cultural sexual scripts for men contain the notion that sexual expressiveness should be primarily physical, consist of a specific sequence of acts, be accomplished through the genitals, oriented toward the goal of orgasm, and accomplished in a reasonably short period of time.[19]

Women, on the other hand, judging from what they say here and in other research, prefer sexual activity suffused with words, varied actions, and directed to the whole body. They are as interested in the process of sex as in a product, orgasm, and esteem various ways of creating and reaching orgasm. They especially value creativity and spontaneity, rather than relying on a uniform sexual script of any type, whether traditional or modern.

Effect of Extramarital Sex on Marital Sex

Since the experience of extramarital sex more often than not was different from marital sex, does it affect the marital sexual relationship? Only 35% of the women thought it had a negative impact, and this tended to be in situations of deteriorating marriages. A few of these women stopped marital sex completely, but the most usual response was to reduce the frequency of it or to reduce their emotional involvement in it:

> I probably have less sex with my husband since getting involved extramaritally. He has always wanted very little.... So, you know, quite often I would be the initator of sex, and since I'm getting all I want—well, maybe sometimes not all I want—so I don't approach him at all now.

> I don't know whether it's more or less sex with him. I stopped counting. I guess it's probably pretty much the same. And— uh—I can't say that having an affair with somebody has turned me on to my husband. I think in some ways it's kind of turned me off because I know I can get it somewhere else.

> Yes, it does, and as I said, I don't try to lay any trip on him anymore. If I am not totally satisfied in a relationship with my husband, I have learned the masturbation in a bathtub trick. We have an old-fashioned bathtub and I can drape my legs

over the end, and if he hasn't been able to finish the job, I can take care of it just nicely in the tub.

I probably started looking for my sexual satisfaction outside the marriage. When I wasn't satisfied with my husband, I didn't even care because I knew the next night I'd be with Ed and get satisfied.

A noticeable though peripheral theme was that of an increase in women's feelings of sexual independence that did not only occur in unsatisfactory marriages. Having learned that sexual satisfaction could be had from more than one source, women were reluctant to continue their previous dependence on their husbands, particularly on occasions when the marriage was temporarily unsatisfactory. Some even preferred the alternative of masturbation.

In contrast to the above reports of negative impact were the feelings of the majority of the women who reported either no effect on marital sex (40%) or that marital sex had improved while they were having extramarital sex (25%). One postive effect on marital sex was to make it freer and more varied:

Now that the truth is out and he knows I like these things and I wouldn't be horrified, it's amazing. The whole picture's changed.

Yeah, it changed my sexual relationship with my husband for the better. It helped me to loosen up and he noticed the change in my behavior. I also very gradually, very slowly introduced him to new techniques in such a way that he was really convinced that I thought them up.

Another positive consequence for marital sex was to increase its frequency:

Yes, it affected my having sex with my husband. It made us both really horny, really horny to think about me having sex with somebody else, so we usually had more in my marriage. (Open marriage situation)

It certainly affected my sexual relationship with my husband. I became more interested in sex with him, something I really couldn't understand at the time. I was riding high, returning from a visit with my lover. All those feelings needed an outlet. At times I felt this was terribly unfair to my husband, but it was always so good between us when this happened.

When I had the thing with Don, my husband and I had much more sex than we ever do. I was generally in a turned-on state about twelve hours out of every day and I was enjoying myself with my husband much more than I had before I started the relationship with Don.

A traditional interpretation of the increase in sexual activity is that it is inspired by guilt, but this is not supported by a careful analysis of the women's interviews. Rather, increased sexual activity seems to be the result of increased interest. That is, the more sex you get, the more you want. These women showed that their capacity and desire for sex enlarged once they had opportunities for this to happen.

Such experiential evidence supports the theoretical argument of psychiatrist Mary Jane Sherfey and the clinical evidence of Masters and Johnson that women have a virtually unlimited sexual capacity. The exclusivity of monogamy, which restricts women to one man each, is probably not the ideal situation for enhancing the growth of all women's sexuality. On the other hand, having multiple sexual partners may foster the development of sexual potential at the expense of some degree of intimacy with each partner. We have already seen that some women can and do manipulate the extramarital script to foster maximum intimacy with their husbands.

Scheduling of Extramarital with Marital Sex

Associated with the problem of maintaining separate spheres of intimacy with two or more partners is the practical concern of scheduling both sexual relationships. One of the general assumptions underlying social interaction is that there should be mutual and symmetrical involvement by all persons taking part in any activity. The more intimate the activity, the more difficult it will be to conceal the lack of expected involvement.

How, precisely, does one time extramarital with marital sex to avoid being negligent of the social expectations? It seems likely that too closely spaced sexual activity with different partners will pose transitional problems. Not only is there the requirement of a rapid transfer of physical and/or emotional intimacy from one situation to another, but also there is the added difficulty of disguising certain bodily cues and clues.

As Erving Goffman, a sociologist specializing in the study of everyday life, writes:

> The involvement that an individual sustains within a particular situation is a matter of inward feeling. Assessment of

involvement must and does rely on some kind of outward expression. It is here that we can begin to analyze the effect of the body idiom, for it is an interesting fact that just as bodily activities seem to be particularly well designed to spread their information through the whole social situation, so also these signs seem well designed to provide information about the individual's involvement. Just as the individual finds that he must convey something through the body idiom, and is required to convey the right thing, so also he finds that while present to others he will inevitably convey information about the allocation of his involvement, and that expression of a particular allocation is obligatory.[20]

Exactly half of the women had had sex on the same day with both husband and lover. Most of them reported difficulty in handling the experience. A few expressed concern about the cues the body idiom could convey:

> I have had sex with my husband and "X" on the same day and even within a few hours time. And it was always when my husband did not know about my having sex earlier with another guy, and I would always come in somehow and manage very subtly to clean up, because I had a fear of his being near me in the bed and all of a sudden having him say, "Aha! Here's the evidence. You've been out fucking with somebody else!" And just simply because maybe I'd have that kind of odor about my cunt or something.
>
> So I've always been careful to clean up afterwards immediately, so in case my husband and I did jump in the sack, there would be no, quote, evidence, unquote. But it's really humorous to me that I would think this because, of course, there's no way that they can prove anything.

> Once I did. I took a thorough shower when I got home, before I got in bed with my husband. It was a very eerie feeling; I was sure somehow he'd know. I think that was the only time, though. It really takes away from my enjoyment, because if I have had a good time with somebody, I like to savor and enjoy it yet afterwards. The person still is with me emotionally for several hours afterward, at least.

> With this new relationship, I guess—there would be times when I would come home from a whole day of making love and have to make love with my husband. Umm—I sort of accepted this. I didn't feel good about it. But he's so inept and it's rather—all so quick. A couple of twicks (sic) on the clit, if I'm lucky, with his hand. No oral sex. So, I really had no trouble with him discovering maybe, that I had been having

sex. Sometimes I was very sore and it wasn't even pleasant physically. I didn't feel good about it.

Others focused on the inward feelings which lingered from the previous situation and the necessity of forcibly transferring them to a different person:

> I would rather not have sex with my husband or with this other person, whoever he might be, within a few hours of each other, say, because I need more time, I like to reflect on meaningful experiences, and I haven't—I probably haven't come down enough from that thinking and reflecting and enjoyment to all of a sudden be thrust into something with somebody else.

A dancer who had been away on a tour sensitively described the problem of transition:

> Sex with both on the same day? *Oh*, yes, I did! That was the day I came home. He came to see me the night before, we made love that night, we made love in the morning. And I knew I shouldn't do that. I knew it was going to make it harder with my husband, but I couldn't let go a single moment that I could have with Frank. And I got on the plane, and I came home, and I was very tense and very grief-stricken....
>
> Then we went to dinner. We came home, and I kind of walked around feeling things, everything looked so dear because it was home. And I knew I had to make love with my husband. I mean, it had been a long time, of course that was what we'd do. If I hadn't had an affair— ah, gruesome details—and I got in the shower and took a shower and came out, and we made love. And I just said to myself the whole time, "Just relax, just let it happen. And don't think about this morning and don't think about Frank. Just—this is the moment that you have to get through and you will get through it." And I got through it and I had an orgasm with my husband, too. But I don't think I would want to live through that day again very often. It was very, very hard.

And another woman tried to solve the problem of confusion which arose from a too rapid transfer:

> Yes, I did, but not a whole lot. I tried to avoid it. It was not good. I often had the feeling, especially in the beginning—I had gotten into the habit of keeping a candle or a light on while making love, because I wanted to make sure which one I was with.
>
> Interviewer: Did you ever make any mistakes in names?

No, it became fairly obvious who you were with once you started making love. But—I didn't feel good about doing that. It was like I was too close from being with another person to hop right into bed with someone else.

It was surprising to find a few women who, while not troubled about stepping outside sexual conformity, found themselves unexpectedly feeling guilty after violating the time norms of social conformity:

I did have sex with him and my husband on the same day, within a few hours. The one time he and I had sex—uh—I felt—umm—like I had cheated on my husband, although I did not feel that way before.

There was a time when I did have sex with both my husband and Mike on the same day, and actually, at the beginning, strange as it seems, it was Mike's suggestion. He didn't feel that I should—quote—cut down. But I tried it and I felt terrible afterwards, I felt a betrayal on both sides but more so I think with Mike than with my husband. I felt very uncomfortable with my husband and I felt as if I was just doing a duty.

It appears that sufficient time serves to insulate us from the effect of competing social and sexual situations, as Goffman has suggested. It should be pointed out that a few women were having extramarital sex with their husbands' approval, but even these women felt uncomfortable. Even without the need to conceal the previous extramarital activity, the emotional residual seems to create distress if it must be transferred to a new, similar, intimate situation. Most women felt that they would not be troubled by sex with a different partner on the next day.

There were several women, however, who had sex on the same day with both husband and lover and enjoyed the experience. In only one case was this enjoyment motivated by revenge toward the husband:

I have no hang-ups about it. If anything, I sometimes feel the slightest bit vengeful, like, "You don't know, do you?"

For the others there was the factor of increased sexual drive, and enjoyment, of a higher libido, that emerged before in our discussion:

Yes, I have. It was only that I was still turned on and I liked it and it was great. I felt a momentary glee that, "Hey, gee, this is cool." It's just a kind of laugh; it's a giggle. There isn't anything retaliatory in it. It's just enjoying. I like sex.

> In my first marriage I did have sex with both my husband and my lover on the same day in a few hours. I found it very exciting and so did my husband. Of course he didn't know what was going on. He found exciting the fact that I was so well-lubricated and I found it exciting the fact that he didn't know why I was so well-lubricated.
>
> After I had sex with Robert I had sex with my husband because my husband, in knowing that I was having sex, got very horny thinking about people having sex in his house and him not there. So he'd come—when I'd finish, then he would come and want sex. I was so happy about things that I thought, "Yea, all right." I was really grinning about everything. How did I feel? Well in having sex in a few hours time with two people, I learned a new term, "sloppy seconds," that I didn't know before. Which was funny, I thought.
>
> With my husband it was much better after I had sex with the other person. I was really, really, I don't know—high—it was really great.

Others had discovered that it was possible to love two people at the same time, contrary to our romantic and cultural myths about the exclusivity of love. This occurred when extramarital relationships lasted for a year or more:

> Yes, I have had sex on the same day with both. I feel no guilt about it. I can't believe it. The guilt must be someplace, but I can't bring it to consciousness. I just feel these are two men I love and if I have sex with them both on the same day, I just do.
>
> Yes, I have. I have felt very good about both of them because I love and I care about and I enjoy expressing my love with these two different but important people.

A distinctively contemporary theme here is the philosophy of personal pleasure that transcends both the norm of monogamy and the difficulties of transferring involvement between competing situations. Although most women did not find a "two-men-a-day" sexual script to be preferable, it is significant that almost one-quarter of these women did so. It provides dramatic evidence of the dimensions of sexual development possible in contemporary scripts for female sexuality.

Most of the discussion in this chapter has so far focused on the positive aspects of extramarital sex, because that is how women perceived and reported their experiences. It is entirely possible, as noted earlier in this book, that women with more positive experiences would be more likely to want to talk about them; thus, this report may not fully explore all the possible negative consequences. Nevertheless, women did voice some concern about the sexual aspects of their extramarital relationships, ranging from pregnancy to physical attractiveness.

Contraception and Pregnancy

Nearly all the women used the same method of birth control for both their marital and extramarital sex. However, in a few situations in which the husband had a vasectomy, this meant using a different form of contraception for extramarital sex. The management of two kinds of contraception sometimes created a problem:

> Since my husband had the vasectomy, I use a diaphragm when I'm with someone else. This is a bit of a problem, since I have to make sure, of course, that he does not know I still keep my diaphragm.

> Eleven years ago Raymond had his vasectomy and that leaves me now with protection at home. But I can't take the pill because if all of a sudden my period got very regular it would be noticeable, an IUD I would be afraid that he would be aware of the string. I have a diaphragm but that's only good if I'm away overnight because of having to leave it in. It's been suggested to me that if I wanted to I would say no to sex that night, but that's not my habit to do that and I would just be afraid that it would be noticeable in one way or another. That leaves me with using a condom or being with another man who has a vasectomy, which has happened also.

Perhaps because of modern contraception and expertise with using it, the women generally were not worried about possible pregnancies occurring through extramarital sex. Only a few women expressed concern. One woman reported:

> I was very concerned about the possibility of pregnancy with Robert not because of anything, but because I don't want to get pregnant. When he was here those two weeks, after he left I didn't have a period for, well, about three months and I was sure that I was pregnant, and I was absolutely up a wall. First of all, I didn't want to be pregnant and my husband and I have an ongoing argument about, quote, if you get pregnant, and we have these huge arguments about what's going to happen when, if, I get pregnant. I've never been pregnant and we realize how ridiculous it is but it still goes on. If I get

pregnant I want an abortion. My husband doesn't want me to have an abortion.

Then I thought I was pregnant and I didn't even know whose it was.... So I thought that I was pregnant when I wrote to Robert, and I told him that if I was pregnant—and he wrote back and said that if I was pregnant, he would claim half and support half (chuckle) and he was all against the abortion idea. My husband was all against the abortion idea and then I found out that I wasn't pregnant. So that's the only reason why I'm worried about pregnancy, because I'm worried about pregnancy in general. These kinds of things are much easier to deal with when your husband knows what's going on.

This woman and her husband had an open marriage, and her husband both knew of and approved of her lover. Problems such as possible pregnancy are more easily resolved in such a situation, when partners not only are aware of the other's outside sexual activities, but have also gone through a transitional process to reach emotional acceptance of them.

Another woman had a birth control failure and became pregnant by her lover. Her experience is a vivid reminder that much work remains to be done to assure birth control efficiency and safety for all women:

The possibility of pregnancy very much looms around our mutual heads because the fact is—it occurred despite the fact I was on the pill. I secured an abortion the first time, and just this Thanksgiving I had a miscarriage—I'm pretty certain of that. The pill and I don't seem to agree, but I don't trust anything else. I had an experience with an IUD and I almost died, so the possibility of pregnancy now is very—is probably one of my paranoia, the prime paranoia now that runs through my mind. Also the fact that the whole abortion experience was like minus, minus, negative to me.... I don't really think that it puts a strain on our sexual relationship; I think that I think of it outside that. I don't think of it really when we are in bed together. I think about it other times. But I don't think the element of strain is there.

Two other women also became pregnant during a period of extramarital sex. One spontaneously aborted and the other chose to have an abortion. Except when women have difficulty or failure with birth control methods, concern over pregnancy is not generally a part of the extramarital situation.

Venereal Diseases

Similarly, women were rarely troubled by fears of venereal disease. Only a few responded affirmatively to the question of whether they were concerned about it:

> I'm always worried about the possibility of venereal diseases which I have checked every so often. My husband and Robert both have sex with other people so I don't know whose germs I'm getting from where. The VD problem is a very strange one. I go to a nice, middle-class, bourgeois gynecologist who's always shocked to death when I tell him I want a VD test. And he can't say it out loud, like I do (chuckle). I think he keeps wanting me to lower my voice every time I ask him for one. He asked me why I wanted one, and I told him both my husband and my lover sleep with other people, and he got very upset.

> Once in a while I was worried. But I would have invented a story to cover it if necessary.

It might be expected that women who were relatively well-educated would not be unduly worried about disease. Often they stated they knew what symptoms to be alert for and would immediately seek medical care. Several mentioned that they also felt free to discuss any possible symptoms with their partners:

> If any kind of disease should result, since he is a doctor and we are adult human beings, I'm quite sure that I would call him up and say, "What do you think I've got and what do you think I should do? Who should I go see? What's happening?" I think I would just share it with him because in no way do we ever lay an exclusive trip on each other.

Thus, concerns over pregnancy and possible exposure to disease were only peripheral items in these extramarital relationships because of the health knowledge of the participants, their willingness to discuss any problems with their partners, and probably, also, the number of relationships that had evolved to open awareness contexts. Robert Thamm, writing on this topic, asserts that when relationships are conducted openly, "the transfer of venereal disease would not seem to jeopardize our relationships."[21] Matters like sexually transmitted diseases and unwanted pregnancies cease being major sources of concern when people have built-in and normalized ways of handling such problems.

Other Problems

The interviews were conducted in a semi-open style, and women were encouraged to include any topic they wished to discuss. A number of items, therefore, surfaced too late to be included in all of the interviews.

The most frequently mentioned of these items was the question of physical appearance. About one-quarter of the women expressed some anxiety about their physical attractiveness. In my observation there was no correlation between a woman's actual attractiveness and her concern over it. And the anxiety was not confined to older women, but included women from every age group.

Two women in their thirties recalled their reactions:

> The first obstacle—the first obstacle was having—was being—having my body observed by a man whom I thought was very attractive when I wasn't thinking that my body was very attractive. That was the great obstacle. I was embarrassed—uh, uh—not embarrassed to be naked, but embarrassed that I would appear ugly naked.
>
> It didn't have anything to do with modesty. Paul was and still is, absolutely marvelous about it. I had decided, uh, about six weeks ago that I was going to have surgery on my breasts, cosmetic surgery. And I called him and I told him about it, and he ah—he just flew off the handle. He said there's nothing wrong with my breasts and—uh—my breasts attract him and excite him and they're soft and they're nice to touch and so forth—and you know—I shouldn't be a dope, and the fact that I've had children and this has left me with stretch marks, he didn't think—he thinks that my body is beautiful and he made that known to me right away. So there—so that was the first obstacle that I had to overcome—a personal, psychological thing.

> When I first had a relationship (at age 28), I was worried about exposing my body. I have stretch marks from having a big baby, and besides that birth control pills had a bad effect on my legs and broke down the veins. So I thought I was very unattractive because I didn't measure up to some ideal that women should—but I have found that the men I've been with don't seem to feel that way. I think maybe mass media have overstressed this "perfect ideal" and a lot of us suffer from it because of it.

And one in her fifties remarked:

> I've always enjoyed my own body, but I don't enjoy it as much

today, because I'm too fat. I think I'm ugly, sort of—you know—there's no doubt about that, in the mirror today, I am, forget it. And I get upset with myself because I don't diet and slim right down to some nice lovely, attractive—like I can never wear a bikini, and oh boy, I would be the bikini-wearer. I love all these nice, sexy clothes and I think if I were only thirty years younger...but you know, my body is all out of shape. But if you can enjoy your own body in bed, I think maybe at this age I have to settle for that.

As the second woman has observed, the mass media have a great deal to do with the representation and formation of ideal standards of physical beauty, presenting a picture of what should be versus what is.[22] The women who are presented on TV, in films, on magazine covers, and in newspapers are primarily physically perfect women, untouched by such real blemishes as sagging breasts, stretch marks, noticeable veins, fat, or wrinkles. Since the symbolic images of women greatly outnumber the real-life images we see, these symbolic images come to dominate our own personal standards. And since physical beauty is still more emphasized for women than for men in our culture, women can be expected to develop anxiety as to whether or not they meet the cultural standard.

Such anxiety is not peculiar to individual women, but must be understood as resulting from the pervasive emphasis on physical attractiveness and youth for women in our society.

For only a few women this anxiety became part of the motivation for extramarital activity:

> There's this terrible thing about age, you know. I was just thirty; gulp! That, you know, you're old and wrinkled and awful the minute you're not eighteen any more. I mean, it creeps up on all of us.... I really think that we're totally intimidated by this age thing. And I'm sure one of the things driving me was, I wanted to prove that I could attract and seduce a man, you know.

Some found it surprising that a man would be interested in them:

> I think maybe, I get a little let down after each relationship because I think that every time I feel that it was my fault, that I was not attractive enough or good enough in bed or something really to have someone interested in me. It really always blows my mind when a man is interested in me. I guess that's just something that will have to work its way out.

Women most often found their extramarital partners did not evaluate their attractiveness by stereotypical standards of female beauty; that men, at least the men they were involved with, were supportive and appreciative of their physical appearance. This feedback served as welcome counterpoint to the unrealistic standards perpetuated by the mass media.

Another topic introduced by a very few women was feelings of inadequacy concerning sexual technique. As one woman in her fifties mentioned:

> I never knew much about fellatio—am I pronouncing it correctly?—so I read about it after starting to date. *The Sensuous Woman* was helpful in terms of technique. A lot of books skirt around it.

Most women were not troubled about technique, however. In fact, it was evident from the interviews that several women took pride in their capability as knowledgeable sexual partners. As models of contemporary female sexuality continue to emerge, it may well be that we will see women feeling increasingly responsible for the possession of sexual expertise.

A final concern brought up by some women was for the wife of the man with whom they were involved. As one woman commented:

> I told him that the only thing I felt bad about was his wife, that women had been screwing other women for centuries, you know, over some man and that I didn't like that aspect of it.

Most of the women made an attempt to resolve their uneasiness by some kind of supportive activity or discussion. In the first instance cited here, the woman was acquainted with the wife of her lover:

> I didn't like the kind of person she was...meanwhile she was unhappy trying to break out of her Mah-Joong and hairdresser mold. Ironically, she turned to me for help because I seemed liberated to her. While I felt I wanted to help her—I want to see women change in general—the more I help her, the more I'm hurting myself, which was hard. But I would invite her when we'd go to these lectures. She'd want to read what I was reading. The first time she stood up for herself as a woman (getting a credit card; they wanted her husband's signature), the first person she called to tell was me.

The following woman did not personally know her lover's wife but knew of her situation through discussions with her lover:

I felt guilty about her. She was also trying to break out of the "happy homemaker" thing and I would find myself defending her to her husband, my lover. It was very strange; I felt divided. It wasn't until I found out she had become active in a local political campaign and was out every night that I figured everything was O.K. because now she, too, had other resources and wasn't totally dependent on her husband.

Finally, in a situation of open marriage, this conflict was again resolved because of the common understandings all the parties had:

I also had his wife's blessings. She in fact felt very good about our relationship because it took a lot of pressure off her extramarital relationship that she was having at the time. I guess it made her feel good to allow him the freedom to do this kind of thing, and she and I continued to be very good friends and even discussed this relationship I was having with her husband.

For the women who had not resolved this issue, it was clear they were concerned and felt it was something that contemporary women would have to deal with more thoroughly and openly in the future. As more knowledge of extramarital behavior becomes publicly and sociologically known, other solutions besides direct and indirect support between women, the lover's wife, and open marriage situations will undoubtedly be added to extramarital scripts.

Conclusion

There was virtually no evidence of the traditional model of female sexuality in the descriptions women gave of their extramarital sexual activity. Rather, women demonstrated an evolving script of female sexual expression with a common theme of female-centered sexuality, of enjoyment for oneself, of not living vicariously through one's partner. Women emphasized the gratification that could be obtained through variety in partners. This variety was defined by relations with younger partners (for both physical and expressive reasons), sexual involvement based primarily on erotic attraction to the male body, and, especially, an emphasis on particular sexual activities like cunnilingus, extensive body contact, and kissing.

This female-oriented sexual script contrasts sharply with the traditional script and its assumptions of passivity, lack of autonomy, family-oriented expressions of sexuality, and sexuality as service to others. Subthemes in the traditional script also rejected by these women were conventional age norms in choice of sexual partners and sexual interactions based solely on love.

Although these women significantly altered the traditional female script in their extramarital sexuality and adopted some behavior conventionally considered to be masculine, they did not duplicate stereotypical male sexual behavior. They still retained the female interest in the social context surrounding the sexual relationship and preferred sexuality with expressively satisfying interaction.

Women also valued the potential for self-discovery and self-definition through their sexuality which they found in their extramarital experiences. The diversity that most women encountered in extramarital sex gave them the opportunity to continue their sexual development and often resulted in changes in their definitions of their sexual selves. In the next chapter we will explore further these unexpected transformations in personal identity.

Chapter Six

After Involvement: Identities and Attitudes

Identity development during and after extramarital relationships was one of the central issues in the reactions of these women.[1] Although they never originally intended to have involvements outside of marriage, they all did and, for most, the experiences were both positive and significant.

Sociologist Anselm Strauss points to the transformational possibilities of playing "a strange but important role and unexpectedly handling it well."

> Whether you had considered this an admirable or despicable role does not matter. The point is that you never thought you could play it, never thought this potential "me" was in yourself. Unless you can discount your acts as "not me" or as motivated by something not under your control, you bear the responsibility or the credit for the performance...more subtle are those instances where you find yourself miraculously able to enact roles that you believed—at least as yet—beyond you...the net result is that you wish to experiment with this new aspect of yourself.[2]

Three out of four women accepted responsibility for their involvements—they did not discount them as something that "just happened"—and incorporated the new experiences into their identities or self-definitions.

Women had often reacted (as illustrated in the interview material in Chapter Two) to evidence of self-discovery or recognition of changed identity in their very first extramarital sex. Althea, in particular, whose initial experiences were described at length in that chapter, was an especially dramatic example for personal change. She said, "I realized that in what I was doing I had become an adulteress," but she was also pleased with this new aspect of her behavior, for she felt she "had taken a giant step forward." As will be recalled, she went on to change significantly her whole life style. Evidence of aspects of self-discovery, threaded throughout the other chapters on intimacy and sexuality, strongly support the transformational possibilities of women's involvements.

There is yet another reason to probe further into this question of identity development in extramarital relations. Sociologically, we know that people form their identities through interaction with others. In the course of social life we associate with many people, and the social reflections we get from the people who are significant to us count most in forming our definitions of ourselves.[3] In childhood, our most significant others are parents. As we mature, parents are supplemented and then replaced by our peers who become the most important influence in defining who we are and who we will be.

In adolescence and young adulthood, with the onset of sexual behavior, our lovers—and later spouses—enter the realm of important people contributing to our definitions of self.[4] Although social scientists originally thought that by the time we became young adults we had fully developed our identities, more recent work sees identity formation as a rather continuous process with substantial change possible as we move through the life cycle.[5] Our sense of self is open to modification, then, whenever we engage in situations or interactions with people we consider meaningful. Becoming involved with people in a new job, perfecting an athletic skill, developing a different hobby—in whatever manner we meet new people who become important to us—all contribute to the possibility of reflecting new and different visions of ourselves. These new visions may either reinforce or modify our previously developed and carefully nurtured definitions of ourselves.

Because of this potential for self-growth and self-discovery in their extramarital situations,[6] women were asked specifically if they thought their attitudes toward themselves had changed as a result of their extramarital experiences. Nine out of ten women reported not only that they had changed, but also that they had changed in a positive and permanent way. The few women who did not feel this way had had only one very brief extramarital relationship.

One of the most common changes mentioned was an increase in self-confidence:

> Yes, it built up my confidence and ego seeing that other men were attracted to me, things that I really didn't know before.

> It's given me a whole new way of looking at myself. It changed my whole way of dress, just my whole appearance. I felt attractive again. I hadn't felt that way in years, really. It made me very, very confident.

> Yes, it has changed my attitude toward myself. It has heightened my self-confidence in myself as a person and in my abilities.
>
> I think I'm more sure of myself and I don't think I have to prove any kind of sexiness like I used to....
>
> I worried about my body for a couple of years in the middle of my marriage that—uh—it was too long and my ass wasn't big enough and my waist small enough and my breasts which were very large were beginning to sag too much. I think now I understand because of my lover that these things aren't extremely important.

Most of the change in self-confidence was rooted in a sense of being more physically appealing because they knew other men were interested in them. This reaction is predictable because of the traditional role men have always played in validating women's worth as sexually attractive people. A husband can do this for his wife within marriage, of course, but even if the marriage relationship is good, he may not be able to provide additional rewards to self-esteem as his ability to reward may already be at maximum levels for him. The dailiness of marriage, and the repetition of tasks and conversation within it tend also to create a built-in level of rewards. People accommodate themselves to this habitual level, making any change difficult.

If a woman feels the need for increased emotional support, either because of the strength of her needs or because of her husband's perceived inadequacy in meeting them (it will be remembered that all of the women specified "expressiveness" as the least satisfying aspect of marriage), she may feel the only choice may be to go outside the marriage. If the husband-wife relationship is deficient, relating to other men not only makes up for a lack in rewards, but also gives a woman multiple sources of rewards from which she can choose the most satisfying.

Women conventionally have been socialized, from childhood on, to seek the approval of others. They are taught to rely on their appearance to obtain that approval, for appearance is a visual cue which others can quickly evaluate and respond to. Women begin hearing "What a pretty little girl you are!" as children and are told "You are so beautiful to me." as adults.

Rather than perceiving these personal rewards from extramarital relationships as just another successful round in the continual traditional female search for male approval, this feedback was seen to have had more than just a transitory effect by most of these women. This was especially so for those in their twenties and thirties who, because of their younger age, probably had the greatest potential for self-development. It is not that women just substituted their lovers' approval for their husbands'; rather, they seemed to progress to a more internally rooted sense of their attractiveness and value as persons.

This new perception of themselves also produced a heightened sense of self-confidence that was not only based on physical attractiveness. Women also reported feelings of being more independent, forceful, self-reliant, and resourceful:

> I have more self-confidence, a feeling of independence and self-reliance that I didn't have before...an understanding that I have resources and abilities too to meet those needs if I have to, and that I could call on them again if I need to.
>
> Yes, a lot more independent, even more sure of myself than before. I think maybe I think more about, care more about me than I ever did. I was the real mother and the real wife and I never thought much about my happiness. Now I do.
>
> I learned how I felt about myself...that I could be forceful, that I could go up to my husband and talk to him and tell him what I wanted and just to be—I don't know—different.

From the accounts presented, I suggest that these may be more permanent changes in self-definition or identity because of the way in which women implicitly defined their participation. Although extramarital relationships resemble other forms of male-female interaction in many respects, these were situationally different, as women consciously decided to have them against prevailing norms. The very act of consciously deciding to *do* this rewarding activity, even if socially disapproved, may have altered the entire dynamic of the social feedback received from extramarital partners.

In an incisive analysis of the essential difference in male-female gender roles, sociologist Nancy Chodorow points out that girls are rewarded for "being" (e.g., nice, feminine, pretty), while boys are rewarded for "doing" (e.g., physical and athletic activities, mechanical skills).[7] The ultimate outcome is that boys grow to rely less on the appraisal of others for their self-esteem because they have internalized faith in their own abilities. It can be suggested that the very same psychosocial mechanism may be operating here in creating the increased self-confidence and autonomy that women reported they had gained. Because the women defined their activity as "doing" something rather than "being" something, the effect on self-esteem may be more self-reinforcing and, therefore, more likely to be permanent.

A supplementary or alternative explanation can be gleaned from other comments of the women. Comments often focused on the role of wife, as women reported new feelings of "personhood" rather than being "just a wife":

> It made me feel much more like a real person, that people saw me as me and not just Michael's wife.
>
> Yes, my attitude toward myself has changed. The primary attitude toward myself is that I no longer think of myself as a middle-aged housewife. That's changed considerably. I think of myself as being younger and more interesting in almost every way, and attractive and fascinating and exotic and—you know—all the good things.
>
> Yes, I realized I was a person in my own right, with my own needs and desires.

Why did women feel this change from "wife" to "person"? Psychologist Erik Erikson, in his explanation of psychological development through the life cycle, states that women tend to develop their identities as persons later than men do, deferring part of that development until after marriage.[8] After marriage women incorporate the role of wife and mother into their self-concept and, in effect, complete their sense of self through their social and emotional attachment to their husbands.

Moreover, Jessie Bernard's research on marriage indicates that women have a lesser probability of developing a mentally healthy identity within marriage than do men. The traditional role of wife, with its emphasis on subjugation of one's personal desires and rights to the welfare of others, is not conducive to the growth of a positive personal identity.[9] These women were more autonomous in shaping the quality of the extramarital interaction to their own needs, especially in the expressive and sexual areas; it is likely that this increased autonomy in the relationship contributed to the positive impact on identity.

Marriage can also result in the arrested development of selfhood for both parties, as husband and wife throw their energies into the building of couplehood.[10] As the couple relationship becomes secure and they return to work on their own self-development, the marriage partner may not be able to perceive, let alone respond to, the growth in the spouse. Several women referred to marrying when young and the negative effect this had on them. As one woman phrased it, "In a new relationship you get a chance to be the new person you think you are."

Women also emphasized the self-development made possible through associating intimately with a variety of people, instead of just one person:

> Yes, in getting to know other people, it's an affirmation of you that's just been mind-blowing to me. Because marrying young and not having had many close relationships with men or women, that has just been a wonderful free thing to get to know other people—it's just changed the nature of my personality.

> Yes, I saw that I could handle myself in a variety of situations, that I could be attracted to and attractive to very different kinds of men. I learned a great deal about the kind of person I was and could become by being with these different kinds of men. I certainly don't think this was the only thing responsible for my self-growth in recent years, but it definitely was an important factor.

> It has added a great deal to what was absent before, in that it filled up my rooms, so it can't help but make me feel better about myself. I appreciate a lot of different people where I used to appreciate a few people, because when you meet on a social level, everything is shallow. You get into people's bodies and minds, it's deeper, it's longer lasting, it is more valid, it is honest, it is more candid and exhilarating. I don't want it to stop.

> You get so much from another person. You find so many facets to your own personality. For instance, I didn't know I was at all athletic (my husband isn't) until I started to do all kinds of sports with this other man.

Their comments reflect the frequent criticism that one of the negative aspects of monogamy is that it promotes isolation from any social contacts except the spouse. This is especially so when married persons practice a couple-intensity that permits only superficial friendship with others.

A final impact on the self that some women reported was an autonomy they had not experienced before:

> I felt more in control of my whole life.

> I'm much happier with myself. I'm happier because I think it gave me the confidence to know that I can do what's right for myself, despite the fact that people will say it's wrong.

> Yes, I do feel having a relationship has changed me. How could it do otherwise? I have evolved a moral code of ethics that is mine and right for me and my way of life. It is not one that has been imposed on me by others, conditioned, religious, parental, and, boy, I carried that yoke for a long, long time. I have become more of a woman and I like being a woman and like being myself.

Women felt a new personal freedom in throwing off old patterns of socialization and in developing their own code of ethics. To be able to reject conventional norms and substitute a personal moral structure is certainly indicative of an increased sense of autonomy and a changed identity. If the goal of human growth is to become self-actualizing—to become all that we can be—as psychologist Abraham Maslow[11] has asserted, then it may be said that many of these women feel they have made progress toward that goal as a result of their extramarital experiences.

Of course, it is not being asserted here that all extramarital encounters will lead to human growth, or that one cannot grow without becoming extramaritally involved. But it is true that we no longer can conclude the opposite—that all intimate relationships outside the marriage bond are necessarily destructive to individuals. Though a majority of persons say they disapprove of extramarital relationships this does not automatically prove that all consequences of those relationships are negative. Despite our attitudinal bias against extramarital behavior, a scientific approach demands that we recognize all possible aspects of this behavior.

Part of our bias has meant that in the past studies looked primarily at the effect on marriages, not on individuals. Morton Hunt, in his study of "affairs" published in 1969[12], focused briefly on this previously unrecognized positive impact on identity. While he did not discriminate the reasons for men's and women's reactions, I am suggesting that the impact on women is related to their socialization as females, including the social construction of the wife role in adulthood. Rejecting the socially imposed constrictions and constraints of these identities—of traditional wife and female—can support growth toward an independent and autonomous personhood. This "breaking out" has already occurred in a number of other social areas for women—jobs, education, politics, religion. Advances in equalizing social opportunities for women has led to dramatic improvement in their mental health in the 1970's, according to a longitudinal study begun in 1952 and conducted by Columbia University researchers Leo Srole and Anita Kassen Fischer.[13] While extramarital sex is probably the area in which people would least approve "equalizing opportunities," the impact on self-image and self-esteem is apparently similar to that in other areas of social life.

As far as is yet known, there is no systematic evidence as to whether a similar personal growth for men occurs in extramarital circumstances. It is less likely that it does, as most males don't begin with the same socially induced base of passivity, constriction, reliance on others as women do, or have done in the past. Most writers on men's extramarital sex, including Hunt, have confined their remarks to the increase or restoration of self-esteem when the marital sex has been unsatisfying, with a resulting confirmation of self-confidence or pride in the sexual area primarily. In general men already have had a variety of arenas—economic, physical, educational, and political—in which to develop their self-esteem and pursue personal growth, so that their overall development of selfhood has not been arrested as it has been with women.

It is possible that as women gradually advance toward full equality, the positive impact of successful extramarital relationships on their self-growth will diminish. The greatest effect on self will probably be found during the present transitional era, in which both the transformations in women's roles, as well as the current flux in sexual norms, coalesce to form supportive conditions for this outcome.

Definitions of the Sexual Self

Since their extramarital activity was sexual as well as social in nature, I also questioned women on any perceived changes in their attitudes toward their own sexuality. Here, again, the response was overwhelmingly positive; nine out of ten women responded that they had changed for the better. Of the remaining few who did not report change, they either had always defined themselves as very sexual, or had had only one brief extramarital encounter.

For about two-thirds of the women, change centered on more awareness and acceptance of themselves as sexual beings, of feeling more sexual:

> Extramarital relationships did help my own sexuality, my feelings about it. They're more positive, I know my own sexu-

ality better. Because my husband had hangups about sexuality, some things he did not want to do that I did experience with other men I enjoyed very much.

I've accepted my own sexuality and feel comfortable with it. I am over forty; I would not want to be any other age, because I know that I have the sureness of self that I never had when I was younger. That's the most wonderful discovery of all—the little country mouse has become sensual and attractive to men.

Oh, yes! When I first started (having relationships) I was extremely shy and wasn't even sure I was sexual. That was an important reason for my doing this. I wanted to find out what and who I was sexually.... Some of it was painful to recognize, especially in the beginning when I was nonorgasmic. But now I'm multi-orgasmic and I consider myself a very sexy and fortunate woman. But it's not just the orgasms—the big difference is that I feel like a sexual *person*. I have integrated sexuality into my being instead of having it exist as a disconnected activity that one plugs into and out of. My whole body is an erogenous zone, and I am much more sensitive to touch, emotion and affection.

My own sexuality has been enhanced. I love being female. I—uh—love my body, I love what it can do, I love what it can feel, I love what it can do to other people.... Defining myself as a sexual being has increased and I realize it's not a dirty thing and it's good and it's part of my—a very important part of my being.

I feel much more sexual. I feel more sexy. At least I know that I'm not a—that I'm pretty good. I feel better about that part of myself.

Women also felt less inhibited:

I've become much more aware of my own sexuality. Just being made to feel desirable, I've been able to perform different acts, to enter into the whole act of lovemaking totally differently.

I feel great about it in a way I wasn't even conscious of with my husband. I like my body more, feel less inhibited, more free to do what I want sexually than I used to.

My sexuality changed in that some of the experimentation in the area of sex first took place outside my marriage.... I then was able to translate that into more freedom in my marriage.

Some women noticed they had become more sexually assertive,

taking the initiative to get what they needed and wanted, even if those needs were unconventional, like a need for variety:

> I think I've gotten a lot more—I'm trying to think of the word—a lot more aggressive, a lot more assertive in—uh—going out after what I want.... When things started to be not so great sexually and not so great in other ways in the marriage, I started to look around for more. Now I think a more honest view of myself is that I enjoy variety from time to time.

One woman in particular had been reared in a family in which her father had exercised the traditional masculine "right" to extramarital sex. Now she refused any longer to see that as purely a male prerogative:

> Yes, I showed myself I can be more aggressive sexually, that I can find another man if I want to, not bad...I felt incredibly masculine having an affair, making overtures, because "Daddy did that but Mother didn't." Yes, this was part of myself saying, "Well, I need it; I want it; I'm going to have it."

Several women specifically mentioned a sense of sexual insatiability that psychiatrist Mary Jane Sherfey and researchers Masters and Johnson have identified as a unique feature of female sexuality:

> I'm really finding no limits to it and finding it delightful and finding it acceptable to men who can handle it. My first husband used to tell me I was a nymphomaniac and almost had me believing it for awhile. I'm not. I am highly sexed.

> Oh, absolutely. In that my sexual responses to me, for me, changed dramatically. For instance, I used to be content with one orgasm, once every two weeks. Everday is fine, now. If I can't get it everyday, I do it myself, 'cause it's just part of what I do.... I think there is an insatiability.... You can sit in the car and drive and just feel nice and warm and you can—I can just let it curve round in my mind and it happens in my body. So I can will an orgasm, just driving along and thinking I'm going to see so and so. And that's where the insatiability comes in. It's always there and you can call on it.... In fact, I've stopped counting orgasms a long time ago.

And, finally, a few women found they had developed the ability to separate the enjoyment of sex from its traditional contexts of love and marriage:

> Yes, I enjoyed it so much with somebody besides my husband

and I never thought I would, in the beginning. Just—I don't know—I always thought that the whole background of acquaintanceship and friendship influenced the nature and quality of sex. But it didn't really. I don't love him in the same deep way I love my husband, and yet the sex was every bit as good, it was really great sex. That said something to me about my sexuality.
Before it was that you only had sex because you loved the person. Here it was—you know—pure sexuality, which was very beautiful. I think now that a purely physical relationship can be really good.

All of these replies concerning the impact of extramarital experiences on women's sexual identity corroborate the reports in the previous chapter on women's extramarital sexual behavior. They dramatize further the possibility of personal change and the dynamics of sexual growth that are involved. When women are able to be autonomous to the extent of choosing multiple sexual involvements, they have access to a variety of sexual experiences and feedback. They are not dependent on the evaluation of only one person, their husband, for their identity as sexual persons as in the traditional sexual system.

Women who do autonomously draw on multiple sources for their sexual feedback discover, as feminine sociologists have predicted, "the extent and degree of their own sex drive instead of having it defined by available resources."[14] Such self-definition allows for the emergence of a new kind of sexual self; from these excerpts we see the new kinds of sexual selves that are discovered and developed: sensual, positive, assertive, experimental, along with the ability to see and experience the body as an instrument of self-pleasure.

This access to multiple sources of sexual feedback is increasingly available to modern women, as it has been to men. Rates of both premarital intercourse and extramarital relations are converging for women and men, although men still tend to have more partners than women.[15] Eight out of ten of this group of women had premarital sex, and half of them also had sex with men other than their future husbands. And yet, even though having premarital experiences, almost every one of these women learned more about themselves through their extramarital experiences.

Such a finding suggests two related conclusions: first, that development of sexuality and identity as sexual persons is a continuous process, subject to modifications whenever and wherever we encounter sexual experiences we define as significant; and second, that sexual development is a more highly prized goal in a post-industrial culture. When cultural values emphasize personal growth and sexual satisfaction, people will behave in ways to reach those goals. Whatever parts of the population have had the least access to sexual expression and development can now be expected to make up for that past lack of opportunity. Consequently, the greatest change in sexual expression is occurring among two groups—women and youth—who traditionally have had the fewest opportunities to express their sexuality.

As women draw upon a larger pool of sexual experience to form their sexual identity, a pool that takes them increasingly outside traditional family experiences, the resulting ripples will affect more than their sexual lives. For women, much more so than men, sexual identity has always been bound to their family roles as wives and mothers, and so the choices they made in other areas of life were constrained by this location of identity. If these roots of identity are now less dependent on sexual experiences within marriage, it means women will feel freer to make choices in other areas, no longer being controlled by their identity of wife and mother. The family, then, will no longer serve as a social control mechanism for women in the same way that it used to.[16]

For instance, if a woman's most significant sexual experiences consists of marital intercourse, pregnancy, and childbirth, all these tend to reinforce the idea that she is primarily a wife and mother. Consequently, in selecting a job she is likely to choose one that will allow her to keep paramount the wife-mother identity. A good example of this is the many women in the past who have chosen teaching as a career, because it is a job that coordinates well with the role of mother. Yet if a woman has significant sexual experiences outside marriage, such as premarital and extramarital sex and sex after divorce, she manifestly is not bound into a wife-mother identity. As we have seen here, women can react to extramarital experiences by feeling like a "person" instead of a "wife." Accordingly, the choices they make in other areas of life will be affected by any change in identity. As one 28-year-old woman, who divorced her husband and was living with a new person at the time of the last interview, commented:

> I think the last couple of years is the first time that I'm actively working toward what *I* want, which is to work with mentally retarded people. I think that's because he (new partner) understands now that I need my time away from him. I've

finally gotten that across. It isn't always that old hassle as it was with my husband, "What do you mean, you want to study?"

Changed Attitudes after Extramarital Experience

Closely related to change in identity is the process of change in attitudes, for people often change their attitudes after gaining new information or having new experiences. For instance, people who have experienced living in interracial neighborhoods tend to be less prejudiced than they were before.[17] According to one study, women who had extramarital relationships were more permissive in their attitudes toward them after their experiences than they had been before.[18] Therefore, I discussed with the women possible changes in attitude on a variety of related issues.

Attitudes toward Female Sexuality

As these women found their attitudes toward their own sexual selves being dramatically changed, it seems likely that these changes may also have affected their views of female sexuality in general.

A few women did not answer the question on attitude changes, and a few thought they learned nothing from which they could generalize. Most felt, though, that they had changed their attitudes toward female sexuality, and all changes were in what they considered to be positive ways.

Most frequently women reacted to the way they had been taught and what they had been taught about female sexuality, and contrasted these with their current views:

> It's made me very proud of my sexuality and the sexuality of women in general. For years women have been taught they didn't have any, or it was something to be ashamed of.
>
> Yes, because I think that female sexuality has really been—if you want to talk about second-class citizens—I think that Freud screwed us all up pretty good. Pardon the pun, I don't even know if it's a pun, but yes, I think it's much more possible for me to view women as sexual beings, to understand a woman's sexual needs.
>
> I think more in terms of women being sexual than I used to.
>
> I suppose I've come to realize that women have really been short-changed in their education of sex and what they have been socially permitted to do in a relationship. Female sexuality should become something beautiful, something that

should be explored, something that should be given reign, the reign of the woman.

What is expressed most saliently in these comments is a sense of anger at the sexual self-determination so long denied women; at a socialization which succeeded to a great extent in suppressing and distorting women's sexuality from what these women now know it can be. Over half of the women spoke very vigorously and at length on the issues of lack of sexual self-determination and repressive socialization.

Several stressed that part of their learning about female sexuality occurred through discussions with other women of their extramarital relationships. Instead of concealing their activities from everyone, women often chose to share certain aspects of their behavior with other women, thereby passing on the knowledge they acquired:

> Yes, because so many of my girlfriends are doing it and tell me about what they do. I think women are probably more sexy than men.... This was something that was kept in the closet, under the rug for so long it's a horrible shame.

> I have learned from myself, from sexual partners, and from other women who've had multiple sexual partners. My ideas have changed drastically as a result of my extramarital activities. I have learned to completely—you know—not to accept all the myths of traditional sexuality, the myths of passiveness, the myths of not needing sexuality to the extent men do, the myths of sexual response that were supposedly ours.

This informal chain of communication is a fertile source of sexual knowledge for women and can contribute to the establishment of sexual autonomy. For so long women have been given biased sexual information in order to support their socialization according to the traditional model of sexuality. Many women spoke of their distrust of knowledge from "experts" that only supports accepted myths about how women are and are supposed to be. Women stressed the need for learning about the real-life activities of other women, of the importance of honest and unfiltered communication among themselves to reduce their pluralistic ignorance about what their sexuality was and could be.

Along with their desire for improved communication among adult women was a concern for the next generation:

> When I think how my mother raised me—you know—"keep your knees crossed" and all of that. I hope that we will be able

to raise the daughters of the upcoming generation—uhmm—better—you know, a little more open-minded.

Several women initiated a discussion about the need to change socialization patterns in the next generation, so as not to repeat the mistakes of their own childhoods. Having changed their concepts of female sexuality, they felt the need to transmit more modern sexual concepts to their own daughters—and sons. How sons will grow up to treat women will also affect women's sexuality in the future.

Attitudes toward Male Sexuality

The experience of extramarital relationships not only provided women with additional information about their own and other women's sexuality, but also served as a testing ground for their ideas about men. About half of the women thought that it had changed their attitudes about male sexuality for the better.

Just as women found the stereotypes about female sexuality being challenged, so too did certain myths about male sexuality come to be questioned. The mystique that men are dominant, impersonal, and sexually invincible was shredded by particular experiences:

> Obviously the best experiences were in finding out that men could also be very sensitive. Probably as much as anything I've learned—"Yeah, there are some men who are only interested in themselves." But before now, I didn't really know. But there are some men who are also in touch with their sexuality and are interested in expressing it in some very nice ways.

> My attitude about male sexuality has changed. With my husband as a role model, it was sex, and he had an orgasm, and that's all there was to it. That, to me, was male sexuality. From my partners, I realized how sensitive and loving men can be—ah—how tender, how fragile, yet how strong, as with female sexuality. And it made me feel good about male sexuality. It doesn't have to be a threatening, dominating thing; it can be a loving sensitive thing.

> Well, it has become a lot less mystifying. That men are people, they have sexual problems and fantasies and desires just as women do.

> It did away with a lot of my stereotypes because I know that all men are not anything in particular and that men need as much reassurance and tenderness as women do.

Women who responded positively to this question about male sexuality perceived what was, for them, a new similarity, a refreshing commonality with men. They found men to be as human as they in their need for tenderness, in their ability to be sensitive, and in their concern for their sexual partners.

One 39-year-old woman spoke in detail about how the idea that men were only interested in making love to "*Playboy* centerfolds" was erased for her:

> Now how can I explain this? When I was younger, and before I had the children—ah—I was always very sure of the way I looked, my body looked, and the way my body performed. And I assumed that that was why men were attracted to me. My breasts were high and firm, and you know—a tight little ass and everything.
>
> Now I find that the men that I'm interested in are not so interested in that. The men that I like and are grown-up, adult men, don't make love to that perfect body; they make love to a person. And that was a shock—you know—the fact that I don't look like a *Playboy* centerfold doesn't seem to discourage anybody. I had always thought that that was very important.
>
> Of course, my thought previously that it was important to look like that, was reinforced by my husband's sexual neglect—you know—that proved it for me. Now, I have a different view of male sexuality. That they—really men are just as turned on to thoughts and ideas and feelings and conversations.

A few women reacted to male-female differences rather than similarities. They saw men as being more sexually self-conscious than women, more vulnerable to "performance anxiety."

> I think I've come to the realization that men are just as worried as to whether they can get it up or not, how they're coming across. I used to think they could just get it up whenever they felt like it. I don't feel that way anymore. I feel they really have to be turned on as much as a woman does, if not more sometimes. And they're always worried about how they're performing. Much more than a woman is.

> Yes, I see more of the pressures on men than I used to, the pressures on them to perform.

One young woman, in her early thirties, located this vulnerability in male biology, turning around Freud's theory of "penis-envy."

> They're much more vulnerable then I'd ever given them

credit for before. Really, I feel so sorry for men to be so bound to that little penis.... I remember noticing this when my daughter was first born.... Every time I babysat for a little boy, I was impressed with how unintegrated his sexual body is with the rest of his body. It really emphasizes his vulnerability, because there it all is, totally separated from everything else, and girls are just so—everything is just folded in a perfect unity and I was very impressed by that and I hadn't really thought about it further until my extramarital experience.

And I suddenly could see that the whole male ethic, the whole machismo, was built up as a defense against this vulnerability. That they had to build something else, because otherwise they were just too—uh—defeatable, too vulnerable. It explains their desire to categorize women as women have been categorized and it also explains women's desire to acquiesce to it, that men are really very fragile and it's much easier to accommodate them than to confront them...which just makes me feel so utterly superior that I almost can't cope with it (chuckles).

Only one woman mentioned learning anything about the "staying power" or penis size of men.

Oh, I realize that men are very different from one another. There's a wide range on how long a man can last. A man can last anywhere from about five minutes to two hours. I didn't realize there was that much variation. And I didn't realize there was variation in size for that matter. I just presumed most men were about the same size.

Although there was no specific question on male sexuality, women were encouraged at each stage of the interviews to speak about any topic they felt was significant. Since only one woman mentioned penis size and staying power it is apparent they are not salient characteristics of male sexuality to these women. As we saw in Chapter 5, in discussing sexual behavior, women do not make judgments on isolated techniques or characteristics. Rather they respond to the gestalt, or entire situation, and then evaluate specifics within the overall context.

As can be seen, most of the information acquired about male sexuality was positive. Several women, however, felt that their extramarital experience gave them a more negative view. One woman reacted to changes in herself toward men with which she was not entirely comfortable:

I see men in a more sexual way now than I did before. I never used to look at a man and think primarily how he would be in bed. I'm afraid I do that now, which is unfair to them because I should be trying to know them as a person first.

The other women, however, reported negative changes toward men. One such person, in her late fifties at the time of the first interview, had had only one extramarital relationship with a man eight years younger than she. It ended unhappily when the man decided unilaterally to terminate the relationship. She said:

> I feel that men, some men, have—the need for sex overwhelms them, that they will say anything in order to achieve satisfaction of their need. I believe that a woman should always discard ninety percent of what is said to her in bed. I don't mean that he does not mean it at the moment, I'm sure he does. But I think it is the same mechanism that causes erection, it's completely involuntary once a certain point is reached.

Her remarks paint a more typical picture of male sexuality, one that has been the traditional sexual script for men. In that script men are interested only in sex and will do or say anything to achieve that end. Since her lover was an older man, it is probable that his behavior was influenced by an era which had more traditional and perhaps more exploitative sex.

Finally, a couple of women thought their learning had included both positive and negative elements. One, in her forties and with more than ten relationships over a period of years, summed up the ambivalence of these observations:

> I've stopped thinking of it as being one thing—of all men being alike. Some men are good lovers and some aren't. They get hung up on the same kinds of things women do, plus some differences. They're very penis-centered. They don't know, with rare exceptions, that their whole body is sexual. They don't seem to have the capacity to be as sensual as women. But happily, as I've said, I have known a few exceptions who are as capable emotionally, sensually, as I perceive women to be. I wish more men could be like that.

Attitudes toward Extramarital Relationships

Nearly all of the women, following the generally positive descriptions of meanings, sexuality, and identity development, considered their extramarital experiences to be worthwhile. In fact, when questioned specifically as to any regrets, only one in four women expressed any. Most of their regrets centered around concerns for their extramarital partner. A few were uncomfortable taking more than they had given, underscoring the previously expressed desire for mutuality in male-female relationships:

> I regret part of it, yes, because even though it was the best, in many ways, love/sex relationship I ever had, in part I know that I was just using it. In part more of my motivation was just for the reassurance that I was getting, than for the actual sharing with him. I do regret that.

> I regret the part about losing part of my natural gift of giving, but I hope that's only temporary.

> I only regret that I was so unfair to the first guy I met, in taking so much from him.

One was concerned over her ending the relationship before her partner was ready to:

> I think I may have been rather abrupt in the way I ended it but that was a kind of function of my own immaturity. I was mature enough to know what I needed but not mature enough to have as much regard or his feelings as I now wish I had.

Or when circumstances, such as moving to another part of the country, made an ending necessary:

> Regret? That's really a hard question. I don't think so. I believe in the same situation, I would do the same thing again. I believe I was going to sleep with someone and I chose the person who made me the happiest. I believe I acknowledged my sexual and personal needs and acted on them in the most constructive way possible at the time. I wish I was different. I wish I didn't need so much. I worry that I hurt Tony, but I'm not sorry that I had him. I'm glad the pain is passing because it sure was awful.

The pain involved in unhappy endings was echoed by a 59-year-old woman whose partner unilaterally withdrew from the relationship:

> The relationship ended about six months ago but the signs were there a few months before that. It was totally the undoing of Mr. X. I don't regret any part of the relationship except, of course, the ending.

And one woman in an open marriage, which ended, in part, because of her overinvolvement with someone, regretted its ending for that reason:

> What I do regret is letting it become an obsession. I don't think I handled it very well. I guess I know what it's like to be sandwiched in between two people and that kind of pressured me and I don't want to get in that situation again. Even in my relationships now with men, I'm very careful.

There were only two women who rated their extramarital experiences as not worthwhile. One had started a relationship with her husband's approval, but ultimately he was unable to accept it emotionally:

> I never would have had my affair if I had known how badly it was going to hurt my husband. He insisted all along that it would not, and I wanted to have it so I wanted to believe him, so I went ahead and had it. But—uh—it hurt him terribly.

And another who had had a traditional "swept away," "in love" affair was very negative:

> It was one of these great affairs—that usually end disastrously. Yes, it was terribly intense. It was probably too intense.... It had no chance to grow into anything more harmonious, which with a little more time it could have. It could have succeeded—I know it.... The impossibility of having one another feeds this romantic thing. If you meet once a year, then you can keep affairs alive. But otherwise they're impossible and so very tragic.

This 31-year-old wife had had an unhappy marriage and became involved with a married man who at first promised to get a divorce and later reneged on his promise.

After all of the women had assessed their experiences, I asked about future extramarital involvements. While only a third of the women with one relationship said they thought they might again get involved, 85% who had had more than one relationship thought they would.[19] The women with only one relationship were more likely to voice some regret, generally. Apparently the greater the amount of extramarital experience, and the more positive the experience, the more likely women are to continue involvements.

Furthermore, the women who had "justified" rather than "excused" their first relationship, as described in Chapter 2, were more likely to have gone on to having additional involvements. The account given as to why a woman had first gotten involved—whether she felt "entitled" to have extramarital sex (a justification) or whether it was "just something that happened" (an excuse)—was associated with whether women continued a pattern of involvements.[20] The women with repeated activity, however, were not always extramaritally involved. Women often had periods of sexual exclusivity with their husbands when an outside relationship ended. Of the third of the women who had separated or divorced at some point after having the extramarital relationships already described, some also varied periods of exclusivity in relations with more than one partner.

When asked, most of the women specified conditions for future extramarital relationships that were based on a modern ideology; themes of the meanings of the relationships were repeated. Expressive satisfaction and personal growth through knowing people were most often mentioned:

> If it's a person I'm friends with first.
>
> If I'm involved emotionally.
>
> If it is the right person.
>
> As long as I feel like reaching out.

Secondarily, there was an interest in extramarital sex:

> Because I like relationships with people and they shouldn't preclude sex.
>
> Because I can't promise fidelity.

There was also a concern for the dynamics of their own marriage:

> It must be an open relationship.
>
> Not someone who would want ties and break up my marriage.

And concern for the other marriage—and the wife of the potential partner:

> NO MORE MARRIED MEN—That's in caps.... I have too much respect for other women now as sisters and as female persons.

I asked the women if they thought their attitudes toward extramarital relationships had changed as a result of their involvements. Three out of four said they had become more accepting:

> I now condone it.
>
> It confirmed what I had come to think. I came to see I don't own somebody's body and mind.

Yes, I no longer think they are cop-outs.

I'm obviously more accepting of others, myself, and extramarital relationships.

I'm more understanding, more tolerant, more accepting.

Yes, I now feel it's O.K. to do.

I just feel it's no big deal anymore.

I see them as a normal part of life. Not that you would always have them, but you could have them and still be living a normal life.

As we would expect, the mostly positive experiences reported resulted in a positive attitude change. This in part represents the natural human tendency to approve of one's own behavior, but it also reflects, I believe, the impact of the successful handling of their involvements. Once most of the women saw their participation did little or no harm either to themselves, others, or their marriages—indeed that they could reap positive benefits—they came to change their attitudes. As one woman described the process of her changing beliefs:

Ten years ago I thought only horrible women got involved. Five years ago I thought only women with guts got involved. I used to be typically female and look down my nose at it. It just was wrong.... Now I'm much more open in my attitude. I'm really coming to the point where anything goes as long as you don't deliberately hurt another person in the process.

Her concern for hurting others was echoed by many other women and may well reflect part of a new ideology of extramarital relationships that is emerging to replace traditional attitudes which define extramarital involvements as always wrong.

Indeed, if we look at these women's marital attitudes after their involvements, we see a decided preference for non-exclusive arrangements.[21] Just over half of the group preferred an open marriage as the ideal because:

...it gives the option of choice if the need arises, but I'm not sure I would utilize the choice.

...I know my needs to have another person with whom to be close.

...I need closeness with many people. No person can live up to being all to one person.

...there should be freedom to do it, but also not to do it.

> ...there must be someone who could touch my husband as I haven't been able to.
>
> ...I prefer honesty and openness to deceit.
>
> ...to grow as a person you need to have friends...with no restrictions.

Moreoever, 16 of the 17 women who had experience with open marriage or open awareness chose this ideal. Actual life experiences with openness were related to a greater preference for openness. This is a group of women who have coped with the problems of transition from conventional marriage, are aware of the difficulties and possible failure, and still chose unconventional marriage arrangements as the ideal.

The ideal choice of marriage for virtually all of the women, in fact, was scattered among various non-traditional forms. There were a few votes each for monogamy with an occasional affair, serial monogamy, group marriage, and even a preference not to be married at all.

Said one 30-year-old woman:

> I would prefer not to be married, so that I would be free to relocate as my career demands, and to plan my life and activities as would most please me. I feel that basically I am independent enough that I will always feel stifled and trapped by marriage. Living together in a very open arrangement might be possible.

And a 59-year-old woman:

> At this stage of my life, it has to be not to be married. If I were younger, it might be different.... I no longer have the patience for tolerating another person around.... I no longer have the impetus to cook or clean, even supposing I were to marry a man who would do his share.

Even the few women who still thought conventional monogamy to be ideal were skeptical about achieving that ideal:

> But realistically it can't be done. Saying a completely monogamous situation with one lifelong mate does not necessarily imply that would be a marriage arrangement. As I've stated before, I'd rather choose to just live with this person. It certainly is an ideal situation because as much as I would want it to exist, I'm really skeptical about the fact that it could.

Another 26-year-old woman who couldn't make a choice explained:

> I'm strongly drawn to marriage because I'm a very lonely person and I don't want to be lonely...but I'm very skeptical as to whether a marriage can work. I wonder how two people can live together—I think always being together in such close proximity, that's just not a situation that two people can survive.

Clearly these women are marriage "veterans" who have become disillusioned, as have many other women, by the gap between their expectations of conventional marriage as a plan for life and the reality they have experienced. With marriage not having met all of their individual needs, they have gone outside its framework to seek answers. What most experienced were satisfying extramarital relationships that came to be potent forces for personal transformation. They found their identities and their understanding of self and their sexuality to be appreciably affected. They discovered their attitudes toward marriage and extramarital relations to have changed.

Although this is a relatively small group of women, the changes in attitude reported here cut across women in a wide age range from the twenties to the sixties, and included a diversity of occupations from homemakers to professionals and variation in educational levels from high school to post-graduate work. The similarity of attitudinal outcomes is a reflection not only of these women's private experiences, but also of the social upheaval in women's roles in the last two decades. The reports of these women speak to the need that many others feel for change in the patterns, structure, and meanings of their intimate lives.

Chapter Seven

Extramarital Relationships With Women

        coming home

    years of alien
bodies confusing mine, demanding
        that i meet
   theirs and touch

   and feel in
thousand of acts of unnatural
        love   my
   child body, torn

   from yours given
a map only of phalluses to find
        the way   but
   now it is

   softly   home
anticipating everything it locks
        into your essence
     slides into your
   sameness dear

   mother/sister
woman/lover   i will never
      leave home
   again

                              Cynthia King

One change in intimacy that has surfaced in the past decade has been the practice of some heterosexual women to have affectionate and erotic relationships with women. The existence of women's bisexual relations was not widely known until the attention given it by the media in the 1970's, when it was frequently linked with the reemergence of the women's movement.[1] While bisexual activity may seem to be of recent origin, there is evidence that married women of the eighteenth and nineteenth centuries routinely created bonds of emotional and physical intimacy with each other.[2]

In our own time, Kinsey's 1953 study found more than incidental numbers of women had had homosexual experience. He estimated that 12-13% of all women had sex and orgasms wih another woman, and that 8-19% of all married women had done so.[3] Approximately 20% of the women in the 1976 Hite report said they were either bisexual or had sexual experiences with both men and women, but this figure was not broken down into married or unmarried women.[4] In the 1975 *Redbook* study of 100,000 women, however, 16% of the wives who had extramarital relations had had a sexual experience with a woman.[5] Of the group of women who participated in the present study, there was a subgroup of nine (18%) who had had an extramarital relationship with a woman.

The others who hadn't had an experience with a woman were asked about their feelings. Only two thought it "unnatural" or "repellent;" these were older women in their late forties and fifties. About half thought the idea was acceptable but wouldn't want it for themselves. The other half were open to the possibility of a sexual relationship with a woman. Of this group many had had fantasies about the idea. Some could not understand how or where the situation could develop into erotic contact:

> It's just something that I don't know what it means. I thought for a long time that if a woman came along where there was a mutual interest that was somehow erotic, I would try to get on with it, try to let some of those erotic feelings, and maybe behavior, come. I don't know what it would involve and I don't know how scared I would be if I was ever in that situation.
> Sometimes I get very annoyed with men. I mean, I have this fantasy that I should turn to women instead but that's never been close to to a reality at all. Sometimes I think that women could never be as painful as men have been in my life. I imagine it would be quite awkward. But maybe if it was—you

know—a properly close and supportive relationship that wouldn't happen. As I say, in general these days, I'm not sure that I understand the difference between—or where the line is drawn between a lot of physical closeness and contact, and how it somehow becomes erotic. And that applies equally to men and women.

This woman voiced the considerations of others who felt that a relationship with another woman might exist outside of the traditional patterns that have shaped women's heterosexual relationships with men in ways often unsatisfying to both sexes.

Others had felt attracted to specific women, but had not acted on their feelings. A forty year-old woman remarked:

I have three women in my life, from different stages of development, different times and places, that I love very dearly, one of whom I was aware that I had an "in love" kind of relationship to. The opportunity was there for physical acting out or consummation of the relationship. But it was something that we just never wanted to do anything more than caress each other "hello" and "good-bye" and hold hands while we walked.... If I should be close enough to her and feel strongly that I wanted to make it into a physical relationship, I think I would do that.

And a thirty-two year-old musician remembered a woman in her past:

There was a woman who I clearly had sexual feelings for. But we never did anything more than kiss each other.... But she loved me and wanted to go to bed with me; I still hear from her all the time.... I believe I didn't make love with her because of inhibition. Because I would have liked to have— my desire for her was not as powerful as my desire for a man. And yet it would have been easy to *accept* being made love to, if I didn't feel inhibited.

The woman above admits to inhibition as being the factor that held her back from fulfilling her desire to "make love with her." Ironically, even in what would have been an uncharted area of sexual activity, the traditional sexual script influenced her behavior. She was operating in the conventional female gender role of passivity since she could have "accepted" being made love to—that is, she could have played the role of passive partner—if she had not been inhibited.

With two previously heterosexual women, the question of who will initiate sexual activity becomes paramount, because both potential partners have been taught to be sexually passive. Unless one person "breaks out" of the gender role and overcomes passivity, nothing will transpire, even in the presence of desire. The sociological question of how sexual activity between women is activated for the first time involves two separate issues. First, how are erotic feelings for women recognized? And second, how do these feelings get transformed into sexual activity? This is another transition some women underwent to become involved in extramarital lesbian activity.

Getting Involved—With Women

There is little known about how adult women who identify themselves as heterosexual become involved with other women. Not much research had been done, partly because awareness of this behavior has grown only during the last several years and, partly, because women's homosexual activities are considered of lesser social importance than men's homosexual activities. Since knowledge is so limited in this area, this chapter will be an initial exploration of the topic and will be primarily a description of women's extramatital lesbian activities. Any conclusions reached are tentative because the data are from a very small group. At times I will use the word "lesbian" to describe the involvement because it is woman-with-woman. However, it is important to note that the women do not define themselves as lesbians. Thus, while we may be talking about "lesbian activities," we are not discussing lesbian women.

One woman in this group who had a relationship with a woman became involved well before public awareness of woman-with-woman relationships. In her situation, the issue of how erotic feelings for another woman are recognized was resolved through an intense emotional attachment. Married in the early 1960's, at the age of twenty, Sandra had her first extramarital relationship—with a woman—a few months after her marriage:

> I got involved in my first extramarital relationship by crying on the shoulder of a close friend and telling her how miserable I was and what was wrong with my marriage.... I really put a very strong emotional bond between me and this other girl.... The emotional bond between us grew into a physical one which I found much more enjoyable than my sexual relationship with my husband.

This gratifying involvement prompted her to separate from

her husband. It did not satisfactorily resolve her situation, though, partly because of the social disapproval she felt toward her behavior:

> My relationship with my friend, who turned out to be a lesbian, which I hadn't known in the beginning, really degraded me, or I had allowed it to degrade me. I thought of it in very bad terms. It meant that I was unfeminine. I could not enjoy sex with my husband; I could enjoy it with a woman. That made me a lesbian—and I didn't like the idea of being something that society did not approve of.

The problem of how sexual activity between two heterosexual women is activated did not apply in this case because Sandra's lover was already a lesbian. Sandra's negative reaction to the relationship and her acceptance of a lesbian identity contrast with the other women who became involved with women during the 1970's. The other women's reactions were all generally positive, and none felt their sexual identity had changed from a heterosexual one. Possibly the fact that Sandra's lover was a lesbian, whereas the other women all became involved with other "straight" women, contributed to her feeling that it "made me a lesbian." Also, Sandra's own words—"I did not like the idea of being something that society did not approve of"—reflect the influence of the less permissive atmosphere of the early 1960's, and its impact on her behavior and her subsequent actions.

Sandra next became extramaritally involved with a man. She returned to her husband while still seeing the man. As she related:

> My affair with this man made me realize that I could be turned on sexually by a man, that I was not necessarily a lesbian and that there might possibly be some hope for my relationship with my husband. If my husband were able to change at all, if he were able to get to the point where this other man was at...with the kind of talk, the kind of actions (that I loved), I could really enjoy him.

Sandra, like nearly all the other women, viewed her husband as being expressively lacking. She also was not pleased sexually with him. Married fourteen years at the time of the last interview, she has continued a pattern of involvements with men during the course of her marriage. One has lasted eleven years. She commented on her reasons for continuing extramarital relationships:

> They are very important to me because they supply my sexual release.... I also became very close emotionally to all of

them.... They're also to add a little excitement to my life. I can't stand boredom. I engage in a variety of activities and a variety of occupations. I keep busy all the time—I like that kind of life. I like a variety of foods, clothes, social events—and I like a variety of men.

While one route to lesbian involvement was that of emotional bonding, as in Sandra's case, a second route—developed as a consequence of the climate of sexual permissiveness during the late 1960's through the 1970's—involved "swinging" or "mate swapping" activities. Only one woman became involved this way, however. As is characteristic of couples who engage in swinging, a man initiated the sexual activity between the women.[6]

This 30-year-old woman in California became part of a group marriage when a relationship progressed from swinging with another couple. She spoke about her lesbian activity:

All encounters have been directed by a male who was participating in the sexual activity at the same time, however. I find this a very comfortable arrangement.

It is somewhat ironic that even in erotic activity between women—an unconventional sexual encounter—a male still assumes the dominant role as dictated by traditional sexual scripts.

There was, however, another more autonomous and more common route to lesbian involvement for these women. It was also linked to the social changes of the past fifteen years and with the evolution of the quality of women's friendships during that time. The background for this evolution is set by certain social values. Namely, women have traditionally been the sexualized gender and are represented as such in the various mass media. Consequently, women learn to view and evaluate themselves and other women in terms of their sexual attractiveness.

Although conventional responses to another woman's sexual appeal have ranged from envy to identification to feelings of superiority, many women have replaced these negative reactions with positive feelings of identification with other women. This transformation in emotional reaction has come about largely as a result of the consciousness raising of the women's movement. Given the fact that our society has always allowed women to touch one another through kissing, hugging, and the like—more so than men allowed to with each other—the initial stage is set for further physical interaction.

Moreover, with women who have already been close friends

intimate topics such as sexuality are very likely to arise. The discussion of sexuality as a legitimate topic of conversation has also been sanctioned by the women's movement. These discussions amid friendship and socially approved physical contact can serve as the lead-in to sexual behavior.[7] Four women became involved homosexually through some combination of the above factors.

The following situation illustrates how these changes in women's feelings about each other, an ongoing friendship, and customary physical contact all contributed to the gradual enactment of erotic behavior.[8]

Helen, a 35 year-old woman who lived in the West, had been a member of a consciousness-raising group for some time. The women in the group had developed a strong emotional bond, particularly in a nucleus of the group. Subsequently, these special friends planned a weekend away at a mountain retreat:

> What happened was I went with a women's group up in the mountains, into one of those mountain hideaways—oh, it was just a super weekend without husbands and little kids and there were five of the members of the group who could go and this was our mini-group really, so we were delighted that we were going to be up there together because we were already so close and had shared so much.

The isolation and natural beauty of the setting were conducive to enjoying a variety of physical activities during the day. That setting and the intimacy that had developed during the period the women's group operated reduced the usual social barriers of self-consciousness that might otherwise have been felt during these activities:

> Here we were in a lovely fantastic modern home, stuck on the side of a completely wooded, untouched, natural setting, on the side of a mountain, away from all kinds of other people. There wasn't even a road nearby. And just below our sunporch there was a mountain creek that we swam in; we took nude sunbaths on the rocks, huge rocks that would accommodate several people at one time lying down. And—uh—the first full day that we had there we spent almost the entire day with wine and cheese and fruit and things down by the mountain stream, and just playing in the water and just thoroughly getting into the whole mountain scene.
>
> You know, it was gorgeous and so peaceful and we all felt thoroughly comfortable doing whatever we wanted to do, whatever that was. And there was a great feeling of closeness,

of course, and tolerance and acceptance and love and just—all kinds of positive things were there with us. And the rest of the afternoon we spent up in the house playing our favorite music and eating and just talking, or being silent or writing and reading, just really relaxing, getting away.

The feelings of sensuous enjoyment, physical relaxation, and emotional closeness evoked a desire to continue the afternoon mood into evening:

> That night Cindy and I decided to sleep upstairs in front of the fireplace with the fire, with the huge windows with spotlights out under the trees. It's just so beautiful there with the glass doors and the spotlights on the trees and yet the fire in this huge stone fireplace. And another gal was going to sleep in the living room with us and the rest of them were going to sleep downstairs in several bedrooms.
>
> The three of us talked a long time in front of the fire and then gave each other quick massages just in the shoulders, or rather around the shoulders and upper back region, the kind that releases tension, that sort of thing, relaxes your neck muscles and shoulder muscles. So then Pat started to sleep, drifting off.

The stage had clearly been readied for sexual interaction. The setting of a lighted fireplace, the intimacy of nighttime, and the suggestiveness of lying down denote sexuality in any script, whether it is conventional heterosexuality or otherwise. With physical touching already established as acceptable and normal in this situation, the removal of the third person allowed an escalation of intimacy that both women accepted with equanimity:

> So there we were; we pulled up the sheets and continued to have body contact in terms of massaging, and nice quiet conversations. And then all of a sudden I think we both realized it was O.K., whatever happened next was probably going to be alright. And we kind of verbalized a bit of it. I can't even remember the way it went, but anyway, she knew that I was enjoying her and I knew that she was enjoying touching me. So we continued to touch each other and became more and more intimate with our touching. And we assumed that Pat was asleep. (I'm not sure she was now that I look back on it and because of a remark that she made later. But I haven't— we just really didn't mind if she was asleep or not because she was such a neat person and such a good friend that it really didn't matter, although we would have preferred for her to be asleep.)

At this point, Helen and Cindy were completly focused on each other to the extent that even the possibility of a third party observing them was not a deterrent. Both had experienced and defined some prior brief physical contact between themselves as erotic so that they had become conscious of the possibility of sexual expression between women. They also had defined their previous contact as positive and enjoyable:

> And she and I had — had kissed before at another time and were amazed at how neat it was just to kiss each other on the mouth — you know, and had talked about it later, how interesing our responses were, about its feeling O.K. and yet we both felt there were sexual overtones to this area of kissing. So — uh — I think this earlier encounter that we had had which just involved a couple of brief kisses — well, I think this earlier encounter made this later touching behavior O.K. Probably laid the foundation for it.

The previous and gradual introduction to erotic contact facilitated traversing a personal sexual frontier:

> So we had touched each other's bodies as we were lying there close together, very close, in fact, just kind of curled up together. And we stroked each other's bodies completely from the waist up, breasts, nipples, everything, and then started exploring down the body. And this was the first time for both of us to have touched another woman this intimately.
>
> But anyway — before I knew it I was exploring the folds of the vagina, the clitoris and was amazed at how different it felt from my own and this was — this was really amazing because she's kind of flat there, and I'm kind of (pause) poufy. Like the mound that is right above the clitoris, she's all flat and I'm poufy.... It was a new experience and an interesting experience and what — we both cared a lot about each other as people. The first thing I knew, I was stroking her clitoris and she was becoming very excited and I realized this and wanted to give her more pleasure. And so she did have a climax.

Just as with the first heterosexual extramarital sex, women also defined the first sexual encounter with another woman as a learning experience. It was different, and yet familiar at the same time. It was different because it represented a hitherto unknown physical and psychological event. It represented a chance to give to another woman what had previously been reserved for men.

It was also familiar because women got a chance to experience their own bodies through the body of another woman. They could compare similarities and differences in a way never possible before. They could also use knowledge of what personally pleased them for the pleasure of another person who was physically similar. It was "mirror-image sex."

Although Helen had just engaged in this unique experience, she had not yet lost all of her sexual inhibitions. She was one of the few women I interviewed who had not experienced orgasm in extramarital sex with men and the same situation prevailed with a woman:

> And then she started to do the same thing to me and I remember being afraid. In other words, like she had—uh—made me feel good by being so free that she could even reach an orgasm that I had induced and that was a stroke for me. And so I cut off her touching behavior because I was afraid that I would not be able to have an orgasm and for some reason I didn't want to spoil it by having her try to give me one and my not being able to to respond the way she wanted. And I think this is a problem for me because I have noticed that this happened a couple of times with men and it's like I—I don't want to disappoint them in not being able to give me one and therefore I just put off the behavior. But this was O.K.; she felt fine about it at that point and I felt good about cutting it off.

Helen later reflected on what had happened and still defined it as totally positive. She experienced no guilt or regret, but instead appreciated both the emotional and physical aspects of the experience:

> We did discuss the whole thing the next day when we were driving down the mountain together, just the two of us in a car, about the positive feelings we still were having about it and—uh—yet the good possibility that it may never happen again. Then this I distinctly remember, how *neat* it was to stroke her breast and nipples and they were so different from mine; her breasts were entirely different from mine, I'm very flatchested and she is *very* full in the breasts, and—it was neat, it was great just to have all this huge breast in my hand.

Interestingly, Helen reacted to the experience of breast touching in the manner of the sexual script typical for men. This script, as we know, prescribes that the larger the breast, the better the experience of touching. At the same time she also placed the sexual situation in a uniquely female perspective by comparing what she felt in her friend's body with the same but dissimilar parts of her own body.

She explained more of her reacton by comparing it to her reacton with men:

> The whole encounter was just as exciting to me as when I have been with a man. It was—in fact, it might possibly have been a little more exciting because of the fact that this was a woman. And it's just really neat to share something like that with someone who has had a woman's experiences.... So— uh—anyway it was just great. I really enjoyed it and I'd like to do it again with her.

Subsequently Helen did have two more sexual encounters with Cindy as their friendship continued.

A last possible way to lesbian involvement, and one of the most interesting from the perspective of sexual development, was reported by three women. It involved a gradual process of self-awareness of bisexual interest. A fifty-three year-old woman recalled a strange experience that signalled her transition:

> It happened at my neighbor's house. I was standing by the kitchen window...on the sill she had plants, and she said, "Look what happened...this plant of avocado seed, it has split open!" Well, here was this shout from this whopping avocado seed—both sexes! And this thought struck me and I got quivery. A shot of quicksilver went from my chest right down past my navel, not quite to the clit, O.K.? (laughs softly)
> But it was so quick and so sudden and so strong that I couldn't look at her. I said, "What is she telling me? Is she telling me something?" And my head was in a whirl.... I went home and thought it over. But Betty is converted to the Catholic faith. She would never even think of touching herself. When I asked her subsequently if she ever did—"Well that's sinful," she said. So she would never have said,"Look at this," and mean something by it. What I was doing was telling myself something. I was telling myself because I would, in the years before, find my eyes caught by a handsome woman. I would love to look at her walk down the street. But—it never connected. I just liked to do that. And I also knew that this was not the thing to do, so it was a surreptitious thought and it was a surreptitious watch on my part of this person. It all came together at one time. It took me a long time to reach that conclusion.

The conclusion she made was that she was attracted to both sexes. She wished to have extramarital relationships but, because of her age and the stereotypes associated with it, found meeting people difficult:

> I had been saying to myself, "What in the world can I do so I can meet people so that I can fill up myself with what I am empty of?" And there was only one way, because of my age.
> One looks at me and automatically assumes she's married, she's older, she is not my style. But I knew I had a style. I knew I could go out in the world and say, "Here I am. I want to be liked and I want to love people." And there was only one way that I could see. It was not going to be with church people, or my ski club; it was not the straight world. It was the swinging world. And there, as a single woman, there things don't make any difference.... I met this lovely couple who invited me to a party where I was touched by a man and a woman, both married, and made love to, and I liked it. That's how I was able to realize the physical aspect of bisexuality.

This woman participated in "swinging" activities for about a year, trying to interest her husband in joining her. He did not because it "was not for him." She then dropped out of swinging because the relationships were not expressive enough to satisfy her needs. During the course of her extramarital career she had both heterosexual and homosexual involvements. About three years after the first interview she left her marriage, which had long been unsatisfactory.

Another woman, Anne, also found her way to bisexuality. She described a transitional process which lasted about five years from her first glimmer of awareness to actual behavior. At the time she had been married ten years and had had several extramarital episodes with men:

> I was about thirty-five years old when I first started having lesbian dreams. At the time I was so naive I wasn't even aware that there was such a thing as lesbianism. I felt very strange about the dreams because I knew such behavior was not normal. Besides I had never had a conscious thought about being sexually attracted to women, so I was really puzzled. I said nothing to anyone about the dreams.
> As the dreams persisted I realized I was beginning to look at women in a sexual way. Women that I saw walking in the streets, for instance—I would suddenly realize I was staring at them because I was very sexually attracted to them. I still did or said nothing about it, because I was quite embarrassed by my own behavior.

Initially, Anne was uncomfortable with this self-discovery, again partly because she had heard nothing about lesbianism except to know that it was not "normal." By the mid-1970's, due to a more tolerant social climate and through personal contact with another woman, she had gradually come to change her opinion and her behavior as well:

> I did begin hearing about lesbianism around this time, and that helped me understand myself better. However, I knew I was not a lesbian because I was still strongly attracted to men.
> Two things happened that really changed me sexually. One was that I fell in love with a woman I was friends with, quite unbeknownst to her and quite unexpected by me. I was struggling with my feelings, not knowing what to do about them, when one day she confided in me that she was gay! I was so taken aback. I had never suspected that. Well we never did have more than a deep friendship, with kissing and sometimes great rushes of erotic feelings. She was involved with someone else.
> Shortly after that a younger woman who was on my softball team started showing me a great deal of attention. I liked her and was very flattered. I was shocked one day when she came up behind me and kissed me on the back of my neck. I couldn't believe how excited it made me.
> It turned out that she was gay and she led me gradually into my first sex with a woman. I was scared but I was also ready for it.

Anne did not greatly enjoy this first sex, because she was "very nervous and scared." Furthermore, she found one aspect to be what she objected to having sex with men:

> She put a great deal of pressure on me to have an orgasm. At the time I never did have one the first time with anyone. So I found that distasteful and not what I would expect from a woman. I thought only men did that.

Nevertheless, the experience was so emotionally moving she wrote the poem reproduced at the beginning of this chapter. Although she vowed in the poem never to have sex with men, she has continued to have relationships with with them and has also come to enjoy sex with women. Her most satisfactory relationships with either men or women, are those with "high expressive quality." At the time of the last interview in 1979, she had left her marriage, gotten divorced, and continued to relate to both men and women, although she described herself as "more attracted" to men.

These, then, are the four principal routes for women's transition to lesbian extramarital relationships—through getting involved emotionally, through swinging, through the assumption of women-positive and sex-positive values that resulted from the cultural changes of the 1960's and 1970's, and through self-recognition. What were the differences between these involvements with women rather than involvements with men? What were the meanings of this additonal transition to unconventional sexuality?

Meanings and Differences

I asked women to reflect on the meanings of their lesbian reltionships. For most it was a further exploration into intimacy, another opportunity to find expressiveness. It existed especially as an alternative to relationships with men when they could not or did not provide the expressiveness women desired. After all, since women are the expressive specialists, who better to turn to for that quality? Women felt there was a different intensity in a relationship with another woman because of that expressive compatability. Also contributing to the intensity was the commonality of life experiences that could be shared.

In the initial attraction to the person, there tended to be a difference between male and female partners. On meeting, women generally viewed men immediately as potential sexual partners, whereas with women partners the sexual attraction built up more slowly, over time, and with repeated interaction.[9] A couple of women, however, had changed this more traditionally female pattern to the immediate sexual appraisal made of men. Of necessity, it was carried out more circumspectly. As a 40-year-old nurse described it:

> I think I've always been very much aware of the fact that when I meet a man that he is a candidate for sex. And I evaluate that; would I like to go to bed with him? I sort of get that squared away in my head. I was not doing that with women, but now I do. I try to evaluate if I am sexually attracted to this woman. If she is a true heterosexual, if she is really uptight about lesbianism, I'm very careful so that I don't blow her mind. Because I'm also aware tht women don't feel attraction for other women even if they are heterosexual.
>
> So, I'm very careful not to do anything that would really turn her on and give her feelings of pulling back. I've become very conscious of people's space. And I'm very quick to identify how close to them their particular individual space is. And, of course, as a nurse I've been educated as to this kind of

territorial rights, and I'm as conscious of it with friends, as with patients.

Despite the different patterns in the initial attraction, most women thought they were attracted to the same qualities in both men and women. There was remarkable agreement about what those qualities were. Women emphasized, as might be expected, the expressive and emotional aspects of the person. A 28-year-old secretary said:

> Once I get to know the person, it's pretty much the same thing: gentleness, understanding, pretty much deep feelings—being capable of having deep feelings, and being able to let go.

And the 40-year-old nurse quoted above explained:

> I think the thing that attracts me to women is the same thing that attracts me to men; intelligence, ability to converse on the levels that I think are interesting, wanting to grow, to change, to become, rather than to remain static and think that they've got their shit together. I think it's the same qualities in women that attracted me to males. And really, there's no difference.

When discussing the physical appeal of a person, an atractive, healthy body was deemed equally important for both male and female partners. Interestingly enough, several women focused on the breast size of women, even though there was no specific question about this. That women also would focus on this in evalutaing other women as potential sexual partners shows the pervasiveness of the emphasis on breast size in our culture. One 28-year-old woman rejected notions of size superiority, and preferred women with breasts similar to her own:

> I do find women with beautiful bodies more attractive than women who do not have beautiful bodies. Don't like big breasts though, I like small breasts, like mine.

One more difference women pointed out was that extramarital relatonships with women were easier to arrange and carry out, for a couple of reasons. There was the different perception of the relationship to husbands:

> A woman seems like a woman friend to other men, it does not seem like a lover. Men do not see other women as potential lovers. It's not that serious to them. So if deception is on your mind, it's much easier to carry out an affair with a woman. You're just going over to see your girlfriend, you're going

shopping, to have coffee, you know, all that usual woman-to-woman stuff, that we're all supposed to do, that our mothers all supposedly did. It's much easier to use that to cover an affair.

The other reason for feeling that extramarital relationships with women were easier to integrate with married life was that such relationships were not likely to lead to an involvement that threatened marriage:

I think a relationship with a woman would affect a marriage less because you're not likely to marry another woman. . . . I mean, you could, in the sense of going away and living with her forever. But for me, you wouldn't marry another woman, you wouldn't have children with another woman.

Sexuality

I asked women if they were aware of any differences in their sexual activity with women as comapared with men. All agreed there were definite and obvious differences. The question of the amount of time spent in sex and the pacing of sexual activity was the principal negative difference women singled out. As a 25-year-old secretary explained it:

I think two women together—you have two people in bed who are really knocking themselves out to try to please each other. There's a definite difference with men. You know, when God designed male and female bodies to fit together, he did a great job. It was a great engineering feat.

There was only one problem. He forgot the nerve endings. Men and women make love differently.... I think men tend to be more impatient. Whereas women—most of us—it took so long to learn our own orgasm patterns and they don't always work, so we're accustomed to taking more time. It's not the performance thing. I think the emphasis is more on the sensousness and pleasure than on performance.

And a 30-year-old dancer echoed the problem of male-female differences in timing as well as goals of sex:

I think women are more willing to be tender and less precipitive about getting down to the main event, as far as sex is concerned. I feel men always want to get right down to fucking. Now I want to get down to fucking, too, but I want to take longer getting there. To feel you don't have to do that if you don't want to. And I feel this is something that women have in common. I don't know whether it's, hmmm, cultural or biological, I don't know. Most women are more—they do that more. More foreplay and afterplay.

A 53-year-old writer emphasized the importance of tenderness in women's lovemaking:

> I think to look into a woman's eyes, and that glance can—you can go farther into that person than you can with a man, because a man is more cock-oriented. He isn't going to lie there for a long time just looking into your eyes, he wants to go elsewhere. That's what really, when you get down to it, is the difference.

Women uniformly agreed they were more likely to find compatibility with a woman than a man on matters of timing, pacing, and tenderness. Female lovers were seen to be, like themselves, more interested in the process of lovemaking, in the touching, gazing, talking, and feeling that were rated equally as important as orgasm. Male lovers, these women felt, were noticeably and distractingly interested in the product of sex. Achieving orgasm was seen as the only satifactory resolution of sex for men. Anything else was not worthwhile, and time spent on any other activity was necessary and enjoyable only if it contributed to the achievement of orgasm.

Bisexual experiences appear to be the ones that most vividly illustrate differences in sexual styles between women and men, for it was here that women had a chance to make a direct comparison. Most women found that their lovers followed the usual sexual script for their sex, and the conclusions drawn from these bisexual experiences support the women's conclusions on male-female differences in sexuality discussed in Chapter 5. It is true that some men are moving toward more tender sex, and some women are moving toward more casual sex. Most men and women, however, are still influenced by the opposing models of sexual enjoyment built into traditional sexual scripts, according to the reports of these women.

Despite this negative comparison, in which male lovers fared less well than female lovers, women also had a positive view of male-female differences. They singled out primarily physical aspects that they thought added to the appeal of bisexual experiences:

> I enjoy the differences, I enjoy the softness of a woman, in terms of her being able to talk about feelings. Just the smell,

the taste, the—just the general softness, the smoothness. When I beome aware of it in other women's bodies, I also become more aware of how I must feel to someone.

But I enjoy feeling the hardness of a man. I enjoy hardness, as I enjoy feeling hair, the penis, I like the way it feels. I love the feeling of penetration. It's just that they're very different.

Also, I found that each sexual experience, whether with male or female, is different. Each person is uniquely himself or herself, in terms of the total personality, which includes their sexuality. I've always been interested in people, and I like the differences.

Here again, as in their extramarital experiences with men, women felt they learned and grew from these relationships. The most obvious area of learning is the opportunity to become more self-aware—"I also become more aware of how I must feel to someone," the woman above says. Women also increased their self-awareness through the opportunity to compare their own bodies with those of other women, to see how they were similar or different. In some of the excerpts quoted in this chapter, women reacted to contrasts in breasts and genital areas. Women's knowledge of their own sexual anatomy has always been more limited that that of men's knowledge of themselves because of the more hidden nature of female anatomy. Not only are female genitalia more physically hidden from view than are men's, but women have also grown up with less opportunity for knowledge. They have not had comparable experiences in team sports, locker rooms, common showers, "skinny dipping," and the like that men routinely have had. Thus, women not only enhanced knowledge of their own bodies but also learned about bodies of other women as a consequence of their lesbian extramarital relatonships.

At the same time, however, women also were able to place themselves momentarily in the role of the male lovers, and to feel what men must feel in touching women. One woman remarked, "When I first started making love to a woman I thought about what men must do and feel in the same situation." Helen, the woman discussed earlier who had a lesbian experience at a mountain retreat, reacted similarly: "It was great just to have all this huge breast in my hand."

Thus, women also increased their perceptiveness of *others'* feelings and reactions through the experience of putting themselves in another—in this case a (usually) man's—role. Putting ourselves in the role of another, either vicariously or actually, is the way people typically learn more about themselves and others, thereby growing in self and social understanding.[10]

Another element of learning that some women experienced was the opportunity to fuse affection with sexuality in a way not experienced before. Our society has fairly distinct rules as to whom we should be affectionate with—parents, aunts, uncles, grandparents, brothers, sisters, perhaps friends—and whom we should be sexual with—non-related persons of the opposite sex within a certain appropriate age range. Consequently people tend to grow up with affection and sexuality linked to specific categories of people. In lesbian extramarital relationships, women often felt freed for the first time of this arbitrary separation of affection from sexuality. A 32-year-old writer described her consciousness of this:

> I was involved with the most open, giving, loving person that I had ever met. She was the person who made clear to me the disparities that had been in my life before about sex and sexuality and just affection. When I grew up there was a certain set of people you're supposed to hug 'cause they're your relatives, and even though you don't care about them you're supposed to hug them and kiss them. I realize I carried a lot of that over to other relationships and that this woman, somebody I really felt great about, I could feel comfortable kissing her and holding her and hugging her. It was the first time I saw the synthesis of really feeling good about somebody as a whole—a real person—and the fact that she was a woman seemed insignificant.

Women tended to view their lesbian extramarital experiences as significant sexual and social events. The only exceptions were isolated cases of lesbian contact through swinging, when no previous friendship between women was involved. The sexual significance lay in opportunities for further sexual exploration and development, and the social impact came through learning about themselves and other women from a totally new perspective.

Identities and Attitudes

Despite having had lesbian experiences, and despite the significance of these relationships, women did not change their basic identities as heterosexuals. Most considered themselves to be primarily heterosexuals. with some bisexual tendencies. Women objected to being asked to label themselves, feeling that labels were inappropriate and innaccurate to designate people's sexual lives.

As a 40-year-old woman commented:

> I've always considered myself primarily heterosexual but perhaps I'm more bisexual. I don't like any of those labelings. Ever since I read Dennis Altman's book on homosexuality, I'm very put off by every word, hetero, bi, or homosexual being used as a noun. I guess I am a person who would consider sex as a dimension of a relationship. I just don't choose to label myself. I don't think there should be adjectives describing behavior. And I see them here as nouns, and I really can't label myself.

Alfred Kinsey, the sexologist, also felt behavior, rather than individuals, should be the subject of classification. He devised a continuum of behavior, using 0 for exclusive heterosexuality to 6 for exclusive homosexuality, with the figures 1 to 5 representing varying degrees of bisexuality.[11] Women intuitively supported Kinsey's idea that heterosexuality and homosexuality were not necessarily identities of people, but categories of behavior.

Wardell Pomeroy, a Kinsey associate, believes "that sexual orientaton is never wholly fixed—that within limits, the range of out erotic interests can be changed at almost any point in the life cycle."[12] Change is more likely to the degree that people are comfortable with their own sexuality. As these women began to experiment extramaritally and grew more accepting of their sexuality, they became more open to the idea of extending their behavior to the realm of bisexual experience. One consequence of women's sexual growth, then, may be to extend the range of permissible behavior for themselves. As noted earlier in this chapter, about half of the women who had not had bisexual experiences were open to the possibilty of a sexual relationship with a woman. Even women who had had relationships with women, however, were not always bisexually involved. They found their interest in women varied over time and depended on whether they met a particular woman they were interested in. Their sexual preferences were fluid and were influenced by the particularities of their living situations. Most felt they would remain open to the possibility of involvements with women in the future even if they were not currently involved.

The last question I asked of women with lesbian extramarital relationships was what sexual orientation they would like for their children. Here, again, there was a dominant preference for heterosexuality. But some women qualified their answers:

> Because of the problems they would face if they weren't.

> But I want them to see sex as only one dimension of a relationship.
>
> But I would like him (son) to be able to be caring and affectionate with men also.

A few women believed that their children should be open to both sexes, and that ultimately their children should make their own choices. Consequently, they consciously made them aware of different sexual alternatives as part of the learning process. The 40-year-old nurse discussed this at some length:

> I certainly am exposing my children to the fact that there is a homosexual cult population. That there are a lot of people whose sexual preference is of the same sex. I've had lesbian friends in the home talking with the children about it—sort of like—don't forget there is a dimension that you can consider too. Both of the children have said that this was one of the best things that I could do to them, was to expose them to this, while they were in the home.
>
> My daughter—our 18-year-old—has said that she would have been really shaken up at some of the things that happened in the dorm, had she not been exposed to a lesbian or a couple of lesbians, and to reading and talking about lesbianism as a choice for a woman. She would have been very shook up at some of the things that she's observed at school. She's been able to handle herself very nicely, been able to change attitudes of some of her classmates.
>
> And I think it's very important, and one of the best things that parents can do to children, is to expose them to as much life while they're still in the nest, and can discuss their feelings with other people who are meaningful to them, with adults, with their parents.

As women choose a life path, then, that veers away from traditional behavior, as they explore all the new options that have been created as a result of the sweeping social changes of the last two decades, we can expect that their new lives will also affect the way they rear their children.

We are already beginning to see studies of the working woman's impact on her children. Most of what we have found to date is that the effects are largely beneficial. Children develop a new sense of responsiblity, a feeling of autonomy, and a belief that they are contributing importantly to family life as they begin taking over household chores. The consequence for girls is especially strong, as they now have as a role model a mother who is strong, accomplished, and self-confident. Boys also develop a different image of what women are like and what they can expect of their future wives.[13]

Although change in women's sexual behavior has a less obvious impact on their childrearing practices, it is another area that deserves observation and study. For among the myriad ways in which women are changing, we cannot afford to overlook the consequences of sexual change that may well filter down to affect the lives of their children. Although studies have shown peers to be major influences on adolescent sexual behavior,[14] this occurs in a relatively closed sexual context between parents and children. The stereotype is that parents are supposed to be non-sexual beings,"uptight" in speaking about sex. As parents, particularly women, alter their own sexual expression and their ability to be open, their influences on their children's sexual development may well increase rather than decrease when children mature into adults. Changes in the development and expression of women's sexuality, then, may also influence their role as the principal socializers of children and, therefore, produce changes in the sexual socialization of succeeding generations.

Chapter Eight

The Extramarital Connection

In the preceding chapters I have presented research findings about the extramarital relationships experienced by the women I interviewed. I interpreted the sociological meanings of these findings and compared and contrasted them with conclusions from other research into extramarital behavior.

In this final chapter, I would like to provide a wider frame of reference for viewing extramarital behavior, focusing on the meanings and consequences for both individuals and society. These interpretations are, of course, speculations to some degree since predicting human behavior is always hazardous. However, the interpretations represent several years of study, consultations with other researchers and theorists, and many conversations with women and men with and without experiences in extramarital relations.

I began the discussion of this book by pointing out the logical inconsistency of sexual exclusivity through monogamy with the contemporary meanings of marriage and the present cultural value of sexuality. Extramarital relations are one piece of social evidence testifying to the inconsistency between two opposing sets of values—the traditional emphasis on sexual exclusivity within marriage and the modern premium placed on sexual consumption in our rapidly changing society. Given the current incidence of extramarital behavior, it can no longer be adequately explained by the weakness or infidelity of particular individuals. Sociologically, it is one of the adaptations to be expected when a society changes values in two major areas of intimate life—marriage and sexuality. And in recognition of its increasing prevalence, there is increasing research attention being given to it.

It was not all that long ago when marriage and sexuality were thought to be synonymous; all approved sexuality was to take place inside of marriage. Our language still reflects that traditional value, for even when sexuality does take place outside of marriage, it is still defined by marriage. For instance, we have premarital sex and extramarital sex. But we have no commonly agreed upon term for sex that takes place after divorce or after being widowed. Nor do we have a label for sex engaged in by single persons who may never marry, or who may not marry until their thirties, as people are increasingly doing. The term "pre-marital sex" is too limited to convey the sense of that long term experience, or of an experience that may not necessarily be followed by marriage.

As ever increasing amounts of sexual experience take place outside of marriage, it is obvious that sexuality is being separated from the institution of marriage.[1] As sexuality becomes a social institution in its own right, a unique set of patterns, values, and rules to cover a variety of sexual situations will emerge. The patterns of behavior in extramarital sex will become part of the separate institution of sexuality, and will also interact with the institution of marriage. Knowledge of extramarital behavior is as vital to understanding modern sexuality as it is to understanding contemporary marriage. Therefore, I will focus broadly on these interrelationships in this portrait of the meaning of the extramarital connections between women and men.

Women and Sexuality

The recent increase in women's participation in extramarital relationships is undoubtedly related to changes in our attitudes about sexuality, but also to the resurgence of feminism that has captured the imagination of many women. The basic issue seems to be that roles which have previously been legitimated for women are now unsatisfactory to them because of the many social changes of the last several decades. Therefore, women are creating, taking, and pressing for new roles that are more fulfilling.

To borrow a hypothesis from the poet James Dickey, he says that:

> It is the most imaginative and vital people who are going to be drawn to adultery. People who are quite willing to give up and give in to conventionality and the *status quo* are not going to be tempted by an adulterous possibility as much as people in whom the life instinct and sense of adventure is extremely strong.[2]

This is the position of many women today; they are no longer so willing to accept conventionality in any area, including sexuality. Influenced by the women's movement, they are more caught up in personal and social change. Very possibly the changing social milieu has sharpened their life instinct by opening up possibilities only dreamed about before.

One of these possibilties, discussed in this book, exists in the extramarital area. Women are breaking out of traditional marriages which have demanded their faithfulness while not demanding it of men. And, women are breaking out of the old roles of sexuality that always evaluated male pleasure as more important than female pleasure.

As social and marriage role-breakers, women will no doubt threaten both men and society. As they move toward more sexual freedom, they may also create envy and provoke an emotional backlash from men, who at the same time will be enjoying the fruits of women's sexual liberation. Conservative women, those who still find traditional patterns of life rewarding, may also be expected to condemn those women who reach out for new roles.

This reaction may be expected because of the unprecedented nature of women's new sexual behavior. Women have always been the keepers of the most conservative sexual standards in society. They have stood long centuries of duty as the moral guardians of our culture. Now they are abandoning their posts and throwing away the very weapon—sexual fidelity—by which they had exerted some small amount of power over men. Now they have more modern sources of power.

In a sense, it is perfectly fitting that women as a group should be influential shapers of the new institution of sexuality. Women's power and influence have always existed more in the sphere of intimate relations than in impersonal institutional processes. And, as I have already mentioned, because women's sexuality has been defined for them by dominant males, women are a group who would be unusually responsive to a chance for sexual autonomy.

Although the traditonal view has been that women were less free to enjoy sex outside marriage, I have suggested instead that extramarital behavior may be an area in which women are now unusually free to establish the kind of sexual patterns they prefer. This is so because the extramarital area is not governed by the social rules and inherited patterns that have long dominated marital and premarital interaction. There is no social pressure to enter and maintain extramarital relationships; women are free to withdraw from them should they be unsatisfactory. Such freedom exists particularly for the large majority of the women who did not "fall in love" with their partners and were not tied by bonds of romance. There is no deep investment, as there is in marriage, that would tend to keep the relationship going if a woman were not getting what she wanted sexually. There is also no long-term institutional pattern, as in marriage, that defines extramarital sex as having purposes other than personal pleasure. For women, as a group, their participation in extramarital sex signals continued liberation from traditonal sexuality, a liberation that began with their participation in premarital sex and is developing into an insistence on equal sexual rights after marriage, both inside and outside it. Women's extramarital sex is the final assault on the "double standard," which, in the current generation of young married women, can be expected to die an unremarkable and overdue death.

What these women got out of extramarital sexuality was a chance to construct a new sexual script that was female pleasure-oriented. The traditional emphasis on sex as a form of service to others was replaced with a primary interest in self-satisfaction. The script women devised for themselves had twin elements of physical and emotional satisfaction. Physical satisfaction centered on variety of partners, extended body contact, the pleasures of cunnilingus, and creative use of other body parts besides the genitals.

The emotional satisfaction of extramarital sex was not derived from traditonal romantic feelings but rather from the expressive aspects of the relationship, with a modern emphasis on communicating emotions, feelings, and reactions. It is, after all, the human ability to speak and feel that distiguishes us from other animals who have sex. Emphasis on these qualities, as well as physical satisfaction, contrasts with the traditional male emphasis on physical satisfaction only.

Women's interest in uniting both physical and expressive aspects of sex was especially obvious in their exploration of bisexuality. It was in these experiences that they found opportunities not only for new physical adventures, but also a way to maximize expressive satisfaction. These adventures into bisexuality illustrate that women, in being liberated from past sexual restrictions, have the potential to be more wideranging in their sexuality than men. Bisexuality, or homosexuality, is still too threatening to most men who cannot, in our culture, even feel free to embrace another man. A further sexual limitation for men is that our institutions more rigidly proscribe male homosexuality than female , because of the male's historic, and still existing, greater social importance.

What we are seeing in the extramarital behavior of these women are the effects of both the sexual freedom movement and the women's liberation movement of the last two decades. Women want to determine their own sexuality, to discover it through their own personal experiences. They are no longer willing to live their lives within the sexual framework provided by marriage and family. They are no longer willing to spend their entire sexual lives pleasing only their husands. They want the potential to achieve optimal sexuality, wherever that may take them. Part of the appeal of extramarital relationships to these women was the opportunity to be innovative, to break with tradition, to create personal change in their own female roles at a time when social change is pervasive and seductive.

One of the places their sexual traveling takes them is to relations with partners of different ages, social classes, races, ethnic groups, genders, and marital status. This opening up of novel classes of partners destroys the rigid queueing system of traditonal sexual selection, in which partners had to be chosen within very narrow boundaries in all those categories. Unleashing the dimensions of selection of sexual partners reduces the structural predictablity of sexuality; if the choice of partner is not scripted, the interaction also becomes more open to spontaneity. For example, women with younger partners found themselves acting as sexual learning agents for men, and women who had greater numbers of extramarital partners were able to learn more about their sexual potential.

Women, because of their newly acquired social power, have the opportunity to be sexual radicalizers and transform a traditional sexual script that was not constructed for their well-being. Although the women in this study succeeded, for the most part, in implementing their definitions of sexuality in their extramarital relations, the larger social question is whether women in general can achieve this in their sexual relations with men, in whatever marital or non-marital situation they find themselves.

To some extent posing this question means seeing men and women as groups of people in conflict because they seek opposing goals. Although this is by no means the entire picture of male-female relationships, there is no doubt that the history of heterosexual interaction can be characterized fairly as "the longest war." Men have a vested interest in maintaining a concept of sexuality that is oriented toward male pleasure and framed in impersonality, while women have much to gain by institutionalizing a sexual script that is oriented to female pleasure and values. What can women do as a group to promote changes which would balance sexual scripts?

In discussing how to equalize gender roles in intimate interaction, sociologist John Scanzoni proposes three principal strategies women can use to promote gender role change. The first is to convince men that it is in their self-interest to change. The second is to appeal to men's altruism and demonstrate that not only will men benefit from adopting innovative patterns in sexuality, but that it will also be better for women. While some men have already been convinced of the benefits sexual equality will bring, more will be reluctant to change because they prefer things the way they are, believe present arrangements are already equitable, or fear change will create personal insecurity and social instability.[3] Thus, Scanzoni feels, women must:

> be encouraged and trained in the use of strategy three—negotiation and conflict. Indeed, so should boys and men. For many years we have been exposed to a great deal of information about communication skills, and very recently about women's assertiveness training. Both communication and assertiveness are important correlates of bargaining but they are not negotiation itself. Negotiation is a process of give and take—in other words, concessions and compromises in exchange for benefits—so that the parties concerned end up with something, but not everything they originally wanted.[4]

Put simply, men will only become more willing to adopt a sexual script which is female *and* male oriented if women demand it. While women and men can learn to negotiate effectively to achieve a more equal interaction in intimate areas, there is a demographic problem that complicates matters. Because of the higher rates of male deaths, imprisonment, homosexuality, and other ineligibilities as compared with females, there are fewer available adult males than females in every age category. The numbers therefore are against women trying to negotiate changes in sexual roles. As there is a numerical excess of females to males, the laws of supply and demand will favor males who wish to maintain their traditional sexual gratifications.

Despite this demographic imbalance, there are still various ways for women to achieve sexual parity in interaction with men. Some of these ways surfaced in the adaptations made by women in this group. One technique is to enlarge the base of potential sexual partners through crossing traditional boundaries of class, sex, race, and primarily age. There is no doubt, though, that the woman in her 50's and 60's is still at the traditional disadvantage. Although age stereotyping is lessening among younger men, older men still hold to it and prefer younger women. In the future, however, older women should find the age discrimination practiced less, as the young men of today move through the life cycle and carry their new attitudes with them. It is also expected that, as sexuality continues to be disassociated from reproduction, the stigmatizing of women past their childbearing years as nonsexual will diminish.[5] In the absence of satisfactory sexual partners women can and have relied on masturbation; as erotic outlets they have substituted other activities such as sports and creative writing, and they have also discovered satisfaction in celibate phases.

Most women, judging from this research and other available information, wish to negotiate and implement new egalitarian sexual scripts, in which women's pleasure is as important as men's, which are total-body oriented rather than genitally oriented, and which are more expressively centered than impersonal or romantic. There is of course a possibility that in their desire to abandon the repressive sexuality defined as traditionally female, women may veer into impersonal, instrumental sex that has been conventionally defined as masculine. It would be risking loss of our uniquely human traits of communication and emotion if women as a group were to elevate the casual, impersonal model of sex as their preferred pattern. It is a danger that women may wish to be aware of as they go about transforming their sexuality.

As the institution of sexuality takes shape, new sexual standards of behavior will emerge from the new scripts that are formed. In premarital sex, sex with affection has emerged as the dominant morality over sex without affection.[6] In extramarital sex, this group of women is saying that they prefer expressive sexuality over impersonal sexuality. But in an era of rapid and extensive change in women's roles, it would be premature to accept any one pattern as dominant. Instead of looking for uniformity in all women's lives, it seems more fruitful to be alert to a variety of patterns. Women of different ethnic groups, social classes, races, or at different stages of the life cycle may well exhibit different styles of behavior.

What is certain is that understanding and identifying women's current sexual scripts will require much more research into all situations of sexuality—single, premarital, marital, post-marital break-up, extramarital, and sequential marriages. We also will need to delve into changes in male sexuality, which cannot remain unaffected as women go through both a private and public transformation.

We need to continue asking questions about the interrelationship of women's altered sexual behavior and their roles in other areas of social life. I have already suggested, as in the experience of some of these women, that more liberal sexuality may result in socialization to a more permissive sexuality for their daughters and sons. There is also research that relates higher levels of education (graduate and professional schooling) with the most successful sexual functioning.[7]

Another important question in understanding the interrelationship of women's sexuality and other roles is how the status level of their occupations might interact with their desire to engage in extramarital relationships. As already noted, the rewards of an involvement are more immediate than that of a career, for which long preparation may be necessary. Would this tend to make an extramarital involvement more attractive to women with low status and boring jobs? On the other hand, would a woman who achieves a high socioeconomic position become more sexually desirable and active because of her status and power, just as men have traditionally? As women gain increased access to their own sources of social power, they will no longer have to use their sexuality as an instrument to get close to power through their intimate relationships with men. Power in men will not be as potent an aphrodisiac as in the past, when women almost always chose as sexual partners men who were more powerful than they. Consequently, we can expect to see women place more emphasis on enjoying sexuality for its own sake. They will place more emphasis on the quality of that enjoyment, if the many comments on sexual interaction in this research are at all representative.

It is predictable that women will increasingly abandon their reliance on the traditional sexual scripts to guide their erotic behavior. They will also rely less on experts, preferring to examine their own experiences as primary to understanding their own sexuality, feelings, and desires. And they will be less influenced by the mass media, which attempt to regulate women's sexual lives through prescriptive advice in stories and articles. Lately, many women's magazines feature articles on women's extramarital sex because it is obviously one of the areas of social life where women are adopting new patterns of behavior. Although some just report data, others feel compelled to tell women what to do. For instance, in the June 1980 *McCalls* magazine, an article presented both positive and negative aspects of extramarital sex quite fairly but, instead of allowing women to draw their own conclusions, ended by advising:

> the risk to marriage of a wife's affair is truly incalculable—and so is the psychological peril.
>
> All things being equal, it seems safer, maybe even saner, to devote one's best energies to the enjoyment and improvement of life on the home front.... As almost every woman knows, the touch of a beloved hand can mean more—even sexually—than a day in bed with a talented technician who does not speak to the heart.
>
> This much at least remains unchanged through the centuries: Nothing is finer, more fulfilling—or indeed, more sanctified—than the inviolate marriage bed...

Many women will undoubtedly agree with this conclusion, many others will want to find out for themselves whether or not it is true, and many others know from their own experiences that it is definitely not true.

Right now we are only beginning to understand the various ways in which women are shaping this infant institution of sexuality, We have far more questions than answers, but since we are liberating ourselves from thousands of years of sexual repression, we will no doubt continue liberating ourselves from our traditional reluctance to ask questions about this important, exciting, and formerly secretive area of human behavior. The future promises a much increased understanding of human sexuality.

Extramarital Relationships and Marriage

Just as women are using their newly acquired power to bring symmetry and equality to sexual scripts, so too will their power tend to balance the social phases of extramarital relations. The extremes of extramarital relations that have been identified as stereotypically masculine—the impersonal one-night stand—and stereotypically feminine—the affair of grand passion—will be supplemented by a variety of other patterns. One major pattern will undoubtedly be the humanistic-expressive one that most of these women experienced, in which sexuality is embedded in expressiveness and friendship. This pattern reduces both the impersonality and romance inherent in traditional definitions. It is uniquely born of the social changes of the 1960's and 1970's, which moved sexuality and intimacy onto the developing frontiers of human behavior.

The contemporary reality of actual extramarital behavior is both more complex and more common than our traditional consciousness of it, which suggests that it is time to bring our consciousness up-to-date. Not only are there extramarital relations of all degrees of emotional commitment, but there are also relationships that exist without sexual intimacy. Using an encompassing definition, some extramarital behavior does not even involve social contact, for it can exist solely in fantasies and dreams.

The different varieties of extramarital behavior can be represented on a line of continuing intimacy, which begins with mental thought processes, extends to conversation, emotions, and continues with beginning physical contact all the way to oral and genital intercourse. The range of possible extramarital behavior might look like this:

dreams — fantasies — thoughts — conversations — emotions — simple touching — kissing — petting — oral and genital sex

Even this representation is not perfect, for genital sex may of course be less intimate than emotions. But at least this allows us to picture the many possibilities involved in a consideration of extramarital intimacy.

In reality every married person has an extramarital life, for who has never had a dream or fantasy of someone other than the spouse? There also are sensual memories of people from our pasts and anticipations of people who will be in our futures. Even the topic of remarriage of one spouse after one's own death is conversationally ruled out in most marriages. The myths of monogamy have not allowed us to exchange these thoughts and experiences with a husband or wife.[9] Ironically, sharing this knowledge of ourselves can increase intimacy and, thereby, strengthen the marriage.

There are also important extramarital relationships that take place on the social level, that never approach the physical. Although this research did not focus on such relationships, they can exist as vital friendship links and deserve to be studied to determine their place in the full-range of extramarital behavior. Undoubtedly many people have or would like to have such cross-sex friendships to supplement their intimate lives, but with the traditional consciousness, these relationships are suspect and probably not tolerated very well in most marriages.

We need to learn much about how to integrate all kinds of extramarital relationships, including sexual ones, into the pattern of successful marriage. It seems less urgent to be concerned about the impact of these relationships on a marriage after both parties have defined it as unsuccessful. In this situation extramarital behavior may be engaged in primarily as a temporary and transitional outlet. We particularly need to revise the "feeling rules" by which we deal with spouses' extramarital behavior within successful marriages, to bring the past negative meaning into line with present-day reality.

The experience of Jim and Peggy Vaughan, a married couple who wrote *Beyond Affairs*, is a good example of how people can learn to transcend inherited feeling rules.[10] Jim had had several "affairs" before telling Peggy about them. She reacted with typical emotions of anger, pain, shame, and distrust. In the feeling rules we have inherited, wives generally also feel shame for they are thought to be, and indeed feel themselves to be, somehow responsible for their husbands' behavior. "If I had only been a better wife, he wouldn't have strayed" is the usual assumption.

Jim reassured Peggy that despite the affairs he loved her and did not want a divorce. In the course of their many conversations about how to repair the damage to their marriage, Peggy became extramaritally involved. This experience was not simply a retaliation or an eye for an eye behavior, but enabled Peggy to understand how it was possible to be extramaritally involved and not have it affect her feelings for her husband. She was able to understand that extramarital activity need not be a rejection of or an attack on the spouse, but rather may be an expression of individual needs that are independent of what marriage does not and perhaps cannot provide. It was a reaction she could not have understood or believed without experiencing it herself. In effect, she had "to take the role of the other"[11] — in this case the role her husband had taken — before she was able to comprehend fully his behavior and reactions. At the same time, her husband also was cast in her former role and was able to feel what her pain had been.

In order to make a transition to new feeling rules which might guide our reactions to extramarital behavior, then, *one* possible route is to test innovative behavior such as the Vaughans have done in exchanging extramarital roles. We can assess the other's experience and determine workable adaptations to the problems, as well as to any positive aspects of extramarital involvements.

Peggy reported that it took her three years to overcome her negative feelings and to be able to trust her husband again. The marriage is now back on a firm footing because the problems they went through convinced them they must be honest with each other in order to trust. While they are human and reasonable enough to realize they are not willing to promise each other total fidelity forever, they have made a promise that they feel they can keep, that of honesty with each other.

The Vaughns' story and their analysis of it suggest that it was the deception and violation of trust that were the most troubling aspects of their extramarital experience. It is likely that many couples share this view. If deception and violation of trust are ingredients in negative reactions we can eliminate at least pain from these sources. Another innovation to be considered then is the open discussion of partners' feelings about extramarital behavior before it occurs. This is a discussion every committed couple should have, preferably before they make a commitment to be sexually exclusive with each other. It should be as routine a discussion before marriage as are careers and how many children to have and where couples will live and how money should be spent. It will be threatening to discuss in advance a topic that so many successfully avoid, but doing so is a step toward changing the built-in structure of extramarital reactions. People can then be better aware of each other's probability of remaining exclusive and of their own probable reaction. At the very least the possibility of deception and loss of trust is lessened.

While no woman in this research had such a discussion before marriage, several did have hypothetical discussions to test their husbands' reactions before beginning outside relationships. Others, as we have seen, brought openness successfully into the marriage after becoming involved. While none of these techniques are guaranteed to be pain-free or successful, immediate solutions, they are initial attempts to solve the dilemma of extramarital activity created by different social forces over time.

These new problems require new behavioral solutions. Clinging to the past practice of denial of the problem and maintaining schizoid attitudes only effectively delays our coming to terms with extramarital behavior. A sociological perspective demands that we recognize when we have created contradictions in our cultural patterns, especially when these contradictions cause us such negative emotions, on both sides of the extramarital coin, as guilt and frustration, pain, insecurity, and distrust. Our unwillingness to recognize and come to terms with dilemmas we have unwittingly created is socially and personally irresponsible. Social reality is after all constructed by us, and we have the power to construct solutions as well as problems.

Fortunately, the recent changes in women's roles promise to propel us more quickly toward possible solutions. Since women are now approaching equal power with men, that in itself will be a force toward breaking the pattern of present intimate relationships. In the area of extramarital behavior, several conseqences can be expected. Women will no longer be the victimized group in extramarital relationships. Their victim status in the past was founded in many ways upon their powerlessness. Fewer women than men had relationships because they were more economically dependent on men, and could not afford to risk losing the financial support of a man. Possibly fewer women than men desired to have affairs, because they were socialized to a romantic love ethic, in which they were taught they could only love one man. Furthermore, it was only in the presence of love that they were supposed to feel sexual desire. Now, married women, when free of economic and romantic dependency, are becoming extramaritally involved at nearly the same rates as men, and with less emotional dependency upon their extramarital partners. As they increase their extramarital experience and change its meaning, women will increasingly compartmentalize their extramarital and marital intimacy, so that one will not necessarily threaten the other and, thereby, damage the marriage. Most men have always succeeded in doing this, and it was thought to be a peculiar and biological property of males. Actually, it is a reaction that flows out of the characteristics of the roles that people play. If each marriage partner has had symmetrical roles in terms of power, work involvement, economic independence, and sexual freedom, we can expect similar reactions from both.[12]

Women who've had extramarital relations willl no longer feel as threatened by their husband's involvements. Husbands whose wives have gotten involved will now be able to experience the insecurities and distress their involvements caused their wives. On an individual level this role exchange may only seem to increase pain and conflict, but these reactions are often a necessary part of human change. Individual distress can in the long run be personally and socially therapeutic. Out of equalization of roles and the exchange of experience can be born new and mutual desires and methods to integrate marital and extramarital life more realistically and successfully.

Women will more likely be the prime initiators in opening this problem to public consciousness and scrutiny. Traditionally, men's opportunities to have affairs was always greater than women's, but they were expected to be covert about such matters so as to hide their unequal privileges. The economic penalties imposed on men whose wives divorced them for adultery also were severe so there was every reason for men to be covert. But women are not under similar restraints now and are forging new social roles in every area. They can afford an openness in extramarital relations that men never could because the structure of society has changed. Although one sociologist had predicted several years ago "that extramaritality must continue to exist in secrecy, surrounded by guilt"[13] despite its widespread incidence and predicted increase, I believe that contemporary women will gradually change this situation. If the feelings of this group of women in my study is at all representative, secrecy is the most disliked aspect of involvements, and these women do not now feel guilty. Many women did something about the secrecy, and many overcame initial guilt they may have felt as they participated more in extramarital activities and did not suffer deleterious consequences to themselves or to their marriages. They have come to know the same truth about most outside involvements that men have known, that they are, under the proper circumstances, manageable and compatible with an ongoing marriage.

I believe that as more people engage in extramarital relationships, as more people talk about them informally with each other, as more research and serious media attention is given to this covert area of human behavior, that a critical mass of involved people and available information will be reached. The convergence rates of male and female extramaritality is also a force which will unite women and men on this issue and contribute to a new consensus. In such a situation we may expect a spontaneous liberation of traditional attitudes, which would change public consciousness about extramarital activities, remove stigma from the behavior, and neutralize our emotional reactions to it. By that I mean that acknowledgement of the existence of extramarital behavior would be commonplace (even Presidents of the United States have them as we have learned). Attitudes would more closely resemble behavior; people who have been involved extramaritally could afford to be selectively open about their lives; and emotional reactions would span the range of positive to negative, depending on the particular extramarital situation. This liberating action is similar to our raised public consciousness about other forms of intimate life styles that surfaced in the 1960's and 1970's. Once uniformly condemned, people who are divorced, or gay, or lesbian, or single parents, have all found increased public support and a new,more postive image for themselves. These people are all carving out new social roles and rules. They are people who have moved out of the protective but rigid traditonal family pattern to find not only new lives for themselves, but also to creative alternative intimacies for others to learn about, understand, and perhaps use as options in their own lives. These people serve as effective transitional models for those of us who may unexpectedly require the security of knowing that others have gone before us in socially *uncharted territory* and have survived. Similarly, the experience of the extramaritally involved can inform the extramaritally "innocent" and provide both positive and negative guidelines in this transitional era of marriage.

A changed consciousness about extramarital behavior could lead to the establishment of support services for those who engage in or have engaged in it, and who feel the strain attached to any socially unapproved role. One example of support services might be peer counseling groups, with or without professional leaders, whose members could advise each other on managing the complexities of involvements. People could offer self-help to each other from their own experiences as to: what are workable and unworkable solutions for integrating extramarital with marital relationships; ways for coping with endings of outside involvements; management of such issues as the effect of involvements on children and extended families (relatives and in-laws). Going to a group session at a neighborhood "Y" or church is a very different experience from defining oneself as having a problem marriage and going to a marriage counselor for professional help. Moreover, even professionals may be negatively biased toward extramarital activity as Masters and Johnson, revealed themselves to be in their 1976 book, *The Pleasure Bond.*

Public acknowledgement and support services for those involved extramaritally is closely related to acceptance of open marriage forms. The basic differences between extramarital involvements and open marriages are few, involving only mutual consent and openness of the partners, in additon to development of norms or rules to cover anomic situations. Most of this research group of women preferred open marriage; it is doubtful that they are alone in their preference. Support groups as mentioned before, plus foundation or government financed research on active open marriages, would provide much useful information to others. While many, if not most, couples might continue to prefer monogamy during part or all of their lives, there apparently are many others who don't. Their individual happiness and contentment might well be increased by having other intimate options available and acceptable as their needs and preferences change during increasingly long and active life spans.

There is every indication that individuals seeking options to marital exclusivity will continue to do so at present or increasing levels, for the appeal of extramarital involvements is strong in our present culture. Extramarital activity is now as culturally American as apple pie. It apparently provides many individual satisfactions that cannot be obtained within marriages because of the very nature of monogamy itself. Individuals who desire or need those satisfactions will continue to be drawn into extramarital relations.

For women, as we have seen, those satisfactions include opportunities for sexual and self-growth and the development of personal identity and resources that are desirable goals in our current value system. Furthermore, women can take back this renewal and exploration of self into their marriage, with positive consequences for the marriage. I recently interviewed a women who had not been extramaritally involved despite years of deteriorating marriage. Now divorced for several years, having had an active sexual and social life since the marriage broke up, she reflected on her "faithfulness" in her marriage to its bitter end. "That was a mistake,"she said, "I now honestly feel if I'd gotten involved during my marriage it would have helped me to feel freer and more open as I've learned to be now. Perhaps if I could have learned that sooner it would have helped me save my marriage."

Men also will continue to be attracted extramaritally for the sexual variety that many are accustomed to having. Furthermore, recent research suggests that "most men participate in extra-sexual relationships because they desire and enjoy the companionship of other women."[14] I have previously suggested that involvements outside of marriage (non-sexual as well as sexual) may contribute to the development of men's expressive abilities, which most women in this and other research consider to be deficient. While extramarital interaction may assist men in developing expressively, their inability is still socialized into them. Since expressive ability is such an important component in contemporary relations between the sexes, and because men could benefit in their human development by being encouraged to live a more complex and varied emotional life, more public attention to this issue is desirable.

Resocialization of males may be one solution, and some attempts have already been taken in a few male consciousness-raising groups.[15] Government grants for such groups and workshops to be run in a variety of settings that would be comfortable for men, such as union halls, professional organizations, athletic centers, and business organizations might well prove effective and appealing to men who desire personal change. One sociologist also suggests such resocialization could occur in 'natural" settings, as men now find themselves in new occupational situations, e.g., nursery and child-care centers, as nurses, and in subordinate positions to women on the job.[16] Mass media could also play a part by furnishing more male role-models that are sensitive, caring, and expressive. Some recent film characters displaying these qualities are Sylvester Stallone in *Rocky*, Burt Reynolds in *Starting Over*, and John Voight in *Coming Home*.

The sociological truth is that extramarital relationships are here to stay. In recent analyses of the causes of extramarital permissiveness, the social factors that appear most influential in setting the extramarital stage include premarital permissiveness, higher marital power of wives, the willingness to satisfy intimacy needs through more than just one person, an emphasis on the pleasurable aspects of sexuality, the freedom and opportunity to meet attractive members of the opposite sex, a belief in gender equality, low religiosity, and higher amounts of education.[17] All of these factors are trends that will likely intensify in any modern post-industrial society.

Extramarital involvements will be an ever more obvious part of marital lives inthe future. They are part of the evolution of the institution of marriage; and they now require us to respond more openly, rationally, and constructively than we have so far. Just as we have managed to adapt to other marital evolutions in the past, so too can we continue to learn to adapt to marital changes in the future. We can begin by demystifying and demythologizing extramarital involvements and coming to terms with the reality of our own and our partners' extramarital desires and behaviors.

In the 1950's, when marital togetherness was the norm, extramarital involvements were viewed as uniformly bad for both marrige and the involved individuals. In the 1960's and 1970's the incidence of extramarital behavior increased, at least in part as a response to the stifling togetherness of the 1950's, and as we began to accept that relationships could be self-enhancing. Our task for the 1980's is to recognize that marriage can also benefit from— or at least not be harmed by—extramarital involvements under certain conditions. These conditions occur when people value their marriage as the primary relationship and use extramarital involvements as supplementary sources of emotional and/or sexual gratification. Most people who become extramaritally involved do have the desire to maintain their marriage, so this condition is already acknowledged.

The second and more radical conditon is ending the deception of faithfulness which is inherent in traditional monogamy. People will again be able to trust their intimate partners when they are able to be truthful and open about the extramarital side of marriage. This will require partners communicating about whether they have extramarital intentions and what each partner's reactions and adaptations are likely to be. Ideally, these negotiations would occur at the time the couples make their initial commitment to each other.

Not only do these conditions promise more honest and more intimate marriages, but also our own individual security is likely to be enhanced. Although the myth of monogamy is that security is obtained through one person supplying all our emotional needs, it takes only that one person disappointing us to destroy our emotional support system. Paradoxically, it is having several sources of possible gratifiction that best assures our security, for if one person temporarily fails us, we have alternative sources to turn to.[18]

Of course, such negotiations will feel risky and threatening to most people. There are no guidelines or role models to follow in this venture. One approach is through the self-help discussion groups I have already suggested. Just as divorced people have formed groups to guide each other through their passage to a new life style, so too can married people do the same.

Radical changes in our intimate life patterns, such as we are experiencing now, are painful, confusing, and likely to cause personal and interpersonal conflict. But people are capable of making the emotional and social transitions that are so frequently demanded in contemporary society. In fact, persons who are most adept at making transitions, whether they are transitions to new careers, new schools, new residences, new mates, or new intimate living and loving styles are probably most successful and happy in modern society.

These passages unto the "social inknown," as sociologist Lucinda San Giovanni has written, all require

> self-reliance and a willingness to take control over the shape and direction of one's life. One needs an ability to tolerate ambiguity, to make critical assessments and to establish guidelines for planning and pacing one's life course. One has to develop skills for risk-taking and decision-making. Most importantly one must value personal change, diversity, and social flux.[19]

Characteristics that enable us to deal with other diversities in contemporary life are also functional for a new marital consciousness that recognizes the possibility of extramarital relationships. People who adopt this new consciouness are not rejecting marriage; rather they are reacting to the more intense and complex individual needs of modern society. Our behavior indicates that we should eliminate our marital hypocrisy and accept the latent extramarital connections we have created to meet some of these needs.

What I have said on these last pages obviously does not apply to the one-half of married people who both believe in and practice sexual exclusivity. But for the other half who don't, the social scenario I have outlined is one logical possibility for resolving the gap between our extramarital attitudes and extramarital behavior. If the gap continues to increase in the future, as is very likely, we will continue to exist with the tensions and emotional turmoil it induces.

A solution will not be obvious or easy, because our emotional reaction to the loss of sexual exclusivity in marriage tends to be as intense as was our former reaction to the loss of permanence in marriage. Further, as I have tried to indicate in this book, the whole question of extramarital behavior must be viewed not only in relation to individuals and marriage, but also within the larger social framework of the revolution in gender roles, and in power relations between the sexes. These in turn are affected by whatever is happening in the rest of society, by social forces creating changes in the various institutions of the economy, polity, education and religion.

This book has attempted to provide new information on the current reality of extramarital behavior, as well as to call attention to the various forces shaping it today. I hope the book will be part of a continuing dialogue and research which will ultimately result in a more satisfactory resolution of our complex needs for sex, intimacy, and identity which lead us into marriage—and often outside of it, as well.

FOOTNOTES

Full identification of sources mentioned in the text and in the following notes will be found in the Bibliogaphy.

Chapter 1

1. National Opinion Research Center, 1977.
2. The data on extramarital relations are very limited. We have no truly representative information on the American population as a whole because of the numerous difficulties in doing this kind of research. In the absence of exact data, we must rely on the existing studies of portions of the population to provide the most accurate extimates available. See DeLora and Warren (1977) for an examination of the problems in sexual research and Libby (1977) for an extensive critique of the literature on extramarital sex.
3. Yablonsky, 1979, p. 16.
4. Pietropinto and Simenauer, 1977, p. 312.
5. Levin, 1975.
6. Bell, Turner and Rosen, 1975; Levin, 1975.
7. Pickett, 1978.
8. Harper, 1961, p. 384. Reiss (1981, p. 289) alternatively suggests that the explanation lies in the child-rearing responsibilities of the female role.
9. Scanzoni, 1972, p. 13.
10. Libby, 1977: xxi-xxii.
11. Kinsey, 1975, p. 433.
12. Yablonsky, 1979.
13. This finding first emerged in Kinsey and has been replicated by others, including Yablonsky, 1979; Hunt, 1969; Cuber and Harroff, 1965; and Levin, 1975.
14. See Hochschild, 1979, for a discussion of the way social structure affects the emotions we display.
15. These scholars include, among others, Robert T. and Anna K. Francoeur, 1974; Rustum and Della Roy, 1970; Lonny Myers and Hunter Leggitt, 1975; Herbert Otto, 1970; and George and Nena O'Neill, 1972a.
16. National Opinion Research Center, 1977.
17. Hunt, 1974.
18. National Opinion Research Center, 1977.
19. See Laws and Schwartz, 1977, for a detailed discussion of a feminist approach to female sexuality.
20. See Bullough and Bullough, 1974, for a historical account of this bias.
21. These sterotypes are/were so well accepted that they formed the assumptions of best-selling marriage manuals from 1950-1970. See Gordon and Shankweiler, 1971.

22. See, for instance, Ehrmann, 1964, p. 600; Gagnon and Simon, 1973, p. 182.
23. Sherfey, 1966, p. 99.
24. Hite, 1976.
25. Kinsey, et. al., 1953, p. 589.
26. Hunt, 1969, p. 131.
27. Bell, 1971b, p. 70.
28. Bernard, 1969, p. 44.
29. Bell, et. al., 1975.
30. Levin, 1975, p. 5.
31. This sample closely resembles a random sample of *Ms.* readers in employment and varies somewhat in education. Statistics supplied by *Ms.* indicate 67% of readers are employed, 27% hold professional-managerial jobs, and 27% hold clerical-sales jobs. In educational status, 30% graduated from college and 31% attended college. Only two women originally selected declined an interview, one because her lawyer advised against it, and one because she found the interview process too difficult emotionally.
32. This procedure is recommended by Glaser and Strauss in *Discovery of Grounded Theory*, 1967.
33. Prior to the initiation of the research project, I conducted informal interviews with approximately 25 women on the subject of extramarital relationships. These women were encountered in college courses on the subject of family, gender roles, and sexuality, as well as through numerous speaking engagements on the same topics. Information gleaned from these informal interviews was used to prepare an interview guide.
34. Unfortunately, not all of the women were available for subsequent interviews because of geographical distance and the lack of current addresses.
35. Bauman, 1973; Kaats and David, 1971.
36. A more serious question of the representative quality of the sample would arise if it were being used to assess the amount of extramarital participation, since there is some evidence (Abernethy, 1978) that feminist-oriented women have more extramarital sex than more traditional women.
37. See Scanzoni, 1978, Chapter 1, for a discussion of this point.
38. Because the data reported in this book are distinctly qualitative in nature, I will avoid the use of exact percentages in reporting results and substitute instead approximations of numbers. For instance, "a few" will mean 3 or 4 women, "more than half" will mean less than 75%, "nearly all" will mean 85-90%. This practice will avoid a quantitative precision which can be misleading in talking about a small group, and will also be congruent with the qualitative nature of the analysis.

39. Neubeck and Schletzer, 1962.

Chapter 2

1. Only two of the women had, in any way, entertained the idea of becoming involved prior to their marriage. In one case this resulted from the insistence of her husband-to-be that they maintain a non-monogamous relationship both during their engagement and after their marriage. In the other case the woman continued a quasi-romantic and sexual relationship with a former boyfriend up to her wedding, and within one month of a disastrous marriage had resumed the briefly interrupted sexual aspect of the outside relationship. She recalls:

   > I just continued sex with Bob after my marriage...I had nothing better to do at the time. I don't think I was consciously looking for an involvement. I don't think I would have gone out with anybody new...

   Since neither of these two women had the intention of conformity at the time of their marriage, the first part of the analysis, focusing on pre-involvement, will not include them.
2. Laws and Schwartz, 1977.
3. Stephenson, 1973.
4. Kinsey et al., 1953, 427; Levin, 1975, p. 40.
5. Hunt, 1975.
6. Linda Wolfe cites a similar example of this in *Playing Around: Women and Extramarital Sex*, p. 73:

   > This man, my neighbor, proposed we sleep together. The most important thing I have to tell you is how shocked I was when he said that. I literally had never given such matters a thought. Marriage was the closing of the door, the ringing down of that curtain. But after that, the idea was never far from her mind. She said, "I began asking myself, why not? Who would know? Why not once?"

7. Nye and Berardo, p. 342.
8. Johnson (1970) and Maykovich (1976) take different approaches to this variable of "perceived opportunities."
9. In a questionnaire study of 291 female college students, 56% reported being offended at least once during the academic year at some level of sexual intimacy. "The experiences of being offended were not altogether associated with trivial situations as shown by the fact that 20.9% were offended by forceful attempts at intercourse and 6.2% by aggressively forceful attempts at sexual intercourse in the course of which meaningful threats of coercive infliction of physical pain were employed." (Kirkpatrick and Kanin, 1957, 53.)
10. Walum, 1977, p. 29.
11. This is true whether we use role models for socialization to uncon-

ventional behavior (Stephenson, 1973, p. 178) or for approved roles (Bandura, 1969, pp. 245-247).
12. Stephenson, 1973.
13. Personal interview with the author, February 7, 1975.
14. See Rubin, 1976, Chapter 4, for one in-depth treatment of the meaning of female decision-making about premarital sex, and see Delamater and MacCorquodale, 1979, Chapter 9, for a report on survey research of contraceptive use in premarital sexuality.
15. Cloward and Ohlin, 1961.
16. Stephenson, 1973.
17. Bell and Silvan, 1970, p. 408; Hunt, 1962, p. 139.
18. Bernard, 1969; Laws, 1970; Schwartz, 1973; Laws and Schwartz, 1977.
19. Kinsey et al., 1953; Hunt, 1969; Cuber and Harroff, 1965; Bell et al., 1975.
20. Bell and Lobsenz, 1974.
21. Laws and Schwartz, 1977.
22. Kinsey et al., 1953, p. 593; Bell and Lobsenz, 1974.
23. Lyman and Scott, 1970, p. 123.
24. Stephenson, 1973.
25. Lyman and Scott, 1970, p. 123.
26. The extent of this woman's transition is reminiscent of the kind of transformation made by ex-nuns as they move into secular life. For an account of the handling of multiple status transitions, see Lucinda San Giovanni, *Ex Nuns*, Ablex Publishing Corporation, Norwood,

Chapter 3

1. See Lisa Kraymer, 1979, "Work: The Intimate Environment," for a discussion of the workplace as a setting for initiating intimate relationships.
2. See Philip Slater, *The Pursuit of Loneliness*, for an analysis of the effects of an exaggerated emphasis on individualism in American culture.
3. Berger, 1973, p. 74.
4. Lyman and Scott, 1970, p. 123; Berger et al., 1973, p. 77.
5. Maslow, 1971.
6. Mead, 1934.
7. See Parsons and Bales, 1955, for a well-accepted functional interpretation of female gender roles. See Bakan, 1966, for a psychological perspective.
8. In her analysis of the function of gender roles in the larger society, Firestone (1970, p. 127) characterizes women as expressive specialists who supply love so that males may concentrate their energies on building a culture and social structure: "Male culture was and is parasitical, feeding on the emotional strength of women without reciprocity."

9. See Burr et al., 1979, Vol. 1, pp. 22-25, for a theoretical summary of this well-documented characteristic of American marriage.
10. See Davidson and Gordon, 1979, or Walum, 1977, for an overview of the socialization process by gender.
11. Scanzoni, 1972.
12. Balswick and Peek, 1971, also agree with this observation.
13. It is probable that women with an interest in expressiveness also expect it of friends and other associates, as well as of husbands.
14. For further discussions of male inexpressiveness, see Farrell, *The Liberated Man*, or David and Brannon's *The Forty-Nine Percent Majority*.
15. Davidson and Gordon, 1979, p. 29.
16. Edwards and Booth, 1976, p. 219.
17. Jourard, 1971.
18. My thanks to Harry C. Bredemeier for this observation.
19. Friendship is one of the neglected areas of sociological research. See Levinson et al., 1978, for an account of the absence of friendship in men's lives. See also Weis, 1980, for a study of the attitudes of college students towards heterosocial extramarital relations not involving expressions of sexuality.
20. See Scanzoni, 1972, 1978, for a discussion of the influence of women's increasing power in male-female relationships.
21. See Feirstein, 1980, for a compelling illustration of the continuation of this pattern.
22. Balswick, 1979, p. 334.
23. See David Allen, 1978, for a corollary argument that the economic role load of modern husbands also functions to depress men's sexual drives in marriage.
24. Balswick, 1979, p. 335.
25. Scanzoni, 1978, p. 78.
26. Gagnon and Simon, 1973, p. 96.
27. My thanks to Bernard Goldstein for this observation.
28. Yablonsky, 1979.
29. See L'Abate, 1980; Balswick, 1980; and Balkwell et al., 1978, for more discussion of research needed on male inexpressiveness.
30. As Jessie Bernard (1972, p. 308) commented: "We have referred many times to the incompatible demands that human beings make on life, for excitement, freedom, new experiences on the one hand, along with security and stability on the other. But they cannot have it both ways. Any commitment, however desirable, imposes restraints. What seems to be reflected here is an inevitable part of the human condition: people shaking their fists at the restraints they need and know they must have. Marriage, whatever form it takes, is for most, therefore, a compromise between conflicting impulses."
31. Cuber and Harroff, 1965.

32. However, Gagnon (1977, pp. 219-220) emphasizes that in Kinsey's data both men and women tend to give self-serving answers when asked the two questions: 1) "Did your extramarital intercourse figure in your divorce?" and 2) "Did your spouse's extramarital intercourse have any effect on your divorce?" Most people denied that their own had any effect, but felt that their spouse's did. However, there was sex role variation in the responses since women were more accepting of their husband's involvement than husbands were of their wives'.
33. For an account of the impact of extramarital involvements on the mothering role, see Atwater, 1979, pp. 517-519.
34. See Firestone (1970) for a discussion of feminism and romantic beliefs; Laws and Schwartz (1977) for a discussion of romance and sexual scripts; and Walster and Walster (1978), for research on romantic love. Additionally, Wilkinson (1978) explores the hypothesis that romantic love is decreasing in the United States because of increasing sexual permissiveness, both premarital and extramarital.
35. Gagnon and Simon, 1973, p. 304.
36. See Thamm, 1975, for a challenging discussion of the inadequacies of monogamy.

Chapter 4

1. Waller, 1938.
2. Scanzoni, 1972.
3. Reiss, 1976, pp. 136-142.
4. Skolnick, 1978, pp. 252-256.
5. The only widely known book, *Open Marriage* (George and Nena O'Neill) does not explicitly deal with sexual openness.
6. Glaser and Strauss, 1967.
7. Skolnick, 1978, pp. 255.
8. Stephenson, 1973.
9. The following excerpt is an excellent example of Mead's (1934) characterization of interaction as developmental and open-ended.
10. Glaser and Strauss (1967, p. 431) state that "the successive interactions occurring within each type of context tend to transform the context."
11. Glaser and Strauss (1967, p. 431) note that it is an empirical question how long a given contract can last before changing.
12. See Scanzoni (1972) for a discussion of bargaining in mate selection and retention, and the exchange of rewards and punishments as a basis for marital stability.
13. See, for instance, Robert T. and Anna K. Francoeur, 1974; Rustum and Della Roy, 1968; Libby and Whitehurst, 1977.
14. Knapp and Whitehurst, 1978.
15. Murstein, 1978, p. 35.

16. Gilmartin and Kusisto, 1973.
17. Knapp and Whitehurst, 1978, p. 41.
18. I use this concept because of its similarity to "cultural lag." When some parts of a culture, usually behavior or technology, change more quickly than other related parts there is said to be a condition of "cultural lag." Similarly, in individuals, they may change their cognitive beliefs and behavior, only to find their emotions lagging behind.
19. Knapp and Whitehurst, 1978.
20. Knapp and Whitehurst, 1978, p. 43; 1976, p. 213.
21. Jessie Bernard, 1972, p. 306, citing the research of Daniel R. Miller and Guy E. Swanson, *The Changing American Parent,* New York: John Wiley, 1958.
22. Stein, 1980.
23. Knapp and Whitehurst, 1978, p. 38.
24. Constantine and Constantine, 1973, p. 27.

Chapter 5

1. Gagnon and Simon, 1973.
2. Laws and Schwartz, 1977.
3. Gagnon and Simon, 1973.
4. For instance, Kinsey et al. (1953) reported some women (14%) could have multiple orgasms; some married women had initiated extramarital sex with younger single men; some accepted extramarital sex "as another form of pleasure to be shared" and so could handle it with equanimity.
5. For example, see Jessie Bernard (1969; 1970); Judith Long Laws (1970); and Pepper Schwartz (1973).
6. Bardwick, 1971.
7. See Reiss et al., 1980.
8. Kinsey et al., 1953, p. 432, reported many women found extramarital sex "particularly satisfactory" because males...had usually engaged in more extensive courting, in more extended sex play, and in more extended coital techniques than the same males had ordinarily employed in their marital relationships."
9. An interesting study could be made of what mature men and women look for in selecting partners for temporary as compared with permanent relationships. Waller (1937) was an early researcher into the "rating and dating complex" but little or no systematic attention has been given to the dating criteria of today's adolescents or of "mature" members of the singles' scene.
10. Kinsey et al., 1953, pp. 417-418.
11. Pietropinto and Simenauer, 1977, p. 137.
12. U.S. Bureau of the Census, Statistical Abstract of the U.S., 1979.
13. In response to the question "What could your partner do to make you more excited?" more men (34.4%) chose "be more active during

sex" than any other of six possible choices. (Pietropinto and Simenauer, 1979, pp. 386-387.)
14. *Statistical Portrait of Women in the U.S.*, U.S. Bureau of the Census, 1976.
15. DeLamater and MacCorquodale, 1979.
16. Hite, 1976.
17. Masters and Johnson, 1978, p. 76. Of course, rejection of cunnilingus may also be rooted in much deeper cultural beliefs and practices about women's genitalia. The defilement and fear of women's sexual organs inherent in clitoridectomies and hysterectomies; the myths of "odor"; and the traditional male emphasis on the "taking" instead of "giving" of pleasure are all examples of this deeper rooting.
18. Hite, 1976, pp. 527-570.
19. See Slater, 1973, or Zilbergeld, 1978, Chapter 4, for a discussion of the characteristics of the traditional male sexual script.
20. Goffman, 1963, p. 37.
21. Thamm, 1975.
22. Tuchman et al., 1978.

Chapter 6

1. Identity is a rather elusive concept to define precisely (Strauss, 1969). However, I am using it in the sense of the individual's cognitive and affective definitions of his/her self as influenced by the perception of others' implicit and explicit social appraisals.
2. Strauss, 1969, p. 96.
3. Mead, 1934.
4. DeLamater and MacCorquodale, 1979.
5. The literature on adult identity transformations had until recently emphasized those changes carried out under institutional aegis (e.g., Becker et al., 1961; Brim and Wheeler, 1966; Goffman, 1961) and through the socialization of professional schools and other forms of social bureaucracy. More attention lately, however (Glazer and Strauss, 1971), has been given to those changes in adult identity which result in individuals who initiate the move into new and previously untried roles, such as persons invoilved in mid-life crisis (Sheehy, 1974), businessmen who change careers in midstream (Levinson, 1978), and nuns who drop out of convent life (San Giovanni 1978). As a result of this broadening of focus to include self-directed as well as institutionally-directed socializations, we are beginning to flesh out our understanding of status transitions and identity transformations in adult life.
6. It is assumed here that extramarital relations are of the class of self-initiated role transitions that carry the potential of allowing persons to test out and discover new aspects of selfhood. It is also assumed they are primary interactions of the kind in which we normally develop and change our identities during the life course. Fur-

thermore, they are events of an episodic but intense and expressive nature. By not being integrated into our usual and legitimated role complex, they are less likely to demand any carry-over from these other roles. Also, given the capacity for adult growth which we now recognize, anyone undergoing such growth is more likely to find acknowledgement of it in interaction with strangers than with familiar others, due to familiar others' preconceived knowledge of us and the habituated patterns of interaction.

7. Chodorow, 1971.
8. Erikson, 1968.
9. Bernard, 1972.
10. Sheehy, 1974.
11. Maslow, 1968; 1971.
12. Hunt, 1969.
13. Srole and Fischer, 1978.
14. Schwartz, 1973, 222-223.
15. For differences in the number of premarital partners, see DeLamater and Mac Corquodale, 1979. For comparison of the number of extramarital partners, see primarily Pietropinto and Simenauer, 1977; Yablonsky, 1979, for men; and Levin and Levin, 1975, for women. Kinsey (1953) questioned only women, not men, on the number of extramarital partners.
16. Laws, 1970.
17. Simpson and Yinger, 1972.
18. Maykovich, 1976.
19. Conversely, only one in ten of the multiply-experienced women said they didn't know if they would have another extramarital relationship. Four in ten of those with single "experiences" (one relationship) didn't know.
20. Among the women with only one involvement at the time of first interview, eight out of ten cited "justifications" for their involvement. Whether or not such women would continue extramarital activities awaits further study. Because the single "experiences" were a small subgroup, and because I was unable to follow up on all of them in the intervening years since the first interview, it is not possible to draw firm conclusions from these data.
21. Choices of marital forms were:
    a. not to be married,
    b. completely monogamous with one lifelong mate,
    c. monogamy with an occasional affair,
    d. open marriage with freedom for both,
    e. serial monogamy,
    f. a polygamous arrangement,
    g. a lesbian marriage, and
    h. other

Chapter 7

1. See, for example, Barbara Grizzuti Harrison in *New York* magazine, April 1 1974, or Loretta Schwartz in *Philadelphia* magazine, October, 1974.
2. See Smith-Rosenberg, 1975, for an account of such relationships. She points out that there has been a historical neglect of this topic, that "it is one aspect of the female experience which consciously or unconsciously we have chosen to ignore."
3. Kinsey et al, 1953.
4. It is difficult to derive exact figures due to the way Hite presented her data. She states "seventy-three (women) identified themselves as 'bisexual,' and eighty-four women had had experiences with both men and women but did not answer as to preference (another 9 percent). (Hite, p. 395.)
5. Unfortunately, the data does not specify whether this experience was before or after marriage. It does say that 8% of wives without extramarital experience had sex with a woman. This presumably was before marriage as the definition of extramarital experience is also not specified, but appears to refer only to heterosexual experience (Levin and Levin, 1975). This, of course, is an example of heterosexual bias in the study of sexuality. See Kayal and San Giovanni, 1980, for an exploration of various biases in sexual research.
6. Gilmartin and Kusisto, 1973.
7. Blumstein and Schwartz, 1976.
8. This excerpt is also an outstanding example of the developmental character of interaction as symbolic interaction theory views it.
9. This is the same pattern that lesbians follow, as compared with male homosexuals (Goode, 1978). Again, this is evidence of traditional gender roles influencing even unconventional sexual interaction.
10. Mead, 1934.
11. Kinsey, 1948 and 1953. However, see Gagnon, 1977, pp. 235-237 and 260-262 for a critique of Kinsey's scheme.
12. Duberman, 1975.
13. Gagnon and Greenblat, 1978, pp. 377-378.
14. DeLamater and MacCorquodale, 1979.

Chapter 8

1. Sprey, 1969.
2. Dickey, 1970, p. 167.
3. Scanzoni, 1979.
4. Scanzoni, 1979, p. 439.
5. Flaste, 1977.
6. Reiss, 1976.
7. Gagnon and Simon, 1969, p. 747.
8. Gittelson, 1980.

9. My thanks to Professor David Abalos for this observation.
10. The Vaughans also talked about their experiences on "The Phil Donahue Show," broadcast June 26, 1980, WNBC-TV, New York.
11. Mead, 1934. "Taking the role of the other" is the sociological process by which we come to understand another's feelings, thoughts, and behavior.
12. For instance, see Richardson's (1979) study of single women involved with married men. Those who were more powerful ended the relationship themselves and suffered less personal devastation. However, Richardson hypothesizes that those with more power feel less intimacy. The hypothesis (and I agree) is that equal power in a relationship assures desirable amounts of intimacy for both partners and lessens the possibility of exploitation by one partner by the other.
13. Jetse Sprey, as quoted in Duberman, 1974, p. 69.
14. Yablonsky, 1979, p. 28.
15. Farrell, 1974; Lewis, 1976.
16. Safilios-Rothschild, 1974, p. 87.
17. See Reiss et al, 1980, for a complete discussion of their preliminary multivariate model of the determinants of extramarital sexual permissiveness. Other important variables in the model which I have not mentioned are willingness to experiment sexually in marriage and sexual happiness in marriage. Bram Buunk (1980), in a study of extramarital sex in the Netherlands, also finds many of these same variables to be significant.
18. Thamm, 1975; of course, we can have too many sources of emotional support and have superficial relationships rather than intimate ones.
19. SanGiovanni, 1978, p. 164.

BIBLIOGRAPHY

Abernethy, Virginia. "Feminists' heterosexual relationships." Archives of General Psychiatry, 35, 1978, pp. 435-438.

Allen, David. "The price of woman." In *Feminist Frameworks*, Allison M. Jaggar and Paula Rothenberg Struhl. New York: McGraw-Hill, 1978, pp. 280-288.

Argyris, Chris. "Some unintended consequences of rigorous research." In *Social Psychology and Everyday Life*. Billy J. Franklin and Frank J. Kohout, eds. New York: David McKay, 1973, pp. 515-532.

Atwater, Lynn. "Women and marriage: adding an extramarital role." In *Social Interaction*, Howard Robboy, Sidney L. Greenblat, and Candace Clark, eds. New York: St. Martin's Press, 1979, pp. 510-520.

Bakan, David. *The Duality of Human Existence*. Chicago: Rand McNally, 1966.

Balkwell, Carolyn, Balswick, Jack, and Balkwell, James. "On black and white family patterns in America: their impact on the expressive aspect of sex-role socialization." *Journal of Marriage and the Family*, 40, 1978, pp. 743-748.

Balswick, Jack. "The inexpressive male: functional-conflict and role theory as contrasting explanations." *Journal of Marriage and the Family*, 28, 1978, pp. 331-336.

Balswick, Jack. "Explaining inexpressive males: a reply to L'Abate." *Family Relations*, 28, 1980, pp. 231-233.

Balswick, Jack O. and Peek, Charles W. "The inexpressive male: a tragedy of American society." *The Family Coordinator*, October 1971, pp. 363-368.

Bandura, Albert. "Social learning theory of identificatory processes." In *Handbook of Socialization Theory and Research*, David A. Goslin, ed. Chicago: Rand-McNally, 1969, p. 213-262.

Bardwick, Judith. *Psychology of Women: A Study of Bio-Cultural Conflicts*. New York: Harper and Row, 1971.

Bartell, G.D. *Group Sex*. New York: Wyden, 1971.

Bauman, Karl. "Volunteer bias in a study of sexual knowledge, attitudes, and behavior." *Journal of Marriage and the Family*, 35, 1973, pp. 27-31.

Becker, Ernest. *The Denial of Death*. New York: Free Press, 1973.

Becker, Howard S. *Sociological Work*. Chicago: Aldine, 1970.

Becker, Howard S., Geer, Blanche, Hughes, Everett C. and Strauss, Anselm. *Boys in White: Student Culture in Medical School*. Chicago: University of Chicago, 1961.

Bell, Robert R. *Social Deviance*. Homewood, Illinois: Dorsey, 1971(a).

Bell, Robert R. *Marriage and Family Interaction*. Homewood, Illinois: Dorsey, 1971(b).

Bell, Robert and Gordon, Michael. *The Social Dimension of Human Sexuality*. Boston: Little Brown, 1972.

Bell, Robert R. and Lobsenz, Norman M. "Married sex: how uninhibited can a woman dare to be?" *Redbook*, Vol. 143, No. 5, September 1974, pp. 75, 176-181.

Bell, R.R. and Silvan, L. "Swinging: the sexual exchange of married partners." Unpublished paper presented at the annual meeting of the Society for the Study of Social Problems, Washington, D.C., 1970.

Bell, Robert R., Turner, Stanley, and Rosen, Lawrence. "A multivariate analysis of femle extramarital coitus." *Journal of Marriage and the Family*, 37, May 1975, pp. 375-384.

Bem, Sandra Lipsitz. "Beyond androgyny: some presumptuous prescriptions for a liberated sexual identity." In *Family in Transition*, Arlene S. Skolnick and Jerome H. Skolnick, eds. Second ed., Boston: Little, Brown, 1977, pp. 204-221

Berger, Peter, Berger, Brigitte, and Kellner, Hansfried. *The Homeless Mind*. New York: Vintage, 1973.

Bernard, Jessie. "Two clinicians and a sociologist." In *Extramarital Relations*, Gerhard Neubeck, ed. Englewood Cliffs, N.J.: Prentice-Hall, 1969, pp. 25-53.

Bernard, Jessie. "Infidelity, some moral and social issues." In *The Psychodynamics of Work and Marriage*. New York: Greene and Stratton, Vol. XVI, 1970, pp. 99-126.

Bernard, Jessie. "No news, but new ideas." In *Divorce and After*, P. Bohannon, ed. Garden City, New York: Anchor Books, 1971, pp. 3-29.

Bernard, Jessie. *The Future of Marriage*. New York: World, 1972.

Bernard, Jessie. "My four revolutions: an autobiographical history of the ASA." *American Journal of Sociology*, 78, January 1973, pp. 773-791.

Block, J.D. *The Other Men, The Other Women*. New York: Grosset and Dunlop, Inc., 1978.

Blumstein, Philip W. and Schwartz, Pepper. "Lesbianism and bisexuality." In *Sexuality Today—and Tomorrow*, Sol Gordon and Roger W. Libby, eds. North Scituate, Mass.: Duxbury Press, 1976, pp. 232-244.

Boylan, Brian Richard. *Infidelity*. Englewood Cliffs, N.J.: Prentice-Hall, 1971.

Bowman, Claude. "Cultural ideology and heterosexual reality: a preface to sociological research." *American Sociological Review*, 14, 1949, pp. 624-634.

Breedlove, W. and Breedlove, J. *Swap Clubs*. Los Angeles: Sherbourne Press, 1964.

Brim, Orville G., Jr. and Wheeler, Stanton. *Socialization after Childhood*. New York: Wiley, 1966.

Bryant, Clifton D. and Wells, J. Gipson. *Deviancy and the Family*. Philadelphia: Davis, 1973.

Bullough, Vern L. and Bullough, Bonnie. *The Subordinate Sex: A History of Attitudes Toward Women*. Baltimore: Penguin, 1974.

Burr, Wesley R., Hill, Reuben, Nye, F. Ivan, and Reiss, Ira L., eds. *Contemporary Theories About the Family: Research Based Theories; General Theories/Theoretical Orientations*. New York: Free Press, Vols. 1 & 2, 1979.

Buunk, Bram. "Extramarital sex in the Netherlands." *Alternative Lifestyles*, 3, 1980, pp. 11-39.

Chesser, Eustace. *The Sexual, Marital and Family Relationships of the English Woman*. Watford: Hutchinson's Medical Publications, 1956.

Chodorow, Nancy. "Being and doing: a cross-cultural examination of the socialization of males and females." In *Woman in Sexist Society*, Vivian Gornick and Barbara K. Moran, eds. New York: New American Library, 1971, pp. 259-291.

Christensen, Harold T. "Scandanavian and American sex norms." *The Journal of Social Issues*, 22, 1966, pp. 60-75.

Cloward, Richard A. and Ohlin, Lloyd E. *Delinquency and Opportunity*. Glencoe: The Free Press, 1961.

Constantine, Larry L. and Constantine, Joan M. *Group Marriage*. New York: Macmillan, 1973.

Cuber, John F. "Adultery: reality versus stereotype." In *Human Sexuality: Contemporary Perspectives*, Eleanor S. Morrison and Vera Borosage, eds. Palo Alto: National Press, 1973, pp. 160-167.

Cuber, John F. and Harroff, Peggy B. *The Significant Americans*. New York: Appleton-Century-Crofts, 1965.

David, Deborah S. and Brannon, Robert, eds. *The Forty-Nine Percent Majority: The Male Sex Role*. Reading, Massachusetts: Addison-Wesley, 1976.

Davidson, Laurie and Gordon, Laura. *The Sociology of Sex and Gender*. Chicago: Rand-McNally, 1979.

DeLamater, John and McCorquodale, Patricia. *Premarital Sexuality: Attitudes, Relationships, Behavior*. Madison, Wisconsin: University of Wisconsin Press, 1979.

DeLora, Joann S. and Warren, Carol A.B. *Understanding Sexual Interaction*. Boston: Houghton Mifflin, 1977.

Denzin, Norman K. *The Research Act*. Chicago: Aldine, 1970.

Dickey, James. *Self-Interviews*. Recorded and edited by Barbara and James Reiss. Garden City, New York: Doubleday, 1970.

Duberman, Lucile. *Marriage and Its Alternatives*. New York: Praeger, 1974.

Duberman, Lucile. *Gender and Sex in Society*. New York: Praeger, 1975.

Duberman, Martin. "The case of the gay sergeant." *The New York Times Magazine*, November 9, 1975, pp. 16-71.

Edwards, John N. "Extramarital involvement: fact and theory." *Journal of Sex Research*, 9, 1973, pp. 210-224.

Edwards, John N. and Booth, Alan. "Sexual behavior in and out of marriage: an assessment of correlates." *Journal of Marriage and the Family*, 38, 1976, pp. 73-81.

Ehrmann, W.W. "Marital and nonmarital sexual behavior." In *Handbook of Marriage and the Family*, H. T. Christensen, ed. Chicago: Rand-McNally, 1964, pp. 585-622.

Ellis, Albert and Albarbanel, Albert, eds. *The Encyclopedia of Sexual Behavior*. New York: Hawthorn, 1961.

Ellis, Albert. "Healthy and disturbed reasons for having extramarital relations." In *Extramarital Relations*, Gerhard Neubeck, ed. Englewood Cliffs, N.J.: Prentice-Hall, 1969, pp. 153-161.

Erikson, Erik H. *Childhood and Society*. New York: Norton, 1950.

Erikson, Erik H. *Identity: Youth and Crisis*. New York: Norton, 1968.

Farber, Bernard. *Family: Organization and Interaction*. San Francisco: Chandler, 1964.

Farrell, Warren T. *The Liberated Man*. New York: Random House, 1974.

Feirstein, Bruce, "A First Avenue romance." *New York*, Vol. 13, No. 22, June 2, 1980, pp. 22-28.

Feldberg, Roslyn and Kohen, Janet. "Family life in an anti-family setting: a critique of marriage and divorce." *The Family Coordinator*, 25, 1976, pp. 151-159.

Firestone, Shulamith. *The Dialectic of Sex*. New York: Bantam Books, 1970.

Flaste, Richard. "Elderly women: myths, stereotypes and positive predictions for the future." *The New York Times*, August 30, 1977, p. 25.

Fox, Greer Litton. "The mother-adolescent daughter relationship as a sexual socialization structure: a research review." *Family Relations*, 29, 1980, pp. 21-28.

Francoeur, Robert T. and Francoeur, Anna K., eds. *The Future of Sexual Relations*. Englewood Cliffs, N.J.: Prentice-Hall, 1974.

Francoeur, Robert T. and Francoeur, Anna K. "The pleasure bond: reversing the anti-sex ethic." *The Futurist*, 10, 1976, pp. 176-180.

French Institute of Public Opinion. *Patterns of Sex and Love: A Study of the French Woman and Her Morals*. New York: Crown, 1961.

Gagnon, John H. *Human Sexualities*. Glenview, Illinois: Scott, Foresman, 1977.

Gagnon, John H. and Greenblatt, Cathy S. *Life Designs: Individuals, Marriages, and Families*. Glenview, Illinois: Scott, Foresman, 1978.

Gagnon, John H. and Simon, William. "On psychosexual development." In *Handbook of Socialization Theory and Research*, David A. Goslin, ed. Chicago: Rand-McNally, 1969, pp. 733-752.

Gagnon, John H. and Simon, William. *Sexual Conduct: The Social Sources of Human Sexuality*. Chicago: Aldine Publishing, 1973.

Gilmartin, Brian G. and Kusisto, Dave V. "Some personal and social characteristics of mate-sharing swingers." In *Renovating Marriage*, Roger W. Libby and Robert N. Whitehurst,eds. Danville, California: Consensus Publishers, 1973, pp. 146-165.

Gittleson, Natalie. "Unfaithful wives: what happens to their marriages." *McCalls*, 107:June 1980, pp.20-26.

Glaser, Barney G. and Strauss, Anslem L. "Awareness contexts and social interaction." In *Symbolic Interaction: A Reader in Social Psychology*, Jerome G. Manis and Bernard M. Meltzer,eds. Boston: Allyn and Bacon, 1967, pp. 429-444.

Glaser, Barney G. and Strauss, Anslem L.*Discovery of Grounded Theory*. Chicago:Aldine, 1967.

Goffman, Erving. *Behavior in Public Places*. New York:Free Press, 1963.

Goode, Erich. *Deviant Behavior:An Interactionist Approach*. Englewood Cliffs, N.J.: Prentice Hall, 1978.

Gordon, Michael and Shankweiler, Penelope. "Different equals less: female sexuality in recent marriage manuals." *Journal of Marriage and the Family*, 33,August 1971: pp. 459-465.

Hacker, Helen. "Women as a minority group." *Social Forces*, 30:1951, pp. 60-66.

Harper, Robert A. "Extramarital sex relations." In *Encyclopedia of Sexual Behavior*. Albert Ellis and Albert Abarbanel, eds. New York: Hawthorne, 1961, p. 384.

Harrison, Barbara Grizzuti. "Sexual chic, sexual fascism, and sexual confusion." *New York*, Vol. 7, No. 13 April 1, 1974: pp. 31-38.

Henley, Nancy and Freeman, Jo. "The sexual politics of interpersonal behavior." In *Women: A Feminist Perspective*. Jo Freeman, ed. Palo Alto, California: Mayfield Publishing, 1975, pp. 391-401.

Henley, Nancy and Thorne, Barrie. "Womenspeak and manspeak: sex differences and sexism in communication, verbal and non-verbal." In *Beyond Sex Roles*. Alice G. Sargent, ed. St Paul: West, 1977, pp.201-218.

Hite, Shere. *The Hite Report*. New York: Dell, 1976.

Hochschild, Arlie Russell. "Emotion work, feeling rules, and social structure." *American Journal of Sociology*, 85: 1979, pp.551-575.

Hunt, Morton M. *The Affair*. New York: New American Library, 1969.

Hunt, Morton M. "Sexual behavior in the 1970's, part IV: extramarital and postmarital sex." *Playboy*, 21:1974, pp. 60-61, 286-287.

Johnson, Ralph E. "Extramarital sexual intercourse: a methodolgical note." *Journal of Marriage and the Family*, 32, May, 1970: pp. 279-282.

Johnson, Ralph E. "Some correlates of extramarital coitus." *Journal of Marriage and the Family*, 32: August, 1970, pp. 449-456.

Jong, Erica. *Fear of Flying*. New York: New American Library, 1973.

Jourard, Sidney M. "The effects of experimenters' self-disclosure on subjects' behavior." In *Current Topics in Clinical and Community Psychology*. C.Spielberger, ed. New York: Academic Press, 1969, pp. 109-150.

Jourard, Sidney M. *The Transparent Self*. New York: Van Nostrand, 1971.
*qbl Kaats, Gilbert and Davis, Keith. "Effects of volunteer biases in studies of sexual behavior and attitudes." *Journal of Sex Research* 7:1971, pp. 219-227.

Kanin, Eugene. "Male aggression in dating-courtship relations." *American Journal of Sociology*, 63:1957, pp. 197-204.

Kayal, Philip M. and San Giovanni, Lucinda. "Sociological biases in the study of sexuality." Unpublished paper presented at the annual meeting of the Society for the Study of Social Problems, New York, 1980.

King, Karl, Balswick, Jack O., and Robinson, Ira E. "The continuing premarital sexual revolution among college females." *Journal of Marriage and the Family*, 9: 1977, pp. 455-459.

Kinsey, Alfred C., Pomeroy, Wardell, and Martin, Clyde. *Sexual Behavior in the Human Male*. Philadelphia: Saunders, 1948.

Kinsey, Alfred C., Pomeroy, Wardell B., Martin, Clyde, and Gebhard, Paul H. *Sexual Behavior in the Human Female*. Philadelphia: Saunders, 1953.

Kirkpatrick, Clifford and Kanin, Eugene. "Male sex aggression on a university campus." *American Sociological Review*, 22: 1957, pp. 50-57.

Knapp, Jacquelyn J. "An exploratory study of seventeen sexually open marriages." *Journal of Sex Research*, 12: 1976, pp. 206-219.

Knapp, Jacquelyn J. and Whitehurst, Robert N. "Sexually open marriage and relationships." In *Exploring Intimate Life Styles*. Bernard Murstein, ed. New York: Springer, 1978.

Kraymer, Lisa. "Work: the intimate environment." *Alternative Lifestyles*, 2:1979, p. 7-32.

Kurtz, Irma. "Creative infidelity." *Cosmopolitan*, Vol. 175, No. 1 July 1975: pp. 130-147.

L'Abate, Luciano. "Inexpressive males or overexpressive females? A reply to Balswick." *Family Relations*, 29: 1980, pp. 229-230.

Laslett, Barbara and Rappoport, Rhona. "Collaborative interviewing and interactive research." *Journal of Marriage and the Family*, November 1975: pp. 968-977.

Laws, Judith Long. "Toward a model of female sexuality." *Midway*, 11, Summer, 1975: pp. 39-75.

Laws, Judith Long and Schwartz, Pepper. *Sexual Scripts: The Social Construction of Female Sexuality*. Hinsdale, Illinois: Dryden, 1977.

Levin, Robert J. "The Redbook report on premarital and extramarital sex: the end of the double standard?" *Redbook*, October 1975, pp. 38-44, 190-192.

Levin, Robert J. and Levin, Amy. "Sexual pleasure: the surprising preferences of 100,000 women." A Redbook Report, 1975.

Levinson, Daniel J. *The Seasons of a Man's Life*. New York: Alfred A. Knopf, 1978.

Lewis, Robert A. "Intimacy without sex: men learning to love men." Unpublished paper presented at the annual meeting of American Sociological Association, New York, New York, 1976.

Lidz, Charles W. "Problems of reciprocal obligations in participant observation research." Unpublished paper presented at the annual meeting of Eastern Sociological Society, New York, New York, 1977.

Light, Donald Jr. and Keller, Suzanne. *Sociology* New York: Knopf, 1975.

Lofland, John. *Analyzing Social Settings*. Belmont, California: Wadsworth, 1971.

Lofland, John. "Styles of reporting qualitative field research." *The American Sociologist*, 9: 1974, pp. 101-111.

Lyman, Stanford M. and Scott, Marvin B. *A Sociology of the Absurd*. New York: Appleton-Century-Crofts, 1970.

Maslow, A.H. *Toward a Psychology of Being*. New York: Van Nostrand, 1968.

Maslow, A.H. *The Farther Reaches of Human Nature*. New York: Viking, 1971.

Mason, Karen Oppenheim and Bumpass, Larry L. "U.S. women's sex-role ideology, 1970." *American Journal of Sociology*, 80, March, 1975: pp. 1212-1219.

Masters, William and Johnson, Virginia. *Human Sexual Response*. Boston: Little, Brown, 1966.

Masters, William and Johnson, Virginia. *The Pleasure Bond*. New York: Bantam, 1976.

Masters, William and Johnson, Virginia. *Homosexuality in Perspective*. Boston: Little, Brown, 1979.

Masters, William H. and Johnson, Virginia E. in association with Levin, Robert J. "The pleasures and penalties of infidelity." *Redbook*, 143: 1974, pp. 53-60.

Maykovich, Minako K. "Attitudes versus behavior in extramarital sexual relations." *Journal of Marriage and the Family*, 38: 1976, pp. 693-699.

Mazur, Ronald. *The New Intimacy*. Boston: Beacon Press, 1973.

Mead, George H. *Mind, Self, and Society*. Chicago: University of Chicago, 1934.

Meltzer, Bernard M. "Mead's social psychology." in *Symbolic Ineraction: A Reader in Social Psychology*. Jerome G. Manis and Bernard M. Meltzer, eds. Boston: Allyn and Bacon, 1967, pp. 5-24.

Merton, Robert K. *Social Theory and Social Structure*. New York: Free Press, 1968.

Mills, C.Wright. *The Sociological Imagination*. New York: Grove Press, 1959.

Murdock, George P. *Social Structure*. New York: Macmillan, 1949.

Murstein, Bernard. *Exploring Intimate Life Styles*. *New York: Springer, 1978*.

Myers, Lonny and Leggitt, Hunter. *Adultery and Other Private Matters*. Chicago: Nelson-Hall, 1975.

National Opinion Research Center. "Cumulative Codebook for the 1972-1977 General Social Survey." Chicago: University of Chicago Press, 1977.

Neubeck, Gerhard, ed. *Extramarital Relations*. Englewood Cliffs, N.J.: Prentice-Hall, 1969.

Neubeck, Gerhard and Schletzer, Vera M. "A study of extra-marital relatonships." *Marriage and Family Living*, 24: 1962, pp. 279-282.

Nye, F. Ivan and Berardo, Felix M. *The Family: Its Structure and Interaction*. New York: Macmillan, 1973.

O'Neill, Nena and O'Neill, George. *Open Marriage*. New York: M. Evans Company, Inc. 1972(a).

O'Neill, Nena and O'Neill, George. "Open marriage: a synergic model." *The Family Coordinator*. October 1972(b): pp. 403-409.

Otto, Herbert. *The Family in Search of a Future*. New York: Appleton-Century-Crofts, 1970.

Parsons, T. and Bales, R.F. *Family, Socialization and Interaction Process*. New York: Free Press, 1955.

Pietropinto, Anthony, M.D. and Simenauer, Jacqueline. *Beyond the Male Myth*. New York: New American Library, 1977.

Ramey, J.W. "Communes, group marriage and the upper middle class." *Journal of Marriage and the Family*, 34: 1972, pp. 647-655.

Reiss, Ira L. *Family Systems in America*, 2nd ed. Hinsdale, Illinois: Dryden, 1976. 3rd ed., New York: Holt, Rinehart and Winston, 1980.

Reiss, Ira. L., Anderson, Ronald E., and Sponaugle, G. C. "A multivariate model of the determinants of extramarital sexual permissiveness." *Journal of Marriage and the Family*, 42: 1980, pp. 395-411.

Reynolds, Paul Davidson. "The protection of human subjects: an open letter to NIH." *The American Sociologist*, Vol. 9, No. 4, November 1974, pp. 221-225.

Richardson, Laurel Walum. "The 'other woman': the end of the long affair." *Alternative Lifestyles*, 2: 1979, pp. 397-414.

Robboy, Howard. *They Work at Night: Temporal Adaptations in a Technological Society*. Unpublished Ph.D. dissertation, Rutgers University, 1976.

Roth, Julius A. "The status of interviewing." *Midwest Sociologist*, December: 1956, pp. 8-11.

Roy, Rustum and Roy, Della. *Honest Sex*. New York: New American Library, 1968.

Roy, Rustum and Roy, Della. 'Is monogamy outdated?" *Humanist*. March, April: 1970, pp. 19-26.

Rubin, Lillian Breslow. *Worlds of Pain: Life in the Working Class Family*. New York: Basic Books, Inc., 1976.

Safiolios-Rothschild, Constantina. "Attitudes of Greek spouses toward marital infidelity." In *Extra-Marital Relations*. Gerhard Neubeck, ed. Englewood Cliffs, N.J.: Prentice-Hall, 1969, pp.77-93.

Safiolios-Rothschild, Constantina. *Women and Social Policy*. Englewood Cliffs, N.J.: Prentice Hall, 1974.

Sagarin, E. "Sex research and sociology: retrospective and prospective." In *Studies in the Sociology of Sex*. J.M. Henslin, ed. New York: Appleton-Century-Crofts, 1971, pp. 377-408.

Saghir, Marcel T. and Robins, Eli. *Male and Female Homosexuality*. Baltimore: Wilkins and Wilkins, 1973.

San Giovanni, Lucinda. *Ex-Nuns: An Exploration of Emergent Status Transition*. Norwood, N.J.: Ablex, 1978.

Sattel, J.W. "The inexpressiveness male: tragedy or sexual politics?" *Social Problems*, 23: 1976, pp. 469-477.

Scanzoni, John. *Sexual Bargaining: Power Politics in the American Marriage*. Englewood Cliffs, N.J.: Prentice-Hall, 1972.

Scanzoni, John. *Sex Roles, Women's Work, and Marital Conflict*. Lexington, Massachusetts: D.C. Heath, 1978.

Scanzoni, John. "Strategies for changing male family roles: research and practice implications." *The Family Coordinator*, 28: 1979, pp. 435-442.

Scarf, Maggie. *Unfinished Business: Pressure Points in the Lives of Women*. New York: Doubleday, 1980.

Schulz, David A. *The Changing Family*. Englewood Cliffs, N.J.: Prentice-Hall, 1976.

Schwartz, Loretta. "Both sides now." *Philadelphia Magazine,* Vol. 65, No. 10, October:1974, pp. 116-119, 202-213.

Schwartz, Pepper. "Female Sexuality and monogamy." In *Renovating Marriages*. Roger W. Libby and Robert Whitehurst, eds. Danville, California: Consensus Publishers, 1973, pp. 211-226.

Sheehy, Gail. *Passages: Predictable Crises of Adult Life.* New York: Dutton, 1974.

Sherfey, Mary Jane. "A theory of female sexuality." *Journal of American Psychoanalytic Association.*, 1966.

Simmel, Georg. *Philosophische Kulter.* Leipzig: Werner Klinkhardt, 1911. As reprinted in "George Simmel's neglected contributions to the sociology of women." Lewis Coser, *Signs*, 2: pp. 869-876.

Simon, William and Gagnon, John. "On psychosexual development." In *Handbook of Socialization Theory and Research.* David A. Goslin, ed.. Chicago: Rand-McNally, 1969, pp. 733-752.

Simpson, George E. and Yinger, Milton. *Racial and Cultural Minorities: An Analysis of Prejudice and Discrimination.* 4th ed. New York: Harper and row, 1972.

Singh, B. Krishna, Walton, Bonnie L., and Williams, J. Sherwood. "Extramarital sexual permissiveness: conditions and contingencies." *Journal of Marriage and the Family*, 38: 1976, pp. 701-712.

Skolnick, Arlene. *The Intimate Environment.* 2nd ed. Boston: Little, Brown, 1978.

Skolnick, Arlene E. and Skolnick, Jerome H. *Family in Transition.* Boston: Little, Brown, 1971.

Skolnick, Arlene E. and Skolnick, Jerome H. *Intimacy, Family and Society.* Boston: Little, Brown, 1974.

Slater, Philip E. *The Pursuit of Loneliness.* Boston: Beacon Press, 1970.

Slater, Philip E. "Sexual adequacy in America." *Intellectual Digest*, November: 1973, pp. 17-20.

Smith, D. "Women, the family, and corporate capitalism." In *Women in Canada*, M.L. Stevenson, ed. Toronto: New Press, 1973, pp. 2-35.

Smith, James R. and Smith, Lynn G. "Co-marital sex and the sexual freedom movement." *Journal of Sex Research*, 6: 1970, pp. 131-142.

Smith, James R. and Smith, Lynn G. *Beyond Monogamy.* Baltimore: Johns Hopkins University Press, 1974.

Smith-Rosenberg, Carroll. "The female world of love and ritual: relations between women in nineteenth century America." *Signs*, 1975, pp. 1-29.

Sprey, Jetse. "On the institutionalization of sexuality." *Journal of Marriage and the Family*, 31: 1969, pp. 432-441.

Sprey, Jetse. "Extramarital relationships." In *Sexual Issues in Marriage.* Leonard Gross, ed. New York: Spectrum Publications, 1975, pp. 131-143.

Srole, Leo and Fischer, Anita K. *Mental Health in the Metropolis: The Midtowm Manhattan Study.* New York: New York University Press, 1978.

Stein, Peter J. "Singlehood: an alternative to marriage." In *Family in Transition.* Arlene Skolnick and Jerome H. Skolnick, eds. 3rd ed. Boston: Little, Brown, 1980,pp. 517-535.

Stephenson, Richard. "Involvement in deviance: an example and some theoretical implications." *Social Problems*, 21: 1973, pp. 173-189.

Strauss, Anslem L. *Mirrors and Masks.* San Francisco: The Sociology Press, 1969.

Symonds, C. "The utopian aspects of sexual mate swapping." Unpublished paper presented at the annual meeting of the Society for the Study of Social Problems, Washington, D.C., 1970.

Talsese, Gay. *Thy Neighbor's Wife.* Garden City, N.Y.: Doubleday, 1980.

Thamm, Robert. *Beyond Marriage and the Nuclear Family.* San Francisco: Canfield Press, 1975.

Thornton, Russell and Nardi, Peter M. "The dynamics of role aquisition." *American Journal of Sociology*, 80: 1975, pp. 870-885.

Toby, Jackson. "Educational possibilities of consensual research." *The American Sociologist*, February: 1972, pp. 11-13.

Toffler, Alvin. *Future Shock.* New York: Random House, 1970.

Tuchman, Gaye, Daniels, Arlene Kaplan and Benet, James, eds. *Hearth and Home: Images of Women in the Mass Media.* New York,: Oxford, 1978.

Turner, Ralph. "The real self: from institution to impulse." *American Journal of Sociology*, 81: 1976, pp. 989-1016.

U.S. Bureau of the Census. *Statistical Portrait of Women in the U.S.,* Current Population Reports, Special Studies P-23, Washington, D.C.: U.S. Government Printing Office, No. 58, April, 1976.

U.S. Bureau of the Census. *Statistical Abstract of the U.S.*, Series P-23, Washington, D.C.: U.S. Government Printing Office, No. 77, 1979.

Vaughan, Jim and Vaughan, Peggy. *Beyond Affairs.* Hilton Head Island, S.C.: Dialog Press, 1980.

Vidich, Arthur J. "Participant observation and the collection and interpretation of data." *American Journal of Sociology*, 60: January 1955, pp. 320-327.

Vogel,L. "The earthly family." *Radical America*, 7: 1973, pp.9-50.

Waller, Willard. "The rating and dating complex." *American Sociological Review*, 2: 1937,pp. 727-734.

Waller, Willard. *The Family: A Dynamic Interpretaion*. New York: Dryden, 1938.

Walshok, Mary Lindenstein. "The emergence of middle-class deviant subcultures: the case of swingers." In *Beyond Monogamy*. James R. Smith and Lynn G. Smith, eds. Baltimore: Johns Hopkins University Press, 1974, pp. 159-169.

Walster, Elaine and Walster, William G. *A New Look at Love*. Reading, Mass.: Addison-Wesley, 1978.

Walum, Laurel Richardson. *The Dynamics of Sex and Gender: A Sociological Perspective*. Chicago: Rand McNally, 1977.

Weis, David L. "Sexual scripting as a factor in attitudes toward projected extramarital behavior." Unpublished paper presented at the meetings of The Society for the Scientific Study of Sex, Philadelphia, 1980.

Whitehurst, Robert N. "Violence potential in extramarital sexual responses." *Journal of Marriage and the Family*, 33, November: 1971, pp. 683-691.

Wilkinson, Melvin L. "Romantic love and sexual expression." *Family Coordinator*, 27: 1978, pp. 141-148.

Wolfe, Linda. *Playing Around: Women and Extramarital Sex*. New York: William Morrow, 1975.

Wolff, Kurt H. ed. *The Sociology of Georg Simmel*. New York: Free Press, 1950.

Yablonsky, Lewis. *The Extra-Sex Factor*. New York: Times Books, 1979.

Zetterberg, Hans. "The secret ranking." *Journal of Marriage and the Family*, 28: 1966, pp. 134-143.

Zilbergeld, Bernie. *Male Sexuality*. New York: Bantam, 1978.

Appendix I

Methodology and Description of Sample

I. Communal Research Model

I utilized what I call a communal research model in doing this study. Communal research seeks to implement a more equal relationship between the researcher and respondent, by reducing the traditional social control of the respondent by the researcher. It also encourages the respondent to contribute to the design of the research, and attempts not only to protect the respondent from unintentional harm, but also to extend some benefit through participation, wherever possible.

The decision to employ a communal research model for this exploratory study of women's participation in extramarital relationships was made because of its compatibility with the chosen approach of the intensive interview and sensitivity of the subject matter. The particular research goal was a symbolic interactionist understanding of process and change in women's roles, attitudes, and identities during and after extramarital relationships. Therefore, it was especially important to maximize rapport with the respondent in order to obtain her complete and uninhibited subjective report.

As the topic and goal of the research precluded use of a random sample, it was necessary to locate a self-selected sample of women with an expressed interest in personal and social change. For this purpose the following advertisement was placed in the September, 1974, issue of *Ms.* magazine:

> Married women involved now/recently in extramarital relationships: feminist sociologist desires personal or mail interview for thesis. Strict confidentiality. Please write Ms. Lynn Atwater, Sociology Department, Seton Hall Unversity, South Orange, N.J. 07079

Although some may object that use of the word "feminist" introduces a bias, this was done deliberately for the purpose of establishing an initial bond of identity between researcher and respondent. In this communal model, traditional sources of bias are used constructively to promote validity instead of diminishing it.

It was not certain initially whether a sufficient number of women would volunteer to be interviewed on such a subject, but the response to the advertisement was extremely positive. Approximately 300 women from 47 states replied, and in their initial letters projected a strong desire for the subject to be researched. From this original volunteer sample, resondents were chosen on the basis of geographical proximity to the researcher and variation in several factors defined as having potential analytical significance to the research. These factors were age, education, occupation, current marital staus, presence or absence of children, and amount of extramarital experience.

I originally selected the research topic because of the lack of sociological data in the area; the number and enthusiasm of the responses suggest that the women were also supportive of the research focus. Many of the letter-writers indicated their belief that research in the area was long overdue because of the many changes in contemporary women's lives. An important preliminary aspect of communal research would seem to be approval of the chosen topic by the respondents. Currently this power to choose almost always rests with funding agencies and/or professional researchers. While obviously it is not always possible for research topics to be chosen or endorsed by respondents, so far there is no evidence as to how many invesigators have attempted to do this. It need hardly be pointed out that doing so would assure greater respondent cooperation as well as help move sociological research toward the humanistic use of the discipline as advocated by C. Wright Mills (1959).

A. First Research Interaction

A letter was sent to all respondents to the *Ms.* ad thanking them for their interest and explaining that, because of the unanticipated size of the response, the researcher would be unable to interview all who wrote. The letter also stated that if sufficient resources became available for a larger project, the respondents would be contacted again to see if they would still be interested in participating.

A different letter was sent to those women selected for personal interviews. This letter included some biographical data on the researcher, additional information on the foci of the research, as well as the names, addresses, and telephone numbers of two personal references located at the universities where the researcher was studying and teaching. The goal was to increase the women's interest and involvement in the project through additional information and to establish credibility through furnishing references. Included with the letter was a reply sheet on which the respondent could indicate whether she was willing to be interviewed personally and the most appropriate times and place at which she could be telephoned for an appointment.

Each respondent was then contacted (or in some cases, they preferred to telephone the researcher), and an appointment was made for the interview. During this pre-interview interaction, I made efforts to increase rapport through informal conversation and by offering reports of the progress of the research. The desire was to engage the respondent, not only as an interviewee, but also as someone who was a partner, albeit a temporary one, in the research.

Every woman was extremely cooperative in scheduling and keeping appointments, and this phase of the study proceeded with no problems. Obviously, the fact that the women constituted a volunteer sample contributed to the outstanding cooperation. However, a frequent pre-interview comment from the women was that they were also interested in appraising the way in which the research was being conducted, and that they would not have participated in any study in which they felt controlled or exploited. Based on these remarks, it is believed that the attempt to build a communal relationship from the first interaction was a significant factor in eliciting respondent cooperation.

B. Interview Structure

In the interview itself, to further a communal atmosphere two goals were incorporated: 1) attempting to equalize status during the research interaction and 2) striving to equalize the benefits of participation for both researcher and respondent. I will first discuss measures taken to reduce status differences and then describe the procedures used to increase benefits of participation for the respondent.

To work toward equalization of status, considerable attention was directed to situational characteristics. My self-presentation was influenced by personal information gained from the respondent during pre-interview communication. I tried to make respondents comfortable by matching styles of dress and vocabulary with them. All interviews took place at a location of the respondent's choice which would assure complete privacy. Actual locations used were respondents' homes, offices available to the investigator, and various restaurants and hotel rooms. The most important consideration was to select settings in which the interviewee could feel as comfortable as possible.

All interviews were tape-recorded with the permission of the respondent in order to allow the interviewer to focus on interacting with the respondent. Ample time was devoted to establishing conversational rapport; then the communal definition of the research situation, with its goals of equality of interaction and benefits, was presented to the respondent for her discussion and reaction.

Although there was a lengthy interview guide prepared in advance to systematize the questions, all respondents were encouraged to participate in the design of the interview by suggesting any questions and important topics that had been overlooked. They were also invited to evaluate any aspect of the interview as it was in progress, as well as given the right to refuse to answer any question. At the close of the interviews, which generally lasted from three to four hours, respondents were given another opportunity to suggest changes in, and report reactions to, the interview experience. As a result of their input, several key questions and topics were added to the interview guide while the research was in progress. Although this made the processing of data and analyses of results more complex, it resulted in a more comprehensive and richer understanding of the phenomenon under study.

Another primary element in the attempt to equalize status during research interaction was the creation of an atmosphere of mutual self-disclosure. Since the interview topic was an especially sensitive one in which the respondent was asked to reveal intimate details of past and present personal history, this potential of unequal information carried the seeds of inequality. (See Jourard, 1969, 1971, for a discussion of the way in which unequal self-disclosure is related to differential social power.) This was a somewhat difficult decision for me to make because of the uncertainty of the outcome. It was unclear whether the response might be unmanageable, in that the respondent might choose to spend an equal amount of time interviewing the interviewer. However, it was felt that the success of the communal approach necessitated an offer of role reversal and answers to any personal questions the respondent wished to ask of the interviewer. This offer was made before the interview began, with the request that questions be deferred until after the interview to avoid biasing the data.

The awareness of a situation of mutual self-disclosure had a considerable impact on my consciousness. The feeling of equal vulnerability created more involvement with the respondent, greater awareness of the need to take the role of the other, and increased sensitivity to the respondents' reactions during the course of what was always a long and often emotionally exhausting interview. No respondent declined to answer any interview question, which may be attributed, at least in part, to the trust-building effect of equal vulnerability and mutually promised confidentiality. Judged by the willing participation during the interviews and by the respondents' self-reports, all felt quite comfortable during the interview. Perhaps the most telling reaction to the communal atmosphere was the comment of a high school educated respondent at the close of the interview:

> Gee, this turned out to be really nice. I was kind of worried. You were a college professor and I didn't know what to expect. But it was like spending an evening talking with my girlfriend.

In addition to eliminating as many aspects of status inequality as possible, this communal research model was based on a second important sociological principle, that of social exchange. Since all cooperative human interaction rests on this basis, it seems axiomatic that seeking to equalize the benefits for both parties in the research situation will help to elicit the respondent cooperation necessary for high quality data. Obviously, the first way in which the researcher can offer reciprocity is through access to research results; accordingly, a special summary of the analyzed data was promised to each respondent.

Beyond this the research interview offers many opportunities for on-the-spot feedback, and information from a professional that can be of significant value. This offer of information was made in the pre-interview discussion to maximize cooperation; actual answers to questions were deferred until after the interview to avoid bias. The researcher, whose sociological expertise was in the areas of gender roles, marriage, and family was able to provide knowledgeable answers as well as make referrals to appropriate books or other sources of information for about one-half the respondents.

Closely related to providing information and feedback was the potential theraputic effect of the interview on the respondent. It was readily apparent from the earliest stages of this project that one of the logical possible outcomes was a positive as well as negative effect on the participants. Research treatment of this question, within the framework of communality, was resolved by confronting it rather than avoiding it.

Accordingly, I held four training sessions with a psychiatrist for two purposes: 1)to refine and develop interviewing skills for use in sensitive and emotional areas and 2) to develop the ability to respond therapeutically when it seemed warranted as a consequence of emotions aroused during the interview. The specific aim was to be able to recognize any need to respond to the psychodynamics of the situation, not to turn the interview into a clinical experience. To guard against contamination of data through transference or countertransference, a number of test and actual interviews were played back and analyzed by a three person team consisting of the researcher, the psychiatrist, and a second sociologist. This interdisciplinary peer feedback also served as a check against over-extending any emerging therapeutic potential beyond the researcher's training.

Based on the self-reports of the repondents, about two-thirds found the interview to be personally beneficial. They cited the cathartic effect of talking about their experiences with a professional, nonevaluative listener, as well as an increase in self-knowledge gained thereby. As Masters and Johnson (1976:220) have stated, "we often do not know what we think or feel until we have a chance to express ourselves and then to decide whether that is actually what we believe." Similar comments from respondents on the therapeutic value of an interview have also been reported by two other researchers (SanGiovanni, 1978; Robboy, 1976) who focused on such disparate subjects as the transitional process of former nuns and the adaptive problems of night workers.

To summarize then, this communal model of research first attempts to eliminate inequalities of interaction in the research interview through minimizing status-displaying situational characteristics, inviting respondents to participate in the interview design, and creating an atmosphere of mutual self-disclosure. Secondly, it strives to maximize reciprocity by providing the respondent with full access to research results, professional response to questions, and realization of any possible therapeutic benefit from the interview experience. As a consequence of operationalizing this model, there was a serendipitous outcome which led to the development of the following new research technique.

II. An Innovative Research Technique: The Self Guided Interview

In response to the invitation to participate in the research design, one respondent suggested that women who lived too far away to be interviewed could tape their own interviews. At first I discounted this, because I assumed it would be unworkable. But the idea began to seem challenging, at least on an experimental basis.

To test this technique, thirty-seven potential interviewees from the original response of 300 were selected on the basis of geographical distribution, high motivation expressed in their letters, or having had some college education. A letter was mailed inquiring about the availability of a cassette recorder and the willingness to tape one's own interview. Twenty-nine persons answered affirmatively, but two of these planned to be visiting the New York area and arrangements were made to do these interviews in person. Again, several suggestions were made by the respondents to make the plan more workable, one of which was to allow the respondent to choose the ultimate disposition of the tapes (i.e., return to respondent erased or in-tact, erasure by investigator), so as to increase feelings of security and control by those participating.

A kit mailed to the remaining twenty-seven volunteers contained: 1) an identification sheet assigning a code number to insure confidentiality, and directions to secure reimbursement for the tapes respondents were to purchase; 2) two pages of instructions concerning the interview itself; 3) a nine page interview guide consisting of open-ended but specific and detailed questions; 4) a one page survey instrument as a partial check on the validity of the interview data; and 5) a self-addressed, stamped envelope for returning the tapes and survey instrument.

Within two months twenty of these respondents recorded and mailed their self-guided interviews to the investigator. As soon as an interview was received, acknowledgement was made and reimbursement mailed. Approximately one-half of the respondents donated the cost of the tapes, knowing that the research was personally funded by the interviewer. Despite the complexity of the interview guides and the length of each interview (average of three to four hours), respondents reported only limited difficulty in conducting their own interviews. It is believed this was because of the extensive testing of the guide in personal interviews, as well as the many inputs made by earlier respondents in designing the questions. When respondents taping their own interviews perceived ambiguity as to the meaning of a question or how extensive an answer was required, they usually chose to provide more than sufficient information. In about one-quarter of the cases, I had further questions after transcribing the interview. Those questions were promptly resolved by subsequent mail correspondence.

This experiment in increasing respondents' autonomy to the maximum through self-recording of interviews was deemed successful on the basis of the 74 percent completion rate of those who originally agreed to record and the general high quality of the interviews. The data compared favorably in both depth and veracity to the personal interviews, and in some ways, were superior. Greater detail tended to be present in the discussion of sexual and emotional material, and there was also a strong suggestion that interviewer bias operated less in the self-guided interivew. A frequent comment on the self-recorded tapes was that "If only you were here now, I would know whether this is what you want me to say or if this is what you are looking for." Obviously, if the interviewer is not present, there are no subtle interactional cues or expectations for the respondent to pick up and try to fulfill. Furthermore, use of the self-guided interviews yields potentially unlimited geographical representation while greatly reducing the researcher's traveling time and expense.

A complete comparison of the two types of interviews reveals problems and limitations. One major problem is a technical one, in that the respondent has to have access to a recorder and the competency to use it. A few women experienced difficulties because they were unfamiliar with borrowed equipment; none failed to complete an interview for this reason. Similarly, in the transcription process, there were mechanical failures in about ten percent of the cassettes; although vexing because of the potential destruction of data, all proved repairable with very small loss of interview time. A second problem is an interactive one, which contains both theoretical and ethical facets. The success of the communal model motivated several respondents to continue a personal relationship with the researcher. Most of this has been by mail correspondence, but several women desired social meetings on visits they made to New York. These relationships have been very enjoyable, but limited available time may restrict researchers' ability to fulfill these personal obligations engendered by the research model.

The principal limitation in the use of self-guided interviews concerns its applicability to particular kinds of samples. There is a need for respondents to be both highly motivated and fairly articulate.

Although the majority of women in this sample had considerable college experience, it should be pointed out that this interview was extremely complex and lengthy, and the technique is too new to establish rigid guidelines for its successful use. It is reported here principally for its value as an alternative to the researcher-conducted interview, and it awaits further testing before a complete assessment of its appropriateness can be made. This initial experiment, at the very least, illustrates the potential fruitfulness of increasing respondent autonomy, as well as the desirability of exploring innovative research uses of communications technology.

III. *Summary and Conclusions of Communal Research Model*

Communal research interaction promises to become increasingly desirable from the respondent's viewpoint as our society moves toward further emphasis on individual rights and autonomy. Establishing communality is also one answer to the investigator's problems of maintaining professional ethics and internal data validity. Communality becomes even more valuable as the duration and intensity of research interaction increases, such as during intensive interviews and lengthy observation of the participant.

The exploratory nature of this research project and the self-selected aspect of the sample facilitated the inclusion of the respondent as a partner in interview design and execution. Since few data were available on the topic and these were possibly outdated, each woman through her personal experience, did know more than the researcher. While it may be argued that the variables of an exploratory project and a self-selected sample are crucial to the success of a communal model, we have scant evidence in favor of this argument. In fact, we do not even know under what conditions it would be workable and advantageous for respondents to participate in research design (Argyris, 1973:528).

The communal model is obviously well-suited to exloratory research, but it would also be useful for study in emerging areas of sociology, such as sociology of the performing arts and the sociology of travel. It can only enhance the opportunity to gather information on topics which are especially sensitive or secretive, such as various aspects of family life, community research, or deviance of any kind. Laslett and Rapoport (1975) also suggest that respondent involvement could be effectively used in studies of work interaction, ethnic group relations, political processes, and leisure activities. Data gathered in a communal manner may be more easily oriented to qualitative analysis, but it is certainly possible to integrate survey instruments for quantitative analysis into the interactive situation as was done here.

More extensive application of the self-guided interview and other autonomous techniques still to be developed seems probable in the future, based on the increasingly higher educational level and technological sophistication of the average person in post-industrial societies. Autonomous techniques would seem to be particularly well-suited for samples that tend to be inaccessible to researchers because they are geographically distant, mobile, or isolated. These would include situations in which a broad geographic sample is otherwise prohibited because of time or expense, the study of persons living abroad for extensive periods, such as oil workers and their families in Arabian countries, travelers, shipboard and military personnel, or occupational specialties that tend to be conducted in isolation or mobility (e.g., forest rangers or professional sports referees). While no one research philosophy or technique is suitable for every situation, the success of the communal model and the self-guided interview in this and the other studies cited suggests their increasing relevance to a contemporary methodology.

IV. Description of Research Sample

A. Demographic Variables

The total sample for this exploratory project consisted of fifty women. Thirty personal interviews (PI) were collected by the researcher from within New York—New Jersey—Philadelphia metropolitan area; an additional twenty were gathered through the "self-guided interview" (SGI) technique form respondents in fourteen states and Canada.

This sample was drawn to fit the needs of an exploratory study intent on researching social and personal change in a particular area of gender roles. The women interviewed represent a range of the major independent variables. As illustrated in Table 1, the age of respondents varied from twenty-five to fifty-nine. Forty-two percent (21) had completed high school or some college; 33 percent (16) held bachelor's degrees, 22 percent (11) held master's degrees, and 1 percent (2) were candidates for a doctoral degree. This is an over-representation of women with graduate degrees but, to the extent this portends the improved future educational status of women, it serves well the goal of the sample.

Occupationally, 30 percent (15) identified themselves as homemakers, with one-half of these working or attending school part-time. About one-third held full-time clerical or secretarial jobs; another third were engaged in managerial-professional employment, and the remaining (3) were full-time students. Seventy percent (35) of the respondents had children varying in age from infants to adults. All of the women without children were in their twenties and thirties.

The sample also contained variation in the women's marital and extramarital situations. At the time of the interviews 66 percent (33) of the marriages were intact; of these cases twenty women were currently involved in extramarital relationships while thirteen were not. The other 35 percent of the marriages (17) had ended in separation, divorce or, in one case, death of the husband. Of the women whose marriages had ended, seven were currently continuing what had been extramarital relationships, but only one woman was living with the person with whom she had been involved. Finally, five women had been married twice; of these two had EMRs in both marriages.

In terms of extramarital relations, there was also considerable latitude in the amount of experience. Thirty-eight percent (19) of the women had only one EMR; 50 percent (25) had experienced from two to six EMRs; the remaining 12 percent (6) had eleven to thirty experiences. The operational definition of an EMR for this research project was "a social interaction in which a married woman participates in sexual relations with a person other than her husband while still living with him." Swinging, or extramaritality in which husband and wife agree to have sexual relations with others at a mutual time and place, was specifically excluded.

TABLE 1
Distribution of Respondents by Age and Educational Level

	AGE 20-29				AGE 30-39				AGE 40-49				AGE 50-59				Grand Total
	HS/SC	BA	GD	Sub Total	HS/SC	BA	GD	Sub Total	HS/SC	BA	GD	Sub Total	HS/SC	BA	GD	Sub Total	
PI	7	3	2	12	3	5	2	10	1	2	2	5	3			3	30
SGI	4		3	7		5	3	8	2	1	1	4	1			1	20
Sub Total	11	3	5	19	3	10	5	18	3	3	3	9	4			4	50

HS/SC — High School or Some College
BA = Bachelor's Degree
GD = Graduate Degree
PI = Personal Interview
SGI = Self-Guided Interview

*20% (N=10) of total sample has completed only high school

B. Feminist Beliefs, Attitudes, Behavior

Since the sample was drawn from readers of a feminist publication, questions were included in the interview (see Section III of Project Interview Guide, Appendix 2) to assess the degree to which these women were involved in feminism. The questions were designed to probe certain aspects of beliefs, attitudes, and behavior.

Respondents were first asked to rate themselves "on a scale of '0' for no support to a high of '10' for full and unqualified support" of their "belief that women and men have the same potential for individual development and are therefore entitled to equal opportunities to pursue this development." The women were also asked to rate their support of "any and all activities by women designed to implement this belief." Of the fifty cases, 88 percent (44) responded with answers in the "8-10" range for both questions, indicating very high support of their belief systems. Another item confirming strong belief in feminist principles was that 90 percent (45) indicated that the women's movement should offer support to lesbians.

In the area of personal behavior we see less evidence of involvement in feminism. Table 2 examines several facets of posible feminist activity, and it shows considerable variation in the degree of participation. Slightly more than half of the sample, 56 percent (28), had been in consciousness-raising groups, and 40 percent (20) were members of other feminist groups. Of these women who were members of other feminist groups, 18 percent (9) had done volunteer work for a feminist organization. What emerges from these data is very high individual support of a belief in equality, but a much lower degree of actual social activity that is defined as feminist.

Further evidence of this emphasis on an individualistic approach to feminism (see Table 2) is the finding that about half the group were avid readers of feminist literature while the other half were not. There was also considerable disagreement on the personal title preferred—Ms.,Mrs., or no title. Finally, although 86 percent (43) reported that the influence of feminism had changed them personally, the changes reported were basically psychological and not political. Thus, comments like feminism "has given me more self-confidence," "made me feel more like a person," "enabled me to understand myself better" were the norm and are more indicative of a therapeutic or growth experience than a radicalizing one.

An additional set of questions focused on preferences concerning the roles of wife, mother, and employee. When asked to rate their importance to a satisfying life style, 66 percent (33) rated all three as equal or almost equal in meaning to them. The dominant picture is one of moderate changes in traditional female life choices, in which most of this group of women wish to combine all three roles. The only evidence of more extreme change is in four women (surprisingly, two of these were in their fifties) who rated marriage as of little importance and two other women who rated parenthood as of little importance, but still included marriage as important to them.

Concerning household roles, there was unanimous agreement that husbands should share tasks, whether or not wives were employed outside the home. Here is prehaps the most widespread rejection of traditional female role norms. Asked who should be responsible for the care of pre-school children, 78 percent (39) felt that this also should be shared by both parents. Five women still believed that the mother should be principal caretaker, and four women mentioned outside agents, such as day care centers and other paid professionals. The image that emerges is a preference for role modification, in which women reduce their household responsibilities to add economically productive roles outside the home. Similarly, they prefer men to modify their roles, adding caretaking functions within the home while no longer being solely responsible for external economic labor. Fifty-eight percent (29) of the women reported that their marriages had, in fact, changed due to the influence of feminism, principally in the direction of a more equal division of labor in the home and more egalitarian personal interaction. Of the remaining (21) cases, eleven marriages ended, in part because the husband refused to accommodate to desired role changes by the wife; two other husbands also refused to change but the marriages remained intact. Eight women rated their marriages as always having been egalitarian.

C. Comparison with National Probability Sample

Although there is no way of measuring the degree to which this analytical sample deviates from a representative sample of women in their degree of feminism, we can compare certain responses with a 1970 national probability sample of ever-married women under the age of forty-five (Mason and Bumpass, 1975), surveyed on their gender role ideology. While the form of questions asked were different, certain topics were similar. For example, in the national sample 49 percent agreed women were entitled to a career as well as marriage and parenthood as compared with 65 percent of this sample who rated all three as equal or almost equal in importance. Nationally, 52 percent felt husbands should share household work as compared with 100 percent of this sample. Nationally, 44 percent believed "there should be free child care centers so that women could take jobs." Only 10 percent of this sample mentioned child care centers, but the question in this research was open-ended, and it was phrased "Who should be responsible for the care of pre-school children?"

Items pertaining to women's labor-market rights elicited very high rates of approval from the national sample; 95 percent supported equal pay, 65 percent desired equal job opprtunities, and 72 percent felt women should be "considered as men for jobs as executives or politicians or even president." These figures compare very favorably with this sample's high belief in equal opportunities for women. The two groups appear comparable in support of women's labor force participation, while differing somewhat in support of more egalitarian household roles.

In painting a summary picture of the role preferences and beliefs for this research sample, it can be said that these women do not differ greatly from the universe of American women. As a group this sample is not radical feminist; rather, they are women who have confronted and decided the kinds of issues in personal life style that more and more American women will be facing in the future. Therefore, it is believed this sample is an appropriate source of clues, insights, and hypotheses for an exploratory study on extramaritality of women in contemporary American life.

TABLE 2

Respondents' Participation
in Selected Aspects of Feminist Activity

Type of Activity	%	N
Consciousness-raising group	56	(28)*
Membership—other group	40	(20)*
Volunteer work for group	18	(9)
Read feminist literature:		
Few (5 or less)	48	(24)
Many (6 or more)	52	(26)
Title preferred:		
Ms. or none	32	(16)
Mrs. or none	38	(19)
Don't care	30	(15)
Feminism changed personal behavior	86	(43)

* Ten women were members of groups in both of these categories.

Appendix 2

Project Guide for Initial Interview

Extramarital Relationships (EMRs)

I. *Personal Data*

(Suppose we begin with some general questions about yourself. Would you mind telling. . .)

1. What kind of hobbies or interests do you have?
2. What is your occupation?
3. What was the last grade you completed in school? If this includes college, what was your major area of study?
4. What is your race? Do you consider yourself to be a member of any ethnic group?
5. What is your religion now (if any)? Do you practice it? In what ways? What religion were you brought up in?

II. *Marital Data*

(In order to fully understand EMR, it is necessary to also understand marriage. Here we would like to begin with some background information on your marriage situation).

1. What was your age, to the nearest birthday, when you were married?
2. What is your age *now,* to the nearest birthday?
3. Are you presently married, separated, or divorced?
4. How many years have you been/were you married?
5. Did you have any previous marriages? (If so, please answer questions 1 and 4 for each marriage).
6. Do you have any children? If so, what are their ages and sex? Whom do they live with now? (To be answered for each marriage, if applicable).
7. What is your husband's age now, to the nearest birthday? (If you are no longer married, you may give his age at the time of your marriage, instead).
8. What was the last grade your husband completed in school? His occupation? His religion now? (To be answered for each marriage, if applicable).
9. Why did you get married? What qualities attracted you to your husband? Do you think he changed any during the course of your marriage? (To be answered for each marriage, if applicable.) Do you still find the qualities that attracted you to your husband to be important or do you look for different qualities in a man now? If you now look for different qualities, what are they?

10. What qualities do you think attracted your husband to you? Did you change in these areas during your marriage? If so, what was his reaction to these changes? (To be answered for each marriage, if applicable.)
11. (To be answered only for first marriage.) Did you have sexual intercourse with your husband before you got married? Did you have intercourse with others before you got married? If yes, can you tell me something about your reasons? What were your feelings (e.g., pleasure, guilt, anxiety) at the time about having premarital sex?

III. *Feminist Attitudes and Behavior*

(In this section, we would like to explore feelings and behavior toward "feminism," herein defined as "the belief that women and men have the same potential for individual development and are therefore entitled to equal opportunities to pursue this development.")

1. On a scale of 0 to 10, which indicates a range of "no support" to "full and unqualified support," how do you rate yourself on your support of feminism? If your answer is less than 10, what aspects of feminism do you have reservations about?
2. How do you rate yourself on your support of the feminist movement, defined as "any and all activities by women that have been taken or may be taken in support of this goal?" If your answer is less than 10, what do you have reservations about?
3. How long ago did you first get interested in feminism? How did you happen to get interested? How has it changed you?
4. Have you ever attended any "consciousness-raising" groups? When? For how long? Do you think that experience changed you? In what way?
5. Are you a member of any feminist organizations like NOW? How long have you been a member? Do you do any work for the organization? How much time do you spend on this work in an average month?
6. Have you read any feminist books or magazines? Which ones?
7. What title do you use, Mrs., Ms., or some other form?
8. Who do you think should be responsible for housework when both a husband and wife work full time?
9. In a married couple, who should be responsible for birth control?
10. Who should take care of children when they are of pre-school age?
11. For a satisfying life style for yourself how would you rate each of the following activities?
    a) Marriage, relationship with husband
    b) Being a parent, relationship with children
    c) Career or occupation
    (Please rate them in one of the following four ways:
    1. *crucially important*-I want my life to center around this area.

2. *very important*-I want to have a major focus of my life in this area.
3. *important*-but I want major investments in other areas.
4. *little or no importance*-in my ideal life, this is not important).
12. There has been some controversy within the feminist movement over the issue of lesbianism. Do you think the issue is good or bad for the movement? Should the movement offer support to lesbians? How come?
13. Has your marriage changed in any way since you became interested in feminism? If so, How?

IV. *Explanation of Involvement*

(The purpose of this section is to understand the process of getting involved in an EMR, regardless of whether the EMR is with a man or a woman.)

1. Are you presently engaged in an EMR? If not, when did your most recent EMR begin and end?
2. Did you have any EMR before this one? (If previously married, relate each EMR to each marriage.) How many EMR have you had in all? Does (did) your EMR involve going with more than one person at a time? (If so, and if you have been married more than once, please answer this question for each marriage.)
NOTE: If you have engaged in more than one EMR, please answer the remaining questions in this section for your most recent and then for your first EMR. All other EMR you may have had will be covered by questions in Section VIII.
3. On a scale of "0" to "10", standing for "totally dissatisfied" to "totally satisfied," how would you rate your marriage at the time you first got involved? If less than 10, how was your marriage unsatisfying?
4. How did you first get involved in your EMR?
5. Would you describe this person (age, sex, marital status, children, education, occupation, race, physical appearance, and anything else you consider important).
6. How did you meet?
7. How long did you know each other before you got sexually involved? Were you also emotionally involved (in love, friends, or what)? If not emotionally involved then, did you later get emotionally involved?
8. Whose idea do you think it was to get involved, his? hers? or yours? How do you know this?
9. What was it about the person that made you go ahead? Do you think it was the person or the situation that was more important in your getting involved? Please explain.
10. Did you think about it much before you got sexually involved?
11. Before you got involved with this person, did you ever talk to anyone about EMR? Did anyone talk to you about EMR? Had you read about it at the time? Did your husband have any EMR before you did? If so, what did you think about it?

13. What obstacles did you have to overcome to initiate and carry on this relationship? (psychological, situational, religious, etc.) How did you handle these obstacles?
14. What was your reaction after or during the first EMR sexual relationship? Did you feel this first EMR was significant in any way?
15. Did you ever have an opportunity for an EMR before you first engaged in one? Why didn't you go through with it? How was this different from the one you did engage in? Did you ever want to have an EMR before you actually had one? If so, what did you do about it?

V. *EMR Activity* (With Men and/or Women)

(In this section the purpose is to gain an understanding of the different types and meanings of EMR relationships from a woman's point of view. Please answer all questions in reference to your most recent EMR; then go back to the beginning and answer each question for your first EMR if you have had more than one. All other EMR besides the first and most recent ones will be discussed in Section VIII).

1. What does having this relationship mean to you? How do you feel about "X"? Like "X"? Love "X"? Ever been in love with "X"?
2. How often do you see one another? Where? For how long? Would you like to see "X" more than you do? Would "X" like to see you more?
3. Who usually suggests getting together, you or "X"? How do you feel about this?
4. Do you call each other on the phone? If no, why not? If so, who usually calls whom? How often? Are you free to call "X" if you wish to? Are there any special arrangements for calling (or writing) one another, such as only on certain days or waiting for certain times? How do you feel about the phone and/or writing arrangements you have? Is there anything you'd like to change about them?
5. What are some of the things you do together? (E.g., dinner, films, walking, going for coffee?) Would you like to do more different things together? Is there any problem with keeping these activities separate from the ones you do with your husband? How do you handle a situation where your husband wants you to see a film with him that you've already seen with "X" (or some similar problem)?
6. Who pays if the things that you do together with "X" cost money?
7. If there are any last minute changes in plans when you are supposed to get together with "X", do you have any special arrangements for contacting each other? If so, did these arrangements ever break down, causing any special problems?
8. What do you talk about when you're with "X"? Is this in any way different from what you talk about with your husband? How important is communicating (being able to express your thoughts, feelings to "X") to your relationship?

9. Have you and "X" given any gifts to one another? If so, what kind of gifts and for what occasions?
10. How would you compare your sexual relationship with "X" with that of your husband? What do you think of "X" as a lover? What do you use for contraception? Do you use the same method with your husband? When with "X", are you concerned about the possibility of pregnancy or disease?
11. How frequently do you have sex with "X"? Are there any things you do in your sex relationship with "X" that you don't do with your husband? (E.g., different positions, oral sex, anal sex, S-M?) If so, how come? Is this an important reason for having the EMR? Are there any things you do with your husband that you don't do with your lover? If so, how come?
12. Are you satisfied with the relationship or are there some things you would like to change if you could? Have you ever thought about marrying "X"? Ever discussed it with him? What were both your feelings about it?
13. How does the relationship differ from your marriage? How does "X" differ from your husband?
14. What do you get out of the relationship? How does that differ from what you get from your marriage?
15. Can you see any way in which the relationship has changed since you started seeing each other? If so, how would you describe these changes?
16. What did you expect EMR to be like when you began your first relationship? How did the actual relationship compare with your expectations?
17. Have there been other opportunities for an EMR while you are having this one? How did you respond?
18. Is "X" involved with anyone else while you are having a relationship? If so, how did you find out? How did you feel about it?
19. What feelings, if any, do you have about the wife of "X"? About any other woman that "X" is involved with?
20. What is the best thing about having an EMR? The worst thing?
21. Have you had EMR only with men or have you had any with women also? Have you ever wanted to? If yes, why don't you? If no to above, how do you feel about women who have EMR with other women?

VI. *EMR Relationships with Women* (Additional Questions)

(If you have had any EMR with women, please answer these questions as well as the previous ones already answered. If you have not had any EMR with women, go on to Section VII.)

1. In what ways does having a relationship with a woman differ from having one with a man?
    a) Are the stages of initial attraction different, and if so, how?

b) Do you feel there is a different intensity, different degrees of jealousy, etc.? If so, please describe.
   c) How do you feel sex with a woman differs from sex with a man?
   d) Is it easier to arrange and carry out EMR with a woman? Does this affect how frequently you see one another?
   e) Do you tend to remain friends with a woman more than with a man after EMR has ended? Why?
 2. How is it you first became attracted to a woman rather than a man? What kind of woman are you attracted to? Does this compare with the kind of man you are attracted to? Are you more attracted now to men or women?
 3. Do you consider yourself to be primarily heterosexual, bisexual, or homosexual? If you had your choice, which would you rather be? Why?
 4. Are you trying to rear your children to be heterosexual, or is it not important to you what sexual preference they might turn out to have? (If you do not have children, please try to answer as to what you think you would do if you did have children.)
 5. Does an EMR with a woman affect your marriage and family life any differently than an EMR with a man? If so, in what ways?
 6. Are there any other differences about EMR with a woman you would like to point out? E.g., differences in your enjoyment, in what the EMR means to you, in the kind of relationship that develops?

(Please go on and answer all other sections of the interview.)

VII. *EMR and Marriage/Family Relationships*

(The objective here is to explore the variety of ways in which being involved in an EMR affects a woman's actions in her marriage and family roles.)

 1. Do you think being involved with someone else changed your behavior toward your husband and/or children? If so, how?
 2. Does it in any way affect your sexual relationship with your husband? Do you have less or more sex with him when you are involved in EMR? Do you ever have sex with both your husband and "X" on the same day or within a few hours time? If so, how do you feel about it?
 3. How do you manage to get out of the house to see "X"? What do you say to explain your absence? What precautions do you take to keep your husband from finding out, if you don't want him to know? Do you have anyone that helps "cover" for you, to support your account of being somewhere else when you're with "X"? If so, how necessary or helpful do you feel this is?
 4. How easy or difficult is it to keep up with your husband's (children's) needs, things around the house, work obligations while trying to carry on a relationship? Are you able to spend as much time with your children as you think you should? Does the age of your children

affect the amount of time spent, or arrangements for EMR in any way?
5. If you desire to keep EMR secret, what do you have to do to make it seem as though everything is the same, as though you hadn't changed? How do you manage this?
6. Do you talk about your relationship with anyone? How did you first tell them about it? Why did you decide to tell them?
7. If you do not talk about your EMR to anyone, would you prefer to? Why?
8. Does your husband or children know or suspect? How did they find out? How do you feel about it? (or would feel if they found out?) What effect do you think this has on your husband or children? On how they feel about you? Was there (or would there be, do you think) any special reaction if your EMR were with a woman, or someone of another race, or someone much younger or older than you?
9. If the EMR was with someone you and your husband both knew, what kind of problems did this create (e.g., everyone attending the same party) and how did you deal with them?
10. Did anyone else find out about your EMR by accident? If so, how did it happen and what was your reaction and theirs?
11. How about your other family members—mother, father, brother, sister, in-laws? If they know or should find out, what difference would it make? How would they react?
12. How would you feel about your husband having a relationship? Would you want to know about it? How come? Would it matter if his relationship were with someone you knew? Why?

VIII. *Outcomes*

(Please select one of the following 4 categories, as appropriate, to answer questions concerning the outcome of your most recent EMR, and also of your first EMR if you have had more than one. Additionally, if you have had more than two EMR, please also answer questions under Outcome 5.)

Outcome 1. Marriage Continuing, EMR Ended.

1. How and when did the relationship end? Who do you think was more responsible for ending it, you or "X"? Why do you think the relationship ended?
2. How did you feel after it ended? What did you do?
3. Do you think being involved in an EMR has changed you? In what ways?
4. Do you think being involved in an EMR has changed your marriage? In what ways?
5. Do you consider the relationship to have been a worthwhile experience? Did you learn anything from it? Do you regret any part of it? Would you do anything differently if you had to do it over? Will you

ever have another EMR? Under what conditions?
6. On a scale of "0" to "10", standing for "totally dissatisfied" to "totally satisfied," how would you rate your marriage right now? What is it that is especially satisfying and/or especially dissatisfying about your marriage right now?
7. Looking back on your EMR, how important an experience was it to you?

Outcome 2. Marriage Continuing, EMR Continuing.

1. Do you think this EMR will end or continue?
2. What do you think will happen to your marriage in the future?
3. Do you think having an EMR has changed you? In what ways?
4. Do you think having an EMR has changed your marriage? In what ways? If one of the changes has been to an "open marriage" situation, how did this happen? Please describe fully how you talked about "open marriage," what you did to change the basis of your marriage, and how the new arrangement is working out.
5. If you have not changed to an "open marriage," would you like to and have you ever tried to make the change? What efforts did you make to change to an "open marrige," and why didn't it work?
6. Do you think you will have any more EMR in the future if this one ends? (If yes:) Under what conditions? Do you think you might have another EMR while this one is still continuing? Why?
7. On a scale of "0" to "10," standing for "totally dissatisfied" to "totally satisfied," how would you rate your marriage right now? What is it that is especially satisfying and/or dissatisfying about your marrige right now?
8. How important to you is continuing this EMR?

Outcome 3. Marriage Ended, EMR Ended.

1. Why do you think your marriage broke up? Did the relationsihp have anything to do with it? Would your marriage have broken up anyway, do you think? How did you feel about your marriage ending?
2. How and when did the EMR end? Who do you think was more responsible for ending it, you or "X"?
3. How did you feel after it ended? What did you do?
4. Do you think being involved in an EMR has changed you? In what ways?
5. Do you consider the relationship to have been a worthwhile experience? Did you learn from it? Do you regret any part of it? Would you do anything differently if you had to do it over?
6. Would you like to get married again?
7. If you do, would you have an EMR (if the opportunity arose) while married? How come?

Outcome 4. Marriage Ended, EMR Continuing

1. Why do you think your marriage broke up? Did the relationship have anything to do with it? Would your marriage have broken up anyway, do you think?
2. How did you feel about your marriage ending?
3. Has the end of your marrige changed the EMR in any way? How?
4. What do you think will happen in the EMR in the future?
5. Do you think having EMR has changed you? In what ways?
6. Would you like to get married again?
7. If you do, would you have EMR (if the opportunity arose) while married? Why?

Outcome 5. To be answered only if you have had more than two EMRs.

1. What factors have been important in your decisions to continue to have EMRs?
2. Where and how do you meet the persons you get involved with?
3. Do you tend to start the EMRs or do the other persons start them? How long does an EMR generally last?
4. How many EMRs have you had in all? Over what period of time? How many have been with men and how many with women?
5. Have any of the EMRs you have had been special or different in any way from the two (your first and last) you've already described? Please tell something about what made them special or different.
6. In general, how meaningful and important were these EMRs to you? Were they principally for love, sex, friendship, or some other reason? (Please try to fully express your opinions and feelings.)
7. Have you developed any "rules of thumb," in terms of appearance, age, marital status, personality, and situations tht helps you decide whether or not to get involved if an opportunity occurs?
8. In general, do other people know of these relationships? How come? How much do they know?
9. Do you think being involved in these EMR have changed you in any way? If so, how?
10. Do you foresee a time why you won't, or can't have EMR anymore? Why?
11. How will continuing EMR affect your marrige (if still married?)

IX. *Attitudes Towards Marriage, EMR, and Female Sexuality*

1. If you could have your choice in an ideal situation, which would you prefer:
   a) not to be married
   b) complete monogamy with one lifelong mate
   c) monogamy with an occasional affair
   d) an open marriage with freedom for both
   e) serial monogamy

f) a polygamous arrangement
   g) a lesbian marriage
   h) other
   Would you comment on your reasons for this preference?
2. Before your own first EMR, what kind of woman did you think got involved in EMRs? Did your opinion change in any way after you yourself had experienced an EMR?
3. Do you think most women would like to have an EMR? Do you think they would participate in an EMR, given the opportunity? Do you think they should? How would you feel if your mother/sister did?
4. What do you think most women you know are doing and thinking about EMRs?
5. Of women who do have EMR, what do you think their reasons are?
6. What do you think are the biggest problems connected with having an EMR? The greatest benefits?
7. Do you think more women will be having EMR in the future? Do you think feminism will have an effect in increasing EMR? If EMR increases, who will this affect marriage?
8. Do you think women can have impersonal sex and enjoy it or do you think they need some sense of emotional involvement with the person? Please explain.
9. If we can specify three types of EMR: a) primarily sexual, b) both sexual and emotional, c) primarily emotional, do you think they affect marriage differently? If so, how?
10. Do you think your attitude toward any of the following changed as a result of your EMR experience? If so, how?
    a) yourself
    b) your own sexuality
    c) female sexuality, in general
    d) male sexuality, in general
    e) EMR
    f) marriage
    g) feminism
    h) lesbianism

X. *Concluding Questions*

1. Have you ever had any therapy or counseling? When, for how long, and for what?
2. Has the therapy or counseling changed your attitudes or behavior concerning either yourself, feminism, marrige or EMR? Please explain.
3. Is there anything else you'd like to discuss that hasn't already been covered?
4. Is there anything you would like to tell other women about your experiences or feelings?

5. Could you tell me why you decided to respond to this interview?
6. What are your feelings and opinions about the interview experience? Please feel free to be honest and say whether it's been difficult, tiring, rewarding, meaningful, or whatever you have felt.
7. Can you make any helpful suggestions for changes, omissions, additions? Is there any particular question you'd like to see answered by this research?

Thank you very much for your time and openness in sharing your experiences, feelings and ideas with me and, ultimately, with other women.

INDEX

age norms, traditional, 114
androgynous personality, 65
autonomy, 68, 152
awareness contexts, 85-86, 88-90, 91, 94

Balswick, Jack, on deception in male-female relationships, 70
bargaining skills, 71
Bell, Robert, on ageing and attractiveness, 24
Bem, Sandra, on androgynous personality, 65
Bernard, Jessie:
    on new women emerging, 24, 25
    on marriage and identity, 146
    see also MARRIAGE
bisexual behavior of husbands, 94
Block, J.D., *The Other Man, The Other Woman*, 20
boys, and sexual socialization, 33

Carter, Jimmy, on lust, 21
child caring role, 71
children, choice to have, 21
    and the sexual learning process, 187
Chodorow, Nancy, on gender roles, 145
class differences, as opportunity, 69
communication theory, 85
consciousness, new, 23
consciousness-raising, 172
contraception, 134-135
cues, verbal and nonverbal, 85
cultural myths:
    love, 133
    sexual exclusivity, 18

decision making, role models for, 36
decisions, unilateral, 99
Dickey, James, on adultery, 189

economic affluence, 61, 98
    coercion, 76
elderly couples, and open marriage, 106

    see also OPEN MARRIAGE
encounters, sexual:
    unmet expectations from, 121
    unwanted, 33
Ellis, Albert, on distinction between sick and healthy behavior, 20
Erikson, Erik, on identity development, 146
extramarital behavior, after, 49-53, 142-165
    attitudes, changed, 154-166
    sexual self, definitions of, 149-154
    socialization, patterns of, 155
    transition to new lifestyle, 53-56
extramarital intimacy, 57-81
    class differences, 69
    communication, 67-69
    cross-sex friendships, 66
    dependency of women, decreased, 75
    equality in male-female interaction, 66
    expressive aspects, 60-63
    female role, traditional, 63
    first encounter, reaction to, 46-49
    guilt, 50-52
    ideology, new, about sex, marriage and monogamy, 52
    intercourse, initiating, 32, 44-46
    male uneasiness, 47
    negative aspects on marriage, 78-80
    personal growth, 53, 56
    positive effects on marriage, 74-76
    religious background, 55
    rewards for marital and extramarital behavior, 74
    situationally expressive men, 70
    thrill seeking, 62
extramarital relationships, 15-26, 188-208
    attitudes toward, 15, 22
    behavioral rehearsal, 34-39
    communication, 69
    conscience, 29
    defined, 35
    economic responsibility, absence of, 71

effects on behavior toward husbands, 74-78
and "falling in love," 41
feminist perspective, 22
fulfillment as motivation, 43
futuristic approach to, 19, 20
and guilt, 24, 25, 50, 52
and happily married women, 25
husband's role, 37
integration of into marriage, 95
intercourse, genital, 35
and liberation, 191
moral approach, 19
partner, as compared to husband, 108
psychological approach, 20
sociological approach, 20
extramarital relationships with other women, 166-187
   consciousness-raising, and emotional bonding, 171
   and emotional needs, 179
   erotic physical behavior, 181-183
   getting involved, 169-179
   historically, 167
   identities and attitudes, 184-187
   learning experience, 183
   meanings to participants, 179-181
   rates of, 167
   sexuality, 179-182
   preference for, after extramarital sex, 185
extramarital sex, 44-49, 122-127, 129-134, 181-184
   belief systems, changes in, 49-53
   cunnilingus, 122, 123, 125, 126
   differences in behavior with partner and husband, 121-127
   effects on marital sex, 127-129
   fellatio, 122, 126
   males, and aggressive role, 32
   and menstrual cycle, 87
   and orgasm, 47
   professionals' attitudes toward, 201
   rationalization for involvement, 49-51
   reactions to first, 47
   responsibility, 50
   self-image of woman, 49
   and sexual coercion of women, 24

   scheduling, 129-134
   spouse reaction to, 19, 80, 86, 94, 105, 198-199
   as therapy, 74-76
   and unhappily married women, 24
   unisexual attitude, need for, 64

feeling rules, 19, 20, 198
Fischer, Anita K., on mental health of liberated women, 149
   see also WOMEN
foreplay, 33
Freud, Sigmund, on female orgasm, 23
   on sexuality, 107

Gagnon and Simon, on construction of female sexuality, 107
Hunt, Morton, on "affairs," 24, 148

gender, and assignment of duties, 99
   role socialization, 34
Goffman, Erving, on everyday life and extramarital sex, 129-130

Hite, S., on homosexuality, 167
   on sexual capacity of women, 24
husbands, women's preference for, 117-118

impotence, 119
intellectual-emotional integration, 101
involvement stage, of extramarital behavior, 40-44
   feelings, 41-43
   and friends, 42-43
   and infatuation, 41
   and love as prerequisite for sex, 41
   and love redefined, 42
   meeting partners, 40
   motivation for, 43, 44
   opportunity structure, 40-41
   and redefinition of sex, 42
   workplace, 40

Kinsey, Alfred, on classificaiton of sexual behavior, 185
   on male sexual behavior, 15

on women and extramarital sex, 16, 110
kissing, see WOMEN

lesbian relationships, meanings and differences, 179-181
lesbianism, and societal reactions, 170,
    and women's movement, 167
    see also WOMEN
Levin, Robert, on satisfied-experimental wife, 25
liberals, and attitudes toward extramarital sex, 25

male insincerity, 69-70
marital sex, and Puritanism, 17
marriage:
    alternatives to exclusivity, 8
    commitment to, changing, 40
    incompatible demands within, 74, 213
Maslow, Abraham, on self-actualization, 148
Masters and Johnson, on sexuality, 24, 123, 151
masturbation, 93, 128
mate swapping, 89, 91
men:
    beauty of body, and Western culture, 111
    clothing, body revealing, 111
    cosmetics, 111
    as dominant group, 190
    expressive competence of, 69-71
    extra marital involvements, 71-72
    homosexual involvement, 93, 190
    inexpressiveness, 69-72
    and masculinity, traditional traits of, 71
    older, and competition with younger men, 114
    and older women, 113-114
    penis size, 158
    property rights, 16
    role-models, and mass media, 204
    role variation, 48
    secretiveness, 201
    as sexual aggressors, 32
    younger, and older women, 111-114, 194

monogamy:
    ancestor's code of behavior, 16, 17, 22
    and external constraints, 17
    failure of, 80-81
    flexible, 81
    in industrial society, 17
    and male expressiveness, 64-66
    myths of, 18
    sequential, 82
    sexual exclusivity, 188
    social need for, 16
    women's attitudes toward, after involvement, 163-165
    and younger men, 45-46
morality, modern sexual, 22
myth of the rigid penis, 119, 123

Nye and Berardo, on discontinuity in male roles, 33

occupations, 21
"one night stands," 57, 70
Open Marriage, (George and Nena O'Neill), 97
open marriage, 37, 82-106, 163
    acting phase, 90
    benefits of, 105
    and children, 97, 104
    closed awareness, 86-88
    disadvantages of, 105
    double standards of, 98
    and elderly couples, 106
    happiness, concealing, 88
    homosexual involvement, 93
    Knapp, Jacqueline, on, 98
    Murstein, Bernard, on female equality, 98
    negotiation skills, 105
    and occupation, 102
    open awareness, 94, 97
    passive phase, 90
    and power, 82
        equalization of, 94
    transformational process, 86
    Whitehurst, Robert, on, 98
    role flexibility, 99
    self-socialization, 105
    socializing device, anticipatory, 101
oral-genital contact, 25, 122-126

penis envy, 157
physical attractiveness as criteria for partner selection, 111, 180
pluralistic ignorance, 84, 155
Pomeroy, Wardell, on sexual orientation, 185
power,
    as independence, 92
    and open marriage, 94, 98
    sexual appeal of, 120, 195
    sources of, 83-84
    women's marital, 75, 77
preinvolvement, 31-40
    female virgins and sexual decisions, 38
    guilt, 31, 35
    intergenerational influence, 36
    premarital sexual behavior, 31
    opportunity, 32
    and time lapse, 39-40
    unwanted pregnancy, 31
premarital sexuality, attitudes toward and behavior, 10
    negotiating, 38

Redbook Magazine study (1975), on homosexuality, 167
religious liberation, 21
risk, and sexual enjoyment, 124
rural America, and marriage, 17

Sattell, J.W., on expressiveness, 69
schizophrenics, sexual, 16
scripts, sexual, and sexual behavior, 107-141
    activity, scripts for, 107
    contraception and pregnancy, 134-135
    extramarital partners, as compared to husbands, 108-121
    foreplay, 125
    genital intercourse, 127
    goal-oriented orgasmic sex, 119
    infractions, punishment for, 107
    husbands, women's preference for, 117-118
    male physique, 111
    men, older, and competition, 114
    myth of "rigid penis," 119, 123
    pairing with younger men, 111-114
    problems encountered, 137-140
    venereal diseases, 136
    secrecy, dishonesty, need for, 79-80
    sex, impersonal, 72
    sexual outlets, opportunity for, 17
sexuality:
    and age of women, 16, 194
    anti-female bias in Western culture, 23
    Beyond the Male Myth (1977), on age of sexual partners, 113-114
    cultural definitions, 23
    and permissiveness, 97
    Redbook Magazine survey on, 25, 167
    secularization of, 79
    stereotypes, challenged, 24
    and survey responses, 24-26
    traditional models for women, 23
    variety, and male validation, 71
Sherfey, Mary Jane, on female sexual insatiability, 24
social myths, and sexual needs, 17-18
    values, and extramarital sex, 17-18
socialization of boys, 33
San Giovanni, Lucinda, on self-reliance, 206
Scanzoni, John, on equalized gender roles, 193
sexual scripts, egalitarian, 194
Skolnick, Arlene, on sexual communication problems, 88
Srole, Leo, on mental health of liberated women, 149
Strauss, Anselm, on self-discovery, 142
swinging, 93, 171, 177

terminology, sexual, 189
touching, and lesbian relationships, 171

Vaughan, Jim and Peggy, *Beyond Affairs*, 198-199

Western civilization, and family life, 16
women:
    bi-sexual (extramarital) relationships with, 166-186

conservative, 190
crying, to coerce, 86
emotional bonding, 171
as equal partners, 88
homosexual activity, as compared to sex with men, 181-183
kissing, between, 174
lesbianism, attitudes toward, 167
and the male body, 111
male-female differences, as perceived after extramarital sex, 157-158
and moral code, traditional, 66
non-traditional, 66
and open marriage, 98
orgasm, pressure to have, 178
pairing, with younger men, 113-114
and passive sexual role, 46
penetration, significance of, 183
person, concern for, 43
rejection fears, 46
sex objects, 44
sexual aggressors, 45-46
  insatiability of, 24, 151
and sexuality, 188-195
as social innovators, 66
and social power, 83-84
socialization of girls, 156
tenderness, 182
validation, 143-149
verbal patterns of, 34
wife-mother identity of, 146
working, and impact on children, 70-71, 186-187
venereal diseases, 136